DICKENS AND THE TWENTIETH CENTURY

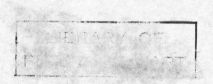

CONTRIBUTORS

Angus Wilson
William Empson
Robert Browning
John Killham
John Bayley
Bernard Bergonzi
Jack Lindsay
Barbara Hardy
Julian Moynahan
John Jones
W. J. Harvey
John Holloway
John Wain
Christopher Ricks
Arnold Kettle
A. O. J. Cockshut
John Gross
Gabriel Pearson

DICKENS
AND THE
TWENTIETH CENTURY

edited by
JOHN GROSS
and
GABRIEL PEARSON

TORONTO: University of Toronto Press

First published 1962
by University of Toronto Press
Published as a paperback 1966

Printed in Great Britain

CONTENTS

ACKNOWLEDGMENTS are due to the *Review of English Literature,* where Angus Wilson's essay on 'The Heroes and Heroines of Dickens' first appeared.

DICKENS: SOME RECENT APPROACHES

John Gross

TWENTY years have now passed since a number of writers, most notably Edmund Wilson and George Orwell, began to transform the traditional picture of Dickens and set in motion a remarkable revival of interest in his work. As well to remark at the outset that this has been pretty much a palace revolution; to the world at large Dickens is still Mr. Popular Sentiment, and his novels a compound of high-spirited caricature, rudimentary social protest, and sickly pathos. Academics may turn their attention to the complexities of Eugene Wrayburn and Miss Wade, but true Dickensians will never desert Mr. Micawber—or stop deriding Little Nell. The nature of Dickens's greatness is bound up with his popularity, but, whatever its merits, the Santa Claus view plainly fails to do him full justice, laying him open much too readily to charges of monotony and facile optimism; and as long as the old hearty Dickens holds the public stage, one isn't inclined to question more sophisticated versions too sharply. But recent writers, including those in the present collection, have begun to voice doubts or reservations about Dickens the gloomy symbolist; the novelty is wearing off, and after two decades it is worth while taking stock.

Of all modern writings on Dickens, Edmund Wilson's essay *The Two Scrooges* (1941) is the most dramatic. Wilson makes a brilliant case for Dickens as Dostoevsky's master, rather than a classic of the nursery, by effecting some simple but basic shifts of emphasis. He presents Dickens as a subversive and uncomfortable writer, inwardly hostile to the age which acclaimed him and seeking relief from the strain of his double life in fantasies of crime and violence. Far more weight is given to the macabre or savage element in Dickens than in any previous account, with the result that his last novels emerge as his masterpieces, while at the same time he is absolved from the familiar charges of exaggeration and cheap melodrama; instead of reprimanding Dickens for his lack of realism, we are recommended to look in his works for symbolism, poetry, and all the devices of an experimental novelist. Biographical material, in particular the Ellen Ternan episode, is not treated as so much musty scandal, but used for the light which it throws on Dickens's character, in an effort to bring together psychological and social insights, to see the baffled rebel and the unhappy husband as one. Above all, Dickens's career is given shape, and the precise sequence of his writings is made to matter: it becomes impossible to go on talking of characters as though they could be transplanted from one novel to another without causing much damage.

That there is a dark side to Dickens was in itself nothing new; earlier writers had pointed the way (most of them are included in Professor George Ford's admirable *Dickens and His Readers*), while Mr. Wilson himself acknowledges a special debt to Bernard Shaw. But *The Two Scrooges* is more satisfying than any previous over-all interpretation, and it has proved extraordinarily persuasive: its influence is plain to see on the full-length studies of Edgar Johnson, Hillis Miller, Jack Lindsay, K. J. Fielding, and Monroe Engel, not to mention dozens of shorter articles. Like all fruitful criticism, it leaves a good many questions unanswered; it was, after all, a piece of propaganda on Dickens's behalf, written at roughly the same time as *To the Finland Station* and consciously tailored to the kind of modern taste which only becomes interested in the Circumlocution Office if Kafka is invoked. In this respect it is revealing to compare Wilson with Orwell. I began, conventionally enough, by bracketing the two names, and certainly they have both played their part in saving Dickens from the lumber-room, but their conclusions point in very nearly opposite directions. Orwell's Dickens is still the old-fashioned radical, not very intelligent, but valuable for his generous anger at injustice of every variety, and chiefly distinguished as an artist by his inexhaustible fertility in piling up lavish but unnecessary detail; his books are 'all fragments, all details—rotten architecture, but wonderful gargoyles'. Orwell makes the traditional picture less fuzzy and more convincing by stressing Dickens's *petit bourgeois* prejudices and limitations, by rapping Chesterton on the knuckles for calling

Dickens a spokesman of 'the poor', for instance, when he really meant the shopkeeping and servant class. Most of Orwell's essay is devoted to a no-nonsense examination of previous assumptions about Dickens, but in the end he is really much closer to Chesterton than he is to Edmund Wilson and his followers. He can still lump together characters or incidents from early and late novels without allowing for obvious differences, and hardly bothers to trace a line of development in Dickens at all, apart from echoing the customary regret that Dickens's social conscience drove him to desert *Pickwick* for 'a form of art for which he was not really suited'.

Depending on one's point of view, the Orwell essay will seem either more sensible or more superficial than Mr. Wilson's. Yet most people have found both approaches stimulating, without worrying too much about the inconsistencies. The literary historians, Humphry House in *The Dickens World* and Professor Kathleen Tillotson and John Butt in *Dickens at Work*, confirm both Orwell in showing how heavily committed Dickens was to his middle-class audience, even at his most radical, and Wilson in showing Dickens's art as maturing and developing towards more unified forms: moving from gargoyles to architecture. That traditional and modern attitudes to Dickens have gone on flourishing side by side will disturb only critical absolutists, but it does suggest some points at which the modernism of an Edmund Wilson or a Hillis Miller needs to be either reinforced or modified.

The notion that Dickens was 'of all the great Victorian writers probably the most antagonistic to the Victorian age itself'—Edmund Wilson's key point—still seems true in the broad sense which was intended, but leads us into difficulties and even absurdities as soon as we try to apply it in systematic detail. Dickens's journalism, for instance, can only be said to be directed against society itself rather than against particular social abuses by stretching the meaning of words, and Dickens the journalist tends to be swallowed up in any account of Dickens the subversive, so that in recent years the journalistic element in the novels has been largely neglected, except by social historians. Certainly Dickens juggles with facts when it suits his artistic purpose, yet at his best he is full of information as well as poetry. Or again, why should it be so readily assumed that Dickens's anti-social tendencies were necessarily progressive in tone? Why not a reactionary Dickens? With his contempt for parliamentary government, his suspicion of blue-book intellectuals, his authoritarianism, his admiration for Carlyle, his fear of the mob, the strongly sadistic streak in his social criticism, it would be easy to make out a case for one—easy, but patently wrong-headed. Yet it is worth asking how he was able to establish himself as a benevolent rather than a destructive figure in the eyes of his contemporaries, and what held him back from following the path of Carlyle. The answer must lie with the age as well as the man. One hardly ever feels inclined to call Dickens a liberal, and it is always a shock to turn from the atmosphere and assumptions of Victorian political memoirs or public debates to Dickens on Boodle and Coodle and the parliamentary cinder-heap. Had he been born a generation later, he would have been ready to join the long, disheartening procession of major artists who have rejected modern democracy and all its ways; there was more of, say, Lawrence than of Galsworthy in his make-up. But as a central figure in his own age, he could hardly help absorbing a measure of liberalism with the air he breathed; his energy is explosive, but his standards are still humane. Nor was he seriously exposed to the romantic temptation of turning his back on his surroundings—he was far too much of a townsman, sentimental about 'the Past' as a kind of Green Belt for week-end excursions, but never about unen-lightened pre-industrial 'History'. And his Christianity is more relevant than one tends to think nowadays. There was undeniably a gulf between his morality, which was Christian in colouring, and his literal beliefs, which were nebulous: hence the embarrassing Biblical language of his operatic climaxes and death-bed scenes. But a formal belief is rarely quite as formal as it appears; one has to allow for childhood memories, emotional overtones, unresolved doubts. Dickens may have thought of Christianity primarily in terms of a diffuse loving-kindness, for instance, but he was also profoundly attracted by the ideas of redemption and resurrection. John Jasper betrays more in Cloisterham than respectability.

If we strain at accepting Dickens as a thoroughgoing rebel or outcast, however, it is, above all, on account of his humour. Only someone who misses the point about Dickens would want to start explaining his jokes; a tactful man like Mr. Wilson simply offers his salute and lets the subject drop. Perhaps one ought to applaud Dickens when one finds him funny and leave it at that, but taking his humour for granted comes after a time to suggest a failure of response. And Dickens without humour is a very lop-sided creature indeed; other aspects of his work are inevitably exaggerated, including the degree of his estrangement from society. His humour may be subversive, even diabolical, but it also helps to dissolve his anger; his laughter reconciles as well as disrupts, and 'satirist' has never seemed an adequate label for him. But comedy which urges us to accept our limitations (not the only kind in Dickens, of course) is, up to a point, urging us to accept the limitations of the world in which we live, just as 'common sense' involves a tacit recognition of what is and what isn't possible within the established social order.

If Dickens's instinctive rebelliousness was often muted or sup-pressed, his conscious worries about his own status were treated with· increasing directness and realism in his later works. Aware of himself as a social anomaly, after *David Copperfield* he produced a series of heroes who weren't quite heroes and wrongdoers who can scarcely be called mere villains. The hoary accusation that Dickens didn't know how to draw a gentleman hasn't been heard for a long time, and at this hour in the day may seem no more than a piece of tire-some and irrelevant snobbery; but neither Dickens nor his con-temporaries would have thought so. The question of what constitutes a gentleman was one of his major preoccupations, as it was of the whole period which saw the middle classes finally wrest power but not altogether prestige from the aristocracy. Luckily he never allowed himself to be bogged down in the finer points of snobbery as thoroughly as Thackeray, but the gentleman, and his insolent half-brother the dandy, loom large in his thoughts. It would be crudely over-simplified to suggest that Dickens began as a dandy aspiring to be a gentleman (or, the unsympathetic would say, a gent) and ended as a gentleman pining to be a dandy—he was at all times far too big a man to be tied down by such flimsy classifications. But Humphry House's remarks on gentility in *The Dickens World*, and the line of development sketched out by Ellen Moers in *The Dandy*, deserve to be pursued further. Dickens understood his own situation more clearly than many admirers are willing to concede, including his need to remain socially acceptable while rejecting society. Dandyism, which had once meant Cousin Feenix and Mr. Turveydrop, came with Eugene Wrayburn to offer one possible mask; confronted with Podsnappery, there was something to be said even for Deportment, while a Twemlow could emerge as the best available arbiter of what makes a gentleman.

Dickens was unable to deal with his role as an artist as directly as he was with his position in society: *David Copperfield* is about

xiii

becoming a gentleman rather than becoming a novelist. But else-where, despite his philistinism and his unconvincing assertions of fidelity to nature (his defence of Krook's spontaneous combustion is a case in point), he shows himself aware of the peculiar nature of his own vision. His art, like that of a romantic poet, struggles to define itself; Sleary's circus in *Hard Times*, for instance, is not so much a slice of Lawrentian 'life' as an image of Dickens's own creative powers, of the imagination which could transform a Coketown steam-engine into 'the head of an elephant in a state of melancholy madness'. The Crummles troupe, Mrs. Jarley's waxworks, Mr. Venus's shop are microcosms of the world in which they appear; Dickens is full of implied comments on his own grotesquerie. He may have been obtuse about the Pre-Raphaelites, but he undoubtedly appreciated Miss La Creevey. There are major characters who can be thought of as artists *manqués*, too—Fagin, Quilp, John Jasper—but with them the element of distortion is less important than the sense of power, the ability to use other people as puppets. In real life Dickens dabbled in mesmerism, and he was always fascinated by the idea of one personality exerting control over another; and while Quilp may be a sorcerer and Fagin a bogey-man, Jasper is an artist. Lke one or two other characters in the last books, he wears a distinctly *fin de siècle* air : a refined neurotic with a dash of Svengali, he already belongs to the Decadence.

Vaudeville, nightmare, folktale—whatever terms we choose to describe the Dickens world will indicate that his place is with the great masters of expressionism : there can rarely have been a less classical, a less mediterranean spirit. Almost everyone now agrees that it is as futile to reproach him for a lack of surface realism as it would be to blame, say, Breughel for not painting like Poussin; characters once dismissed as flat are accorded a quasi-mythological grandeur, mannerisms are seen as motifs and stage-properties as symbols. With the labours of Professor Hillis Miller, one might be justified in feeling that this particular vein has been worked dry, while some writers are growing nervous of using the very word 'symbol' in connection with Dickens. Certainly an approach which attributes to the novelist a conscious, thoroughgoing symbolist method, or fails to allow for the overflow of superabundant detail— Orwell's 'wedding-cake decoration'—is both extravagant and unhis-torical. But the quarrel is largely one over terminology, since even critics who object to loose talk about symbolism recognize what it is meant to convey, and themselves continue to discuss Dickens in terms of imagery, atmosphere, accumulated detail. Professor Miller's total picture may be misleading, but his specific comments give one the feel of Dickens, and even when he appears over-ingenious he is usually only unearthing what was there already (see, to give a random example, his remarks on the theme of suffocation in *Oliver Twist*). It is no secret that Dickens's characters repeat themselves, and in general repetition is one of his artistic principles; symbolic or not, his books are full of recurrent imagery. He still awaits his Wilson Knight, but perhaps the time has passed, and the job has already been done piecemeal. Undoubtedly we have heard rather a lot lately about Prisons and Rivers and Fogs, at the expense of other aspects of Dickens's artistry. No one has ever shown to the full why his language crackles with such electricity, though there have been some interesting observations by Professor Quirk on his dialogue, his choice of words, and even his syntax. The subtlety of his rhythms, too, deserves to be brought out; critics have been frightened off far too easily by jeers at the bogus blank verse. Take, for instance, the description of Lincoln's Inn Fields on the night that Tulkinghorn meets his death:

In these fields of Mr. Tulkinghorn's inhabiting, where the shepherds play on Chancery pipes that have no stop, and keep their sheep in the fold by hook and by crook, until they have shorn them exceeding close, every noise is merged, this moonlight night, into a distant ringing hum, as if the city were a vast glass, vibrating. (*Bleak House*, Ch. 48.)

At the beginning of *Bleak House*, it has more than once been pointed out, the present participle is used to suggest continuous, all-engulfing action; here it serves rather, together with a series of rhymes or half-rhymes, to convey the buzz of suppressed excitement at impending murder—and all this while an elaborate conceit is being worked out!

George Orwell spoke of Dickens as a writer who was 'worth kidnapping'; opposed philosophies of life have claimed him for their own, and widely differing schools of criticism, too. To talk of a Dickens tradition would, not so long ago, have conjured up the idea of a school of primitive comedy, borrowing a few tricks from the all-too-imitable Boz and expiring miserably at the hands of cockney journalists and professional funny men. Since then we have been encouraged to look for the master in more exalted places, to trace his hand in Joyce as well as W. W. Jacobs, Stavrogin as well as Mr.

Polly. Our view of Dickens hasn't been altogether enlarged by this change; the early novels, offering less than the later ones to critics in search of complexity and buried meanings, have suffered comparative neglect, and it was easier for Chesterton than it is for his successors to do full justice to *Pickwick*. But the fact that it has been possible to quarry in Dickens for such a variety of material is one of the surest marks of his commanding position. It has become a commonplace to bracket him with Shakespeare: what other comparison could convey his strength, his scope, his range of sympathy? If the parallel is pushed too far, it inevitably harms him, however, since we are bound to conclude that he *wasn't* Shakespeare, that finally there is something stunted about his genius. Yet one can make too much of the emotional cripple, or of the favourite for children of all ages. After a time, reading Dickens, one learns to catch a certain stern, uncompromisingly serious note: a tone of voice, rather than anything one can easily isolate in terms of character or plot. It is never sustained for very long, but it is enough to make one feel that while an Arnold or a George Eliot consciously strive towards maturity, Dickens is ultimately the most grown-up of the great Victorians: he may be mawkish, hysterical, often not very intelligent, but in the end he knows more. A paradoxical conclusion; but the critic who hopes that he can encompass Dickens's achievement without sometimes contradicting himself would do better to look for another author.

DICKENS: THE PRESENT
POSITION

Gabriel Pearson

A QUESTION to a recent session of *The Brains Trust* asked the team
to account for Dickens's continuing popularity. This evoked the
usual adjectival riot: vital, exuberant, humorous, and so on. One
member of the panel, however, doubted whether Dickens still was
popular and feared that he had been taken over by the academics. It
is tempting to dismiss this as merely another example of quite a
widespread paranoiac suspicion of academic criticism. Yet, however
crudely expressed, this suspicion may not be entirely baseless and
uninformed. Most major novelists of the last century and this now
appeal to a fairly limited section of readers and perhaps always did.
This would certainly be true of George Eliot (with reservations),
Conrad, Henry James, and D. H. Lawrence. This section, of course,
was never limited to professional critics and academics. It included
simply an informed common readership. Nonetheless, it is academics
rather than the more general men-of-letters and literary journalists
who have fostered their reputations and have created, through teaching as much as anything else, a fresh potential readership. Of course,
there have always been one or two novelists with the kind of appeal
that creates addicts. Jane Austen has her Janeites, a jealous and
meticulous following, as well as the attentions of Mrs. Leavis and
Lionel Trilling. Trollope provides endless fodder for relaxing poli-
ticians; though the academic-baiters may gloomily suspect that his
spell in the operating-theatre cannot be long delayed. While Emily
Brontë can still startle the afternoon half-listeners to *Woman's Hour*
with the heroics of Gondal. (Of course, there is no comparable programme to adopt Henry James; but if there were, it wouldn't!)

Dickens, by contrast, has always held a uniquely privileged position as a truly popular classic, indeed as an almost mythic colouring of the consciousness of a whole people. The obverse of this has been a fairly constant sour disrespect among the literary intelligentsia. This account is, of course, only generally true. His champions have ranged from the publishers of children's picture-books to the steely intelligence of Bernard Shaw. Yet it remains broadly the case that from the time of his death until the nineteen-thirties, Dickens has been popularly loved and, from Oscar Wilde onwards, intellectually rather disreputable. It needed the creation of a 'dark' Dickens to restore his reputation among academic critics. And even this restoration, despite the efforts of Edmund Wilson and many others, only became noticeable after this war and irrevocably confirmed in the fifties. So much is old hat.

But what has happened to the popular reputation? This is an enquiry in which statistics (for example, library borrowings, sales of the recent Oxford University Press edition, and programme rating for radio and television serials) would be helpful. Yet in the end hunches and estimates based on personal experience probably have to serve. I myself read Dickens for the first time, apart from a few childhood skirmishes with adapted versions of *Oliver Twist* and *David Copperfield*, in the long vacation *after* completing a degree in English Literature. When Dickens was instituted as a special author in the Keele English Literature course, it became rapidly clear that most students were encountering him for virtually the first time. They came prepared with a handful of notions about sentimentality, coincidence, and caricature. Actual reading and discussion came with the force of a revelation. They found him astonishingly vivid, entertaining, and accessible. Nor was this merely a function of the automatic respect commanded by a place in the syllabus. Arnold, also resurrected for special study, while he aroused some interest, remained very much a text. These are merely straws in the wind. Yet it does seem likely that fewer young people will encounter Dickens in quite the intimate and natural way that, to take random examples, James, Conrad, and Lawrence did. And in this they merely represent their respective generations. Dickens, despite the film and television, is surely losing his hold over the childhood imagination. Even the heroism of Oliver's archetypal request becomes muffled in a world of affluence: it has to be recreated by the mature imagination. Yet there is a compensation. More and more the serious reading public of the future will be made up of graduates who have passed through the English Schools of our universities or at least will have been in contact with those who have. If this seems a dismal prospect, one can only urge that there will be more and more of them. And with Dickens's new-found academic respectability they are at least likely to encounter him and to continue reading him. Perhaps this sounds too optimistic. Yet it seems true that many of the same qualities that once made for Dickens's vast popular following still operate over this new class of readers. One can sympathize with John Killham's anxiety over Lionel Trilling's report 'of a class of students capping each other in pointing out parallels between *Our Mutual Friend* and *The Waste Land*'; yet it is worth recording that many students concurred with the common reader in finding Dickens—to their own surprise—still very funny indeed.

Yet it is true that the Dickens of the modern student is a very different figure from the popular Chestertonian Dickens which made no distinction between 'early' and 'late', which could treat Sam Weller and Joe Gargery as though their respective novels were interchangeable and which generally rejoiced in abundance and humour to the neglect of the more passionate and sinister aspects of Dickens's world. I am inclined to feel that while the one Dickens is no *truer* than the other, the 'academic' Dickens is the product of a more meticulous and discriminating attention. Yet here one must reconsider the fears of the *Brains Trust* panellist. Surely in one respect he is right: academic attention can, and to some extent has, led to distortion and loss. (He did not, of course, say all this. I am reproducing here what I take to be the implications of his remark.) The qualities that held Dickens's audience (and this is really the only word for it) are somehow central to his achievement and constitute the bulk of his effects. Yet this 'bulk' is just the thing most difficult to render in the short critical essay which is the usual academic medium. This is why, leaving aside the permanently fascinating relationship between Dickens's life and art, it is the big books, like Chesterton's, Forster's, Gissing's, Johnson's, and Lindsay's, that seem to get over the feel of Dickens. The shorter essays—Orwell's and Edmund Wilson's—focus the problems or initiate new approaches. What they miss—and it is never their intention to convey it—is the pulse of energy, the extraordinary oscillation of moods and effects, the sheer density of stuff that remains our central experience of Dickens. A critic like J. Hillis Miller can give us a subtle exploration of the underlying connectedness of Dickens's effects, even to the extent of accounting for their frequent disconnectedness. Yet this still falls short of our sense of a teeming creativity, a world-building omnipotence whose language is foison.

There is no way round this difficulty. Modern criticism is a closet-activity, a self-conscious account of a private experience of reading. Yet it has to communicate with the appearance of objectivity. And so it develops a terminology rather than a true vocabulary. Terminology always has at least the appearance of being analytic. The work in hand is conveyed through dissection rather than re-creation. Yet the force of a Chestertonian approach consists precisely in its uninhibited capacity for enthusiasm. We may dissent from particular insights. Yet we recognize in Chesterton something of Dickens's total effect, one that thrives on a shared public excitement, which seems the condition of its success, the way in which it should be read. Clearly, the post-Jamesian criteria of relevance and total design imply a quite different way of reading novels. Jamesian novels work on our intelligence: their emotional impact is delayed by aesthetic distancing. Whereas—the distinction is crude but still worth making—Dickens's novels work very directly on our feelings. They involve our memories, fantasies, our very personality. Sometimes they exploit us and we feel done down. Sometimes they astound us by unexpected subtlety or tact (nothing is ever, in this sense, unexpected in James). But always they exist by virtue of impact and bulk, and these our critical terminology cannot encompass.

Still, anxiety about an academic (or, strictly, 'intellectualist') treatment of Dickens can be broken down in a more accessible way. The 'popular' approach has always dealt in terms of humour, social protest, characters, and plot. The first still, as John Gross points out, remains largely unexplored. The second has at least temporally been exhausted by Edgar Johnson and others. The last two, however, seem to have suffered by neglect in favour of symbolic and psychological readings. But perhaps discussion of character can still yield results in terms of a more directly moralistic account, particularly of the late novels. Hence part of the interest of this collection of essays might lie for the non-specialist reader in discovering how far a group of fairly representative 'academic' critics has succeeded in taking account of the 'popular' view of Dickens. Certainly, they remain academics. They are all aware, in varying degrees, of the current symbolic and psychological interpretations. All, however, have reservations, not only about the more extreme rendering of the 'symbolist' position, but also about whether this position has not now exhausted itself. Even if it has not, it certainly needs working out, with considerably more intellectual thoroughness than has always been applied in the past.

Dickens's plots have tended to be relegated to the level of mere skeletal intrigue. Yet most readers would acknowledge that Dickens can tell a story compellingly. And, if this is so, then clearly a great deal remains to be said about the economics of his narrative. Character likewise tends to an unfashionable concern among critics of the novel. Yet clearly, at least in his earlier novels, Dickens's vitality and that of the characters he creates are inseparable. It has been a prejudice of post-Jamesian criticism to view consideration of character as an abstraction from concern with total design. Yet this abstraction has been one which the popular mind, following the example of Dickens's own public readings, has found remarkably easy to make. Perhaps the popular audience *is* simply unsophisticated. Yet the workings of memory are remarkably similar to it. Even in *Bleak House*—generally considered one of Dickens's 'mature' works—the tissue of plot quickly dissolves and what remains is a great cast of people. Yet this too does not correspond with what happens when we read or re-read that novel. The cast comes magically together again and the performance—in every sense—is once more on.

Edmund Wilson and the critics who followed him felt that they were breaking new ground, that they still had to affirm, in the face of opposition, that Dickens was a major novelist. Few would now question this. The adjective 'Shakespearean' has now become commonplace; it will be found several times in these essays. Now that his greatness has been established, a greater diversity of views becomes possible. The dogma and special pleading have gone. Instead the critic can become more relaxedly the reader, can infuse his criticism with a more personal flavour. It is this, I think, that accounts for the informal, often even casual, style of most of these essays. However, the personal flavour is not merely a matter of relaxation. It also represents a determined effort to come individually to terms with Dickens's achievement and to assimilate it to more traditional notions of what constitutes greatness in art.

Several of these essays seriously tackle the question of plot. In some ways the spatial reading involved in symbolic interpretation has become dangerously facile. It ignores the temporal mode of the novel which still, after all, constitutes our main experience in reading. Two approaches seem to predominate. On the one hand, there are those like John Killham and perhaps Mrs. Hardy who tend to see Dickens's plots in terms of 'episodic intensification'. (Empson also objects to symbolic readings in favour of dramatic intensification.) This view urges that it is often a mistake to apply too rigorously Jamesian criteria of relevance and design. The novels work, sometimes by means of contrast, sometimes by virtue of the vitality of individual scenes. Mrs. Hardy interestingly argues that, at least in *Martin Chuzzlewit*, the breakdown in unity is not so much due to intellectual incompetence, as to a too purely intellectual modulation from the mode of comedy to the mode of melodrama. Other critics—particularly those concerned with the later novels—have argued for the application of criteria of unity to Dickens's novels different from those of James. John Harvey notes that Dickens's use of coincidence subserves his basic insights into the nature of reality. This reveals itself in considerable narrative tact. For example, Dickens does not always, as one might expect, exhaust all the possibilities of dramatic irony. Thus, Esther visits the house in which her father lives, but Dickens indulges in no crude Hardyesque underlining. On the contrary, 'coincidence is so extensive that it becomes natural'. Indeed, Mr. Harvey goes on, 'it expresses our sense that real life blends the casual and the causal, that things are connected and contingent': hence Dickens's form 'is expressive of his deepest sense of what life is like'. On the other hand, John Wain stays with the spatial reading: he sees the form of *Little Dorrit* as an 'outward radiation rather than linear progression'. He is supported in this by Christopher Ricks's remark that 'not a very great deal about *Little Dorrit* is to be left unsaid if The Prison is comprehensively discussed'.

Not everyone would agree. John Killham, for example, objects to the extensive application of the term 'symbol', preferring to speak of 'emblems'. He would tend to argue that such 'emblems' can give no comprehensive account of the novel in which they occur. Moreover, it can be urged that a successful symbolic reading, far from justifying the unity of a novel, may be the index of imaginative breakdown, failure of inventiveness, and incompetence in plotting. Certainly most critics readily accept that even Dickens's most mature achievements are flawed by irrelevant material, conflicts of convention and passages of purely functional and uninspired bridging. What one notices, however, is the increased readiness to acknowledge flaws without being paralysed by them.

Many of these critics are interested in a directly moralistic approach. Emphasis is removed from the nightmare and fantasy aspect of Dickens's creativity and placed more firmly on his attempt to face up to the complexity of moral life. In this reading the criminal is no longer seen as symbolic of both the revolutionary unconsciousness of society and the repressed instincts of the individual, but as a means of focusing moral issues, of facing up to the realities of human relationships beneath the snobbery and money-ethics that dominate society. This view emerges most clearly in Christopher Ricks's article on *Great Expectations*, but it is, of course, much easier to apply to that novel than to the larger, more complex works.

These essays do not bring into prominence any startlingly new view of Dickens; perhaps in that respect they are typically mid-century and post-revolutionary. What they do, however, is to pose questions about Dickens's mind. How philistine and how educated? What sort of man is he—cruel or kind? These questions, though they do not obtrude, none the less continually pose themselves just under the surface. They are raised variously by John Holloway, by John Bayley, by Julian Moynahan, and by others. John Holloway's essay is perhaps one of the most far-reaching attempts to unravel the curious tangle of assumptions, prejudices, and beliefs out of which Dickens's art is born.

What, however, is still missing is some account of Dickens's immense high spirits, his superabundant detail and journalistic *élan* —in a word—once again, the *bulk* of his effects. None the less, several critics in this book have paid their tribute, notably A. O. J. Cockshut and Robert Browning, dealing, significantly, with Dickens's first and last works. Biographical source material, so richly documented and so obviously involved with the novels at all levels—so that it is often tempting to read each novel as a retelling of Dickens's childhood experience—has sometimes threatened to envelop a purely critical approach. This material—which includes not only the Blacking Factory trauma but the Ellen Ternan revelation—seems now to be accepted and thoroughly absorbed. The relationship between children and parents which plays so large a part in Dickens's novels no longer has to be automatically referred back to Dickens's childhood situation. This theme can now be tackled for the insight it yields, not just into Dickens's own life, but into a perpetually recurring human situation. Julian Moynahan's essay takes psychological reading to a much deeper level than hitherto, one which assimilates it to considerations of structure and imagery. This assimilation of biographical material has perhaps helped to overcome some of the inhibitions set up by Dickens's notorious 'sentimentality'. The death of Paul Dombey can now be considered without necessarily asserting the critic's own tough-minded sophistication; Little Nell can die without the accompaniment of raucous laughter. But though this is true, discussion of Dickens's sentimentality, though not taboo, is still not altogether uninhibited. Embarrassment persists. The response remains negative —confining itself largely to the sort of 'explanatory' reading employed by George Ford in *Dickens and His Readers*.

Finally, a tentative attempt is being made to anchor Dickens more firmly to the world in which he lived. Mr. Holloway, again, makes an effort to see him as involved, however inarticulately, in the ideological debates of his age. His essay on *Hard Times* makes a salutary corrective to Dr. Leavis's perhaps too Lawrentian account and does something to rehabilitate the old view of Dickens as a disgruntled middlebrow. This essay continues the work of Humphry House and K. J. Fielding of placing Dickens within an intellectual context. Perhaps opposed in spirit to this sort of documentation is the Marxist approach of Jack Lindsay and Arnold Kettle, who, however, differ interestingly in their emphasis. Lindsay is mostly concerned with the way in which profound social forces interact with the lives of individuals; Kettle with Dickens's conscious rejection of capitalist social relationships. A. O. J. Cockshut, on the other hand, explores Dickens's relationship to Christianity through the symbolism of the decaying cathedral, and suggests the over-all context of Western civilization against which Dickens can be read.

There is no consistent line in this book. Instead, it is a collection of individual responses, uniform, if at all, only in a general level of response to Dickens's vitality and genius. This nobody denies. Beyond that, all is open to exploration and revaluation. Perhaps the early novels will come more fully into favour again. Perhaps we shall return to Dickens's humour. Perhaps this collection even indicates a growing *rapprochement* between the popular and academic view. If so, in the year of the 150th anniversary of his birth, this can only be a sign of the health of our appreciation.

Part One

Part One

THE HEROES AND HEROINES
OF DICKENS

Angus Wilson

To EXAMINE the heroes and heroines of Dickens is to dwell on his weaknesses and failures. Only a strong conviction of Dickens's extraordinary greatness can make such an examination either worth while or decorous; since the literary critic, unlike the reviewer, can always choose his fields and should seek surely to appreciate rather than to disparage. Even in the weak field of his heroes and heroines, Dickens made remarkable advances, for though he matured—or, to use a less evaluating word, changed—late both as a man and as an artist, his immense energy drove him on through the vast field of his natural genius to attempt the conquest of the territory that lay beyond. The development of the heroes and heroines of his novels is indeed a reflection of this change or maturing, and a measure of his success in going beyond the great domain he had so easily mastered. Some of the dilemmas that lay at the root of his difficulties were personal to him; but others were historical, and some perhaps will never be solved by any novelist.

In general, the subject of Dickens's heroes has not received much attention from serious critics. Admirers have preferred to dwell on his excellencies; detractors had found more positive qualities to excite their antipathy. The child heroes and heroines brought tears to the eyes of contemporary readers, and have found equal portions of admiration and dislike in later times. There has been some general recognition that the now highly acclaimed late novels owe something of their declared superior merit to a greater depth in the portrayal of the heroes and the heroines.

I shall not here discuss the child heroes and heroines, except to

3

suggest that as Dickens matured he found them inadequate centres for the complex social and moral structures he was trying to compose. The children too gained in realism by being removed from the centre. The peripheral Jo has a deeply moving realism that is not there in the necessarily falsely genteel Little Nell or Oliver. It is also perhaps worth noticing as a mark of Dickens's rich genius that he could be prodigal with his gifts, making masterly child portraits of Paul, David, and Pip serve merely as fractions of a large structure. Most post-Jamesian novelists would have exhausted their total energies in such portrayals of the childhood vision.

It is, however, the adult heroes and heroines with whom I am concerned. Let me first suggest the limitations which I believe hampered Dickens in successfully creating central figures in his works, and then, by analysis of the development of the heroes and heroines through his novels, throw some light perhaps upon how far he overcame or could overcome these limitations.

The historical limitations of the Victorian novelists are too well known to be worth more than a mention. The happy ending is an unfortunate distortion in Dickens's work as it is in that of the other great Victorians, but, despite the change made to *Great Expectations,* it goes deeper than a mere capitulation to the whims of readers. With Dickens as with Thackeray, though for different reasons, the contemporary idea of domestic happiness as the resolution of, or perhaps more fairly one should say, the counterpoise to social evil, was a strongly held personal conviction. Even more vital to Dickens was the idea of pure love as the means of redemption of flawed, weak, or sinful men. Neither of these beliefs can properly take the weight that he imposed upon them; though the latter, at any rate, is not such a psychological falsity perhaps as many twentieth-century critics have thought. The main destructive effort of this exaggerated view of love as a moral solvent falls upon those characters in the novels who, under any view, could be regarded as heroes and heroines. Closely allied to the popular prejudice in favour of wedding bells and the patter of tiny feet is the contemporary absolute demand for sexual purity. There has been a recent tendency to play down the effects of this on the Victorian novel. True, these effects have so often been discussed as now to be trite, but that does not unfortunately diminish them. This censorship did, in fact, reduce the great Victorian novelists in the sexual sphere to a childish status beside their continental contemporaries. It is surprising how often they can get past the ban by suggestion; it is surprising how often the ban does not matter to an imaginative reader; again, our freedom is only relative and has its own danger of absurdity; all this is true—yet the fact remains that our great Victorian novelists were forced at times to devices that are false, ridiculous, or blurred. And these faults occur too often at the moral heart of their work. In English fashion, and with reason, we may take pride in the degree to which our Victorian novelists achieved greatness in spite of this—but we can't efface it. No characters, of course, suffer so greatly as the heroes and heroines. Once again, however, I would suggest that Dickens had a special personal relationship to this sexual censorship—and that, while it sometimes led him into exceptionally absurd devices, it also produced a characteristically powerful effect. The sexual life of Charles Dickens, like that of most Victorians, has become a shop-soiled subject, but one may briefly say four things of it—he was a strongly sensual man, he had a deep social and emotional need for family life and love, he had a compensating claustrophobic dislike of the domestic scene, and he woke up to these contradictions in his sexual make-up very late. Surely the distressing feature about the famous letter to the press upon the break-up of his marriage is not so much the tasteless publicity, but the tasteless publicity sought by a man of Dickens's years and standing. He acted at best like a young man blinded by new fame. His emotional life, in fact, for all his many children, was by most standards immature. Thackeray, very percipient where his dislike of Dickens was concerned, hit the right note, when he said of Kate, 'the poor matron'. Dickens behaved not as a middle-aged man but as a young fool or as an old fool.

The contemporary censorship, in fact, went along with, rather than against, Dickens's natural inclinations. His submerged, but fierce, sensuality was to run some strange courses from the days of John Chester until it came to light in the diverging streams of Wrayburn and Headstone. Seduction withheld, deferred, foiled—at any rate never accomplished—produced many interesting and complex characters, who would not have been born in a fiction that reflected the real world where men are more resolute and women are weaker.

Perhaps even more important in its effect on his heroes and heroines than the imperfect view of love and the impossible view of sex that Dickens shared with his readers was the ambiguous view of Victorian society that he shared with so many of the artists and intellectuals of his age. Broadly speaking, one could say that the young

Dickens aspired to a respectable middle-class radicalism attacking particular social evils, and ended as a middle-aged revolutionary with a peculiar hostility to the middle classes. Such an evolution in a man not given to intellectual self-analysis inevitably produced ambiguities in his portrayal of every social class at one time or another. And in no group of characters is this unconscious evolution with its accompanying contradictions more clearly displayed than in the young men who stand at the heroic centre of his books. This uneven course in his social opinions, now veering, now tacking, yet for all its changes moving in one final direction, affected his attitude to the future and to the past, to all classes, to education, to money, to ambition, to work, to play, to conformity, and to rebellion. This strange and complex pattern of life may be observed working out in various ways among his heroes and heroines.

Any account of Dickens must start with *Pickwick Papers*, the novel which announces an age of innocence before the course has begun. Perhaps Dickens never produced so satisfactory a hero as Mr. Pickwick again—a man who, like his author, imperceptibly changes; but not from hope to despair, rather from nullity to positive goodness. None of the problems of Dickens are met in this book: Mr. Pickwick developed in the garden of Eden before the fall, the next step from him was to Oliver and Nell—children, at least, have their measure of original sin. Yet no article on Dickens's heroes should fail to salute the perfection of Mr. Pickwick before it goes on to the real story.

Apart from the children, the first group of heroes may be seen leading up to the self-portrait of David Copperfield. Like Mr. Pickwick, this 'walking gentleman', genteel hero group begins in near nullity: one cannot discuss Harry Maylie or Edward Chester, for they are not there. Nicholas and Martin advance us a few steps: they are haters of hypocrisy, cant, and cruelty; sharp-tongued and humorous; hot-tempered; inclined to selfishness; a bit weak and spoilt; pale reflections, with their eye for the absurd, of the unintrospective young Dickens as he saw himself. Martin, with Jonas and Chevy Slyme for his relations, can hardly claim gentility; but Nicholas is a born gentleman of a somewhat ill-defined kind, although his uncle is a money-lender. The young, socially unsure Dickens had need not only of false gentility and of hatred of the aristocracy, he needed also a suffused and vague love of the past—a mark of the genteel. So Nicholas's first act, when he became a rich and prosperous merchant, was to buy his father's 'old house . . . none of the old rooms were ever pulled down, no old tree was ever rooted up, nothing with which there was any association of bygone times was ever removed or changed'.

It is something of the same undefined traditional gentility which so endears to David Copperfield Dr. Strong's vaguely traditional old school and the aroma of scholarship given off by his improbable dictionary. David is the culmination, in fact, of these purely genteel heroes for whom Pip was later to atone. Of course, being a self-portrait, David has more life, but, after childhood, it is a feeble ray. To begin with, who can believe that he is a novelist? Indeed, although he is said to be a model of hard work, we never have any sense of it except in his learning shorthand. Dickens was far too extrovert in those days to analyse the qualities in himself that made for his genius. It is notable that David is no more than 'advanced in fame and for-tune', where Dickens was advanced in literary skill and imaginative power. It is also notable that after childhood, nothing happened to David himself except the passion of his love for Dora and the shock of her death—and these, which should be poignant, are somehow made less so by being smiled back upon through the tears as part of youth's folly and life's pageant. *David Copperfield* is technically a very fine novel of the sentimental education genre, but the mood of mellow, wise reflection is surely too easily held; and, when we think of Dickens's age at the time of its writing, held all too prematurely. 'Advanced in fortune and fame', as a result, has inevitably a smug sound, and 'my domestic joy was perfect' seems to demand the Nemesis that was to come in real life.

Nor is this smug, genteel, conformist quality of David helped by Agnes. A successful novelist guided by her 'deep wisdom' would surely become a smug, insensitive, comfortable old best seller of the worst kind. Agnes, indeed, is the first of the group of heroines who mark the least pleasing, most frumpy, and smug vision of ideal womanhood that he produced. Agnes, in fact, is betrayed by Esther Summerson, when Dickens in his next book so unwisely decided to speak through his heroine's voice. It is not surprising that this wise, womanly, housekeeping, moralizing, self-congratulating, busy little creature should have needed a good dose of childlikeness, a dose of Little Nell to keep her going when she reappears as Little Dorrit. If we cannot believe in the child-woman Little Dorrit, at least we are not worried as we are by Agnes or Esther Summerson about her

7

complete lack of a physical body—a deficiency so great that Esther's smallpox-spoilt face jars us because she has no body upon which a head could rest.

But if nothing happens to David himself after Mr. Murdstone goes off the scene, something does happen in the novel, about which David (Dickens) uses language that suggests that there lies the real drama —as well he may, for with Steerforth's seduction of Em'ly, and indeed with Steerforth himself, we are at the beginning of all those twists and turns by which Dickens eventually transforms a somewhat stagy villain into a new sort of full-sized hero. From Steerforth to Eugene Wrayburn is the road of self-discovery. Of all the would-be seducers in Dickens's novels, James Steerforth alone gets his prey; yet he is the only one, until Wrayburn, whom Dickens seems to have wished to redeem. If we look at the facts of Steerforth's character, it may be difficult to see why. From the moment that he so revoltingly gets Mr. Mell dismissed at Creakle's school until his carefully planned seduction of Em'ly he *does* nothing to commend himself. Yet David (and surely Dickens) uses language that would save if it could—'But he slept—let me think of him so again—as I had often seen him sleep at school; and thus, in this silent hour I left him. Never more, oh God forgive you, Steerforth, to touch that passive hand in love and friendship. Never, never more!' . . . 'Yes, Steerforth, long removed from the scenes of this poor history! My sorrow may bear involuntary witness against you at the Judgement Throne; but my angry thoughts or reproaches never will, I know.' And at the last—'among the ruins of the home he had wronged, I saw him lying with his hand upon his arm, as I had often seen him lie at school'. If Dickens could have redeemed Steerforth he surely would have done so. And, indeed, he did; for Eugene Wrayburn is as much a redemption of Steerforth as Pip is a scapegoat for the falsities in David. On the whole, as I suggest, redemption through Wrayburn is a somewhat arbitrary business; but before that redemption came about, the figure of Steerforth had suffered under many guises and, in the course of his translation to hero, had borne witness to many changes in Dickens's social and moral outlook, had even assisted in the birth of a heroine more adequate to Dickens's mature outlook than either Little Nell or Agnes, or indeed the strange hybrid figure of Little Dorrit.

To trace these changes we should perhaps go back before Steerforth to earlier seductions in the novels. At the start the seducer is a cynical rake or libertine—John Chester or Sir Mulberry Hawk. He stands full square for the aristocratic dandy whom the middle-class radical Dickens detests as the source of outdated arbitrary power. Yet we have only to look at Boz in his early pictures to see the beringed and ringleted dandy—or is it the 'gent'? Dick Swiveller is kindly treated. In his adolescence surely it was among the would-be swells of Dick Swiveller's world that Dickens moved—the direct butt, no doubt, of any real dandy's contempt and laughter. The seducer, then, up to *Dombey*, is a crude class symbol.

Dombey and Son brings us farther forward. Carker has some genuine sensuality, of the cold, calculating, rather epicene imitation-Byron kind that the early nineteenth century must often have bred. True, he is vulgar, hypocritical, and apparently subservient—but then, unlike Steerforth, he has to scheme and work for his living. Like Steerforth, his Byronic professional seducing spills over into other sorts of pleasure-loving—a somewhat ornately comfortable villa. There are four things in which Steerforth differs from him, apart from age: Steerforth despises the world, he puts other values above work, he sometimes wishes that he was not wasting his life, he has the vestige of a power to love or at any rate to want to be loved. It is not very much luggage, yet it proves enough to make the long journey to Eugene Wrayburn. Carker fails in his seduction, but then in Edith Dombey he has a much more difficult job than little Em'ly presents to Steerforth. There were two roads open for the Dickensian seducer—glamour (it was presumably this that Steerforth used, though little Em'ly's last note to Peggotty shows small evidence that she has felt it) or boredom. Boredom and self-distaste, these were the marks of the woman who had already sold herself into loveless marriage—Edith, Louisa Bounderby, Honoria Dedlock, if she had not already been seduced before the novel began. Pride saves Edith Dombey; pride would have saved Lady Dedlock; pride and an instinct of self-preservation saved Louisa. Yet it is hardly a fair contest—Mr. Carker emits his faint ray of vulgar sensuality, James Harthouse his rather superior brand of Steerforth's worldly charm. But, if it only takes one to make a rape, it takes two to make a seduction; and there is nothing in Edith or Louisa to respond. They are looking for flight from a desperate situation and indeed they take it; but they are not looking for any species of sexual love. The female equivalent to the sort of professional minor Byronism that Steerforth and Harthouse and Gowan, no doubt, in his relations with Miss Wade, offer, is the minor, rather half-hearted coquetry that is touched on in Dolly Vardon, punished in Fanny Dorrit and Estella, and finally redeemed in Bella Wilfer. But Estella and Bella are more than coquettes, they are proud, frozen, unhappy women anxious to be free of desperate homes, they combine in fact the nearest approach that Dickens gets to a sensually alive woman with the proud cold beauties—Edith, Louisa, and Honoria. *Our Mutual Friend*, in fact, contains the developed hero and the most developed heroine in Dickens's fiction. The one has come a long journey from the seducer-villain; and the other, almost as long a journey from the coquette and the runaway wife. Even so they remain separate, each is re-claimed by a nullity, John Harmon and Lizzie Hexam. Yet in them Dickens had admitted to the saved a degree of sexual reality that argues well for the future.

We may leave Bella on one side; she has brought some frailty, some liveliness and some sexual warmth to Dickens's heroines; but she plays little part in the evolution of Dickens's social or moral out-look—it was not a woman's rôle to do so.

Eugene Wrayburn is a far more interesting case. His salvation is really immensely arbitrary. Even after he has left Lizzie for the last time before Headstone's murderous attack, he has not given up his ideas of seduction entirely—his father's voice tells him, 'You wouldn't marry for some money and some station, because you were frightfully likely to become bored. Are you less frightfully likely to become bored marrying for no money and no station?' It is indeed his rival's blows that save him. Yet we have seen that Steerforth had certain pleas to offer; Wrayburn offers all the same pleas and by this time they have become more urgent to Dickens. First, contempt for the World and for success—this, once a hidden admiration, is now the centre of Dickens's moral values. Private income, public school, and university education, all these may be forgiven if they produce a despiser of bourgeois society. Dandy insolence, once the mark of an arbitrary, outdated order, is now the badge of rejection of Podsnap. Other values above work and duty? This has been amply confirmed by a rather separate but very successful hero, the sad, Calvinist-destroyed Clennam. Then the vestige of regret for a wasted life has gone through many fires since Steerforth's day; it has been purified by Richard Carstone and above all by Sidney Carton, whom Shrews-bury, gentlemanly bohemianism, and the Bar could not entirely destroy. Above all the need for love has also been through Carton's fire so that Lucie can say to Darnay, 'remember how strong we are in our happiness, and how weak he is in his misery'. Loneliness, failure, pride, bitter rejection of all that made up Victorian progress and Victorian morality, a considered rejection of duty and hard work as moral ends, Dickens comes through to acceptance of these in the person of Eugene Wrayburn. And sensuality? Does he also redeem his own strong sensuality? This, I think, is less certain. The thin, calculated sensuality that runs from the Byronic Steerforth to the Yellow Book Wrayburn is not surely of the obsessive, tortured kind that we suspect in Dickens. Does not this real sensuality peep through in more sinister places? In Pecksniff's scene with Mary Graham, in Jonas's wooing of Mercy, in Uriah's glances at Agnes—there is more real lust there than in all the wiles of Steerforth and Harthouse, in all the brutalities of Gowan. And now the lust comes up again on the wrong side, in slavery to the Victorian doctrines of hard work, of fact, of ambition, and of self-betterment—all things that had played a large part in Dickens's own life and which he had now rejected. The obsessive lust of Bradley Headstone finds no redemption. Yet as he rolls on the ground, after Charlie Hexam has left him, I believe that Dickens feels as strong a pity for him as David had felt for Steerforth. Would Dickens perhaps have left from here on another long pilgrimage deep into the holy places of his own soul? Can Jasper be the next strange step in that new pilgrimage?

THE SYMBOLISM OF DICKENS

William Empson

A POINT about *Oliver Twist* seems to me where one needs to
start in considering this topic. Oliver, though a gentleman by heredity and heir to a property, has been brought up from birth in an
orphanage with no other contacts; it is a wicked place, but he is
uncorrupted by it. This is very believable; but also, unlike the other
orphans, who are represented as talking some kind of dialect, he
talks the stilted grammar of a hero of Scott or a 'juvenile lead' in
Victorian melodrama, which he has had no opportunity to learn. I
suppose the readers never quite believed in that, but many would
regard it, if they had it pointed out, as a convenient simplification
carrying the essential truth; it could also be recognized as a fairy-
story tradition, and like the immediately recognizable royalty of the
shepherdess Perdita, but they would rightly feel that this kind of
explanation was not what was needed. Dickens would impute a
serious meaning even to this first example of his symbolism, though
he probably took the method for granted; he meant that all the little
boys in the orphanage were being robbed of their English heritage,
and he thought the best way to make his readers feel so was to
make them imagine one of their own boys in such a place. The
farcical plot, in which the villain spends his whole time tracking
Oliver to keep him out of his rights, is good enough theatre but can
only be felt as sensible if it is given this symbolical meaning. But
then again, the melodramas Dickens was imitating would regularly
gain weight from social feelings which could only be fitted on to the
plot through an unconscious use of this kind of symbolism; the
method was all around him, and his great power of sympathy gave
him an easy intimacy with it. He seems to have become interested in
the theory later, when he found churning out plots more of an effort.

13

However, after recognizing the naturalness and force of the symbolic process, we should also recognize that it is liable to have unintended side effects. The great protest of *Oliver Twist* is somehow less alarming than it sets out to be. After all, for a reader looking at it in a practical way, and wondering what to do about the sad cases which the new novel is exposing, the detail of the story is likely to offer a very soothing reflection. All you need do, really, is go through these workhouses and pick out the little gentlemen, because all the other little boys are just pigs. Dickens would have been indignant if anyone had told him that this was what the book meant, but the method is always liable to be caught out in some such way. It might be argued, indeed, that Dickens was deeply in tune with his audience, and himself scarred by the memory of the few months in the blacking factory, so that unconsciously he intended this effect, as part of the symbol which he found a satisfying whole. Perhaps this is true in a way, so far at least as he was determined to let no shadow fall on his young hero; but if he had been warned of this possible misreading he would (obviously, I think) have struggled to find a way of getting round it.[1]

Critics tend to invoke symbolism, by a very worthy impulse, when they know that something about the story has been found absurd but none the less feel that the effect as a whole is good. They are often right; but it is never a sufficient justification of one of these strained bits to prove from the rest of the novel that it is symbolic. I think, indeed, that the history of literary controversy, especially about Dickens, has led to a rather comical false distinction. Many people in his time, and even more people just after his time, said that the old vulgarian was theatrical; as for example in the fierce parody of Dickens by Trollope in *The Warden*. To be theatrical was part of being crude and popular, though the real accusation of Trollope was that it meant lying political propaganda. Scholarly critics at last spoke up in favour of Dickens, after such different authors as Ibsen and

[1] I was so confident of this that I did not check it as I should have done; Dickens is an author we are prone to re-write in our own minds. Since then I have found he *did* 'take precautions', chiefly by using reported speech for all the charity-boys, the hero included. The only sentence from any child at the orphanage is the demand for More, which Oliver has been deputed to speak (however, a dying inmate of the baby-farm which he leaves at the age of nine has spoken with high poetry). Oliver and Noah are allowed direct speech after they have run away, when the contrast feels mainly one of character; even so, the characteristic rhetoric of Oliver is delayed till farther on in the novel. He is then very little older; and the arrangement, I submit, is a matter of precaution rather than of realism.

Mallarmé had been praised for some kind of symbolism; they felt, no doubt, that the great reputation of Dickens on the Continent must be a warning sign that previous English critics had been wrong in disagreeing with the English people about him; so they began finding he was full of symbolism. This technique was intellectual or aesthetically advanced, so it gave Dickens class. But really the devices which are called symbolic are precisely the same as those which were called theatrical; I agree that they are often good, but calling them by the new name does not give any help in deciding which of them is good.

It seems to me a misfortune that the literary theory about symbolism has developed so much without thought of the tradition of fair-minded public controversy. To take what is perhaps the most prominent case, I find the injustice altogether too tiresome when D. H. Lawrence expects us to believe Chatterley had always been psychologically impotent because he has got wounded in battle; but, for that matter, if I were a negro I would be very cross with the excellent work of Conrad, *Heart of Darkness*. After presenting the wickedness of the whites towards the blacks very firmly, he uses all his power of 'atmosphere' to suggest that the primitiveness of the blacks somehow seduced the whites into treating them wickedly, an idea which is quite undemonstrated even if he could have found some defence for it. The symbolism of Dickens, I think, is often fully justified as well as dramatically or poetically very impressive; but the bad bits in Dickens come where it isn't. I find the rhetoric over the death of Jo ('and dying thus around you every day') very good, chiefly because of the argument that epidemics are no respecters of class; this makes it quite different from the death of Little Nell, which is made worse by a falsity in the religious position. A literary critic who thinks he is forbidden by aesthetic theory to consider the beliefs of the author naturally cannot tell the difference between one bout of sentiment and another. Such at least is the position I would wish to take up, though I realize that it would take a great deal more work to offer a sustained argument about Dickens.

Part Two

Part Two

SKETCHES BY BOZ

Robert Browning

WRITING TO John Forster from Lausanne in 1846, Dickens declared that he found it difficult to write fast when away from London:

I suppose this is partly the effect of two years' ease, and partly of the absence of streets and numbers of figures. I can't express how much I want these. It seems as if they supplied something to my brain, which it cannot bear, when busy, to lose. For a week or fortnight I can write prodigiously in a retired place (as at Broadstairs), and a day in London sets me up again and starts me. But the toil and labour of writing, day after day, without that magic lantern, is IMMENSE!! [1]

The *Sketches by Boz* is Dickens's first published work, and it is appropriate that it should record his intimacy with London and its citizens.

In 'Thoughts About People' (Characters, I), where Dickens describes a group of London apprentices on a Sunday jaunt, we can discern the stimulation the want of which he felt in Lausanne:

We walked down the Strand, a Sunday or two ago, behind a little group; and they furnished food for our amusement the whole way. They had come out of some part of the city; it was between three and four o'clock in the afternoon; and they were on their way to the Park. There were four of them, all arm-in-arm, with white kid gloves like so many bridegrooms, light trousers of unprecedented patterns, and coats for which the English language has yet no name—a kind of cross between a great-coat and a surtout, with the collar of the one, the skirts of the other, and pockets peculiar to themselves.

Each of the gentlemen carried a thick stick, with a large tassel at the top, which he occasionally twirled gracefully round; and the whole four, by way of looking easy and unconcerned, were walking with a paralytic

---

[1] W. Dexter, *The Letters of Charles Dickens*, 1938, Vol. I, p. 782.

swagger irresistibly ludicrous. One of the party had a watch about the size and shape of a reasonable Ribstone pippin, jammed into his waistcoat-pocket, which he carefully compared with the clocks at St. Clement's and the New Church, the illuminated clock at Exeter 'Change, the clock of St. Martin's Church, and the clock of the Horse Guards. When they at last arrived in St. James's Park, the member of the party who had the best-made boots on, hired a second chair expressly for his feet, and flung himself on this two-pennyworth of sylvan luxury with an air which levelled all distinctions between Brookes's and Snooks's, Crockford's and Bagnigge Wells.[2]

The stimulation was bred partly of familiarity and partly of the variety of spectacle, the sheer thickness of impressions. In different sketches, Dickens drops in at the bar of a large gin-shop and watches the washerwomen and Irish labourers taking their quarterns of gin, he calls at Bellamy's, the dining room of the Houses of Parliament, and marks a gourmet peer gloating over a Stilton, he joins the coal-heavers 'quaffing large draughts of Barclay's best' in the old pub in Scotland Yard, and he peers between the blue curtains of a West-end cigar shop to see the well-dressed malcontents relieving their boredom by flirting with the young lady 'in amber with large ear-rings' who sits behind the counter 'in a blaze of adoration and gas light'.

The London of the *Sketches* is not fictitious. Dickens's realism, unlike the superficial realism of Pierce Egan's *Life in London*, does not confer glamour on the sordid and squalid. And whereas Egan confines his regard to central London, St. James's to St. Giles, Dickens takes in the whole metropolis with its rapidly extending suburbs, such as Stamford Hill, Camberwell, Norbury, and Richmond. He chronicles much that is small in scale and dull-toned with such fidelity, that it is the distinction of the *Sketches*, as it is that of Joyce's *Dubliners*, that the reader senses the life of a whole city.

Just as the London of the *Sketches* is, despite changes, recogniz-ably the London Hogarth drew, so it is recognizably the London we know today. Small eating-houses and taverns have not changed as much as might be thought. Their ambience is much the same. The chaffing humour of Dickens's cabmen and omnibus cads is still to be met with in their modern counterparts, taxi-drivers and bus

[2] Quotations are from *Sketches by Boz* in the New Oxford Illustrated Dickens, Oxford University Press, 1957, the text of which is that of the later, considerably revised, editions of the work.

conductors, when those are Cockneys. The British Museum still knows readers like the one described by Dickens in 'Shabby-Genteel People' (Characters, X):

He was in his chair every morning, just as the clock struck ten; he was always the last to leave the room in the afternoon; and when he did, he quitted it with the air of a man who knew not where else to go for warmth and quiet. There he used to sit all day, as close to the table as possible, in order to conceal the lack of buttons on his coat; with his old hat carefully deposited at his feet, where he evidently flattered himself it escaped observation.

About two o'clock, you would see him munching a French roll or a penny loaf; not taking it out of his pocket at once, like a man who knew he was only making a lunch; but breaking off little bits in his pocket, and eating them by stealth. He knew too well it was his dinner.

And the contents of junk-shops in the suburbs answer very well to the description in 'Brokers' And Marine-Store Shops' (Scenes, XXI).

On a board, at the side of the door, are placed about twenty books, all odd volumes; and as many wine-glasses—all different patterns; several locks, an old earthenware pan, full of rusty keys; two or three gaudy chimney-ornaments—cracked, of course; the remains of a lustre, without any drops; a round frame like a capital O, which has once held a mirror; a flute, complete with the exception of the middle joint; a pair of curling-irons; and a tinder-box. In front of the shop window are ranged some half-dozen high-backed chairs, with spinal complaints and wasted legs; a corner cupboard; two or three very dark mahogany tables with flaps like mathematical problems . . .

Of course, Dickens is more than a good observer, even in this his first book, but he was, in Henry James's phrase, 'one of the people on whom nothing is lost', and it is the first recommendation for this volume, that in it he gave such a lively account of what he saw and heard in London. At the time of writing most of the papers here collected, Dickens was a press reporter; and, whatever the deficiencies of his formal education, it is clear that he could hardly have had a better training for the craft of novel writing.

Modern reprints of Sketches by Boz follow the Chapman and Hall edition of 1839 in the disposition of material, most of which had previously appeared in journals and in the two issues by Macrone (First Series, 1836; Second Series, 1837). In 1839 the papers were distributed into four groups: 'Seven Sketches from our Parish', 'Scenes', 'Characters', and 'Tales'. This arrangement is perhaps regrettable inasmuch as the Parish sketches, with which a new reader is likely to begin, are too consciously droll for modern taste.[3] The age was one of popular humorists, and the proliferating journals of the day were crammed with comicalities and *facetiae*. The Regency love of punning had not abated; both Theodore Hook and Thomas Hood were, at their worst, gravely funny. Dickens did not altogether escape the infection, and a few of the sketches are disfigured by tasteless drollery. The Parish sketches are not without merit, but they are much inferior to others in the collection.

Dickens owes not a little to the ephemeral publications of the eighteen-twenties and eighteen-thirties. Mr. Pickwick and (in the *Sketches*) Mr. Minns may be related to the literature of comic discomfort. But granting that, the differences are as remarkable as the affinities. It is instructive to compare John Poole's paper on 'Early Rising'[4] with Dickens's 'Early Coaches' (Scenes, XV). Poole exaggerates:

Two towels, which had been left wet in the room, were standing on a chair, bolt upright, as stiff as the poker itself, which you might almost as easily have bent. The tooth-brushes were riveted to the glass in which I had left them, and of which (in my haste to disengage them from their stronghold), they carried away a fragment; the soap was cemented to the dish; my shaving-brush was a mass of ice. In shape more appalling Discomfort had never appeared on earth.

Dickens is notably more restrained and more truthful, and leans not at all on tired figurative language:

You proceed to dress yourself, with all possible dispatch. The flaring flat candle with the long snuff gives light enough to show that the things you want are not where they ought to be, and you undergo a trifling delay in consequence of having carefully packed up one of your boots in your over-anxiety of the preceding night. You soon complete your toilet, however, for you are not particular on such an occasion, and you shaved yesterday evening.

It says much for Dickens's taste that he eschewed the kind of extravanganza that Hook and Poole affected. If Dickens exaggerates,

---

[3] The Parish sketches were placed at the beginning of the first series of *Sketches by Boz*, Macrone, 1836, so they may be said to have occupied this position from the earliest publication in volume form.

[4] *Sketches and Recollections*, 1835.

as he does in the 'Tales' and in later fictions, he does not do so pompously. The writing is brisk and nimble. The contemporary writer whose influence was strongest and most beneficent is Leigh Hunt. This is the third paragraph of Dickens's 'Greenwich Fair' (Scenes, XII).

The road to Greenwich during the whole of Easter Monday, is in a state of perpetual bustle and noise. Cabs, hackney-coaches, 'shay' carts, coal-waggons, stages, omnibuses, sociables, gigs, donkey-chaises—all crammed with people (for the question never is, what the horse can draw, but what the vehicle will hold), roll along at their utmost speed; the dust flies in clouds, ginger-beer corks go off in volleys, the balcony of every public-house is crowded with people, smoking and drinking, half the private houses are turned into tea-shops, fiddles are in great request, every little fruit-shop displays its stall of gilt gingerbread and penny toys; turnpike men are in despair; horses won't go on, and wheels will come off; ladies in 'caravans' scream with fright at every fresh concussion, and their admirers find it necessary to sit remarkably close to them, by way of encouragement; servants-of-all-work, who are not allowed to have followers, and have got a holiday for the day, make the most of their time with the faithful admirer who waits for a stolen interview at the corner of the street every night, when they go to fetch the beer—apprentices grow sentimental and straw-bonnet makers kind.

With this we may compare Leigh Hunt's paper, 'A Now: Descriptive Of A Hot Day': [5]

Now blinds are let down, and doors thrown open, and flannel waistcoats left off, and cold meat preferred to hot, and wonder expressed why tea continues so refreshing, and people delight to sliver lettuces into bowls, and apprentices water door-ways with tin-canisters that lay several atoms of dust.

I think that Dickens learnt from Hunt this technique of a congery of simple sentences (often in the passive). From Hunt, too, he may have acquired a feeling for the poetry of the urban scene. This influence, if influence it is, is completely digested in 'The Streets—Morning' (Scenes, I). That sketch is written with a tact and delicacy that Dickens did not always command, and it called forth one of George Cruikshank's best designs in illustration, that of a street breakfast. A reader unacquainted with *Sketches by Boz* would do well to begin with it.

[5] *The Indicator*, June 28, 1820.

In 'Astley's' (Scenes, XI), the sketch of a visit to the circus, a family party in the audience is described with a simplicity and economy that looks deceptively easy:

> The first five minutes were occupied in taking the shawls off the little girls, and adjusting the bows which ornamented their hair; then it was providentially discovered that one of the little boys was seated behind a pillar and could not see, so the governess was stuck behind the pillar, and the boy lifted into her place. Then pa drilled the boys, and directed the stowing away of their pocket-handkerchiefs, and ma having first nodded and winked to the governess to pull the girls' frocks a little more off their shoulders, stood up to review the little troop—an inspection which appeared to terminate much to her own satisfaction, for she looked with a complacent air at pa, who was standing up at the further end of the seat. Pa returned the glance, and blew his nose very emphatically; and the poor governess peeped out from behind the pillar, and timidly tried to catch ma's eye, with a look expressive of her high admiration of the whole family.

It is as fine a distillation of early Victorian England as any of the genre paintings it so much resembles. From the family group Dickens turns his regard to the clown, the riding-master, and the bare-back rider, with a digression on what such performers look like beyond the glamour of sawdust and flaring gas-jets. By this means Dickens neither ignores nor dispels the illusion. His viewpoint is neither naïve nor cynical:

> Nor can we quite divest ourself of our old feeling of reverence for the riding-master, who follows the clown with a long whip in his hand, and bows to the audience with graceful dignity. He is none of your second-rate riding-masters in nankeen dressing-gowns, with brown frogs, but the regular gentleman-attendant on the principal riders, who always wears a military uniform with a table-cloth inside the breast of the coat, in which costume he forcibly reminds one of a fowl trussed for roasting. He is— but why should we attempt to describe that of which no description can convey an adequate idea? Everybody knows the man, and everybody remembers his polished boots, his graceful demeanour, stiff, as some misjudging persons have in their jealousy considered it, and the splendid head of black hair, parted high on the forehead, to impart to the coun-tenance an appearance of deep thought and poetic melancholy. His soft and pleasing voice, too, is in perfect unison with his noble bearing, as he humours the clown by indulging in a little badinage; and the striking recollection of his own dignity, with which he exclaims, 'Now, sir, if you please, inquire for Miss Woolford, sir', can never be forgotten. The

graceful air, too, with which he introduces Miss Woolford into the arena, and, after assisting her to the saddle, follows her fairy courser round the circle, can never fail to create a deep impression in the bosom of every female servant present.

We must hesitate, even as Dickens does, to find the riding-master ridiculous. The description of the man and his deportment, though ironical, is respectful. This man personates the idea of a circus riding-master to perfection. As such he cannot be false, even though he owes his manly chest to a table-cloth stuffed inside the jacket of his uniform.

Dickens is viewing the circus with evident nostalgia, as the first paragraph of the sketch avows. The circus and its personnel were to the child the very enshrinement of beauty, grace, and wit. For the grown man the enchantment has fled, but not the affection. Such illusions and such impostures are beneficent.

Dickens digresses, as he says, to describe the misery and squalor of 'the class of people, who hang about the stage-doors of our minor theatres in the daytime' hoping for employment:

That young fellow in the faded brown coat, and very full light green trousers, pulls down the wristbands of his check shirt, as ostentatiously as if it were of the finest linen, and cocks the white hat of the summer-before-last as knowingly over his right eye, as if it were a purchase of yesterday. Look at the dirty white Berlin gloves, and the cheap silk handkerchief stuck in the bosom of his threadbare coat. Is it possible to see him for an instant, and not come to the conclusion that he is the walking gentleman who wears a blue surtout, clean collar, and white trousers, for half an hour, and then shrinks into his worn-out scanty clothes: who has to boast night after night of his splendid fortune, with the painful consciousness of a pound a week and his boots to find; to talk of his father's mansion in the country, with a dreary recollection of his own two-pair back, in the New Cut; and to be envied and flattered as the favoured lover of a rich heiress, remembering all the while that the ex-dancer at home is in the family way, and out of an engagement?

The poor player has an almost symbolic rôle. Many of Dickens's fictional heroes are suspended between poverty and riches, between comfort and squalor, between respectability and crime. The actor of bit parts in minor theatres is, in a special way, of their number. He, and the circus personnel who resemble him, acquire a moral signi-ficance for Dickens: they act a lie, as (more subtly) Oliver Twist, William Dorrit, and Pip act a lie. The riding-master who personates a gentleman is a figure whom Dickens will not ridicule, partly from sentimental regard, but partly, too, from an unspoken, and probably unconscious, identification with the man. There are subtler and less amiable frauds than a table-cloth thrust into a jacket.

'The Mistaken Milliner' (Characters, VIII) is not completely successful. The story is a little huddled. But it opens brilliantly:

Miss Amelia Martin was pale, tallish, thin, and two-and-thirty—what ill-natured people would call plain, and police reports interesting. She was a milliner and dressmaker, living on her business and not above it. If you had been a young lady in service, and had wanted Miss Martin, as a great many young ladies in service did, you would just have stepped up, in the evening, to number forty-seven, Drummond Street, George Street, Euston Square, and after casting your eye on a brass door-plate, one foot ten by one and a half, ornamented with a great brass knob at each of the four corners, and bearing the inscription 'Miss Martin; millinery and dressmaking, in all its branches'; you'd just have knocked two loud knocks at the street-door; and down would have come Miss Martin herself, in a merino gown of the newest fashion, black velvet bracelets on the genteelest principle, and other little elegancies of the most approved description.

If Miss Martin knew the young lady who called, or if the young lady who called had been recommended by any other young lady whom Miss Martin knew, Miss Martin would forthwith show her upstairs into the two-pair front, and chat she would—*so* kind, and *so* comfortable—it really wasn't like a matter of business, she was so friendly; and then Miss Martin, after contemplating the figure and general appearance of the young lady in service with great apparent admiration, would say how well she would look, to be sure, in a low dress with short sleeves; made very full in the skirts, with four tucks in the bottom; to which the young lady in service would reply in terms expressive of her entire concurrence in the notion, and of the virtuous indignation with which she reflected on the tyranny of 'Missis', who wouldn't allow a young girl to wear a short sleeve of an arternoon—no, nor nothing smart, not even a pair of earrings; let alone hiding people's heads of hair under them frightful caps. At the termination of this complaint, Miss Amelia Martin would distantly suggest certain dark suspicions that some people were jealous on account of their own daughters, and were obliged to keep their servants' charms under, for fear they should get married first, which was no uncommon circumstance—leastways she had known two or three young ladies in service, who had married a great deal better than their missises, and *they* were not very good-looking either; and then the young lady would inform Miss Martin, in confidence, that how one of their young ladies was engaged to a young man and was a-going to be married, and Missis was so proud about it there was no bearing of her; but how she needn't hold her head quite so high neither, for, after all, he was only a clerk. And, after expressing due contempt for clerks in general, and the engaged clerk in particular, and the highest opinion possible of themselves and each other, Miss Martin and the young lady in service would bid each other good night, in a friendly but perfectly genteel manner: and the one went back to her 'place', and the other to her room on the second-floor front.

The first paragraph consists of three sentences. The first two are statements made with almost epigrammatic incisiveness. The third is a long elastic sentence that interestingly develops a borrowed idiom, that of such a young lady in service: 'you would just have stepped up . . . you'd just have knocked . . . and down would have come Miss Martin herself'. Even in this mildly oblique way, the narration acquires actuality.

The second paragraph is made up of three long sentences. Here Dickens mingles third-person narration with *oratio obliqua* in the most fluent manner. The first sentence modulates into the serving-girl's speech 'and chat she would—*so* kind, and *so* comfortable'. From this mixed tissue there emerges an imagined colloquy eloquent of the lives and characters of Miss Martin and her customers. This is done without actually introducing any serving-girl, since none is needed for the story.

As so often in Dickens, the account is minutely particular. The handsome brass door-plate and Miss Martin's elegant costume are the tokens of her respectability, her gentility, and her professional skill. In feminine society the dress-maker may be a kind of leveller. A serving-girl, in her person and in her dress, may have the advantage, or may think she has the advantage, on her employers. And it is to this self-promotion, social and sexual, that Miss Martin ministers. Her understanding of her customers is perfect.

Again we may notice that Dickens is not ridiculing. There is no narrative condescension of the kind George Eliot might have shown.

'Thoughts About People' (Characters, I) is a good sketch, but one that may at first sight seem insipid. The style is restrained, the phrasing modestly telling. The sketch is largely occupied by two generic portraits: the unloved and the unloving. For the first, he takes an unmarried city clerk of middle age. By a judicious selection of glimpses—we see him arriving at the office, we see him at his books, at his eating-house, and at the home of his employer—the man is brought before us, and our sympathy secured. Dickens then turns for contrast to a class of men for whom he feels little sympathy. They are handled with considerable acerbity:

These are generally old fellows with white heads and red faces, addicted to port wine and Hessian boots, who from some cause, real or imaginary —generally the former, the excellent reason being that they are rich, and their relations poor—grow suspicious of everybody, and do the misanthropical in chambers, taking great delight in thinking themselves unhappy, and making everybody they come near, miserable. You may see such men as these anywhere; you will know them at coffee-houses by their discontented exclamations and the luxury of their dinners; at theatres, by their always sitting in the same place and looking with a jaundiced eye on all the young people near them; at church, by the pomposity with which they enter, and the loud tone in which they repeat the responses; at parties, by their getting cross at whist and hating music. An old fellow of this kind will have his chambers splendidly furnished, and collect books, plate, and pictures about him in profusion; not so much for his own gratification, as to be superior to those who have the desire, but not the means, to compete with him. He belongs to two or three clubs, and is envied, and flattered, and hated by the members of them all. Sometimes he will be appealed to by a poor relation—a married nephew perhaps—for some little assistance: and then he will declaim with honest indignation on the improvidence of young married people, the worthlessness of a wife, the insolence of having a family, the atrocity of getting into debt with a hundred and twenty-five pounds a year, and other unpardonable crimes; winding up his exhortations with a complacent review of his own conduct, and a delicate allusion to parochial relief. He dies, some day after dinner, of apoplexy, having bequeathed his property to a Public Society, and the Institution erects a tablet to his memory, expressive of their admiration of his Christian conduct in this world, and their comfortable conviction of his happiness in the next.

There Dickens stigmatizes what, morally, he recoils from. In Mr. Minns (Tales, II) and Mr. Dumps (Tales, XI) we see more of such life-haters. Mr. Minns is unfavourably shown in contrast to his vulgar, but genial relations. Scrooge is the best known of Dickens's life-haters.

The sketch concludes with another generic portrait: that of the London apprentices. They are the 'anti-type'. Dickens remarks that 'they are usually on the best terms with themselves, and it follows almost as a matter of course, in good humour, with everyone about them'. For much the same reason Dickens likes hackney-coachmen, cabmen, and cads. He relishes, in especial, 'their cool impudence and perfect self-possession'.

The types are nicely brought into conflict in 'The Bloomsbury Christening' (Tales, XI). The cold and irritable Nicodemus Dumps is chaffed by the omnibus cad:

'Don't bang the door so,' said Dumps to the conductor, as he shut it after letting out four of the passengers; 'I am very nervous—it destroys me.'

'Did any gen'lm'n say anythink?' replied the cad, thrusting in his head, and trying to look as if he didn't understand the request.

'I told you not to bang the door so!' repeated Dumps, with an expression of countenance like the knave of clubs, in convulsions.

'Oh! vy, it's rather a sing'ler circumstance about this here door, sir, that it von't shut without banging,' replied the conductor; and he opened the door very wide, and shut it again with a terrific bang, in proof of the assertion.

In 'Omnibuses' (Scenes, XVI) Dickens enlarges on the mischievous enterprise and ready wit of omnibus cads, and in 'The Last Cab-Driver, And The First Omnibus Cad' (Scenes, XVII) he introduces a notable individual, Bill Barker ('Aggerawatin Bill'). Barker belongs to the sub-criminal class, but Dickens can no more withhold admiration from him, than from the Artful Dodger.

At the end of the last-mentioned sketch, Dickens writes regretfully, 'Slang will be forgotten when civility becomes general'. As Pip's history shows, civility is, for Dickens, a doubtful good. Characters like Bill Barker or Sam Weller are enviably uninhibited. They are like a gust of fresh air in bourgeois society. They spoke out, as—on a very different level—Dickens himself spoke out in his writings.

What Dickens spoke out against was Victorian civility: a civility based on the pursuit of wealth and status, and riddled with snobberies and fetishes.

In 'Horatio Sparkins' (Tales, V) the Malderton family have the still-recognizable English weaknesses:

Mr. Malderton was a man whose whole scope of ideas was limited to Lloyd's, the Exchange, the India House, and the Bank. A few successful speculations had raised him from a situation of obscurity and comparative poverty, to a state of affluence. As frequently happens in such cases, the

ideas of himself and his family became elevated to an extraordinary pitch
as their means increased; they affected fashion, taste, and many other
fooleries, in imitation of their betters, and had a very decided and becoming horror of anything which could, by possibility, be considered *low*.
He was hospitable from ostentation, illiberal from ignorance, and prejudiced from conceit. Egotism and the love of display induced him to
keep an excellent table: convenience, and a love of good things of this
life, ensured him plenty of guests. He liked to have clever men, or what
he considered such, at his table, because it was a great thing to talk
about; but he never could endure what he called 'sharp fellows'. Probably
he cherished this feeling out of compliment to his two sons, who gave
their respected parent no uneasiness in that particular.

The family were ambitious of forming acquaintances and connexions
in some sphere of society superior to that in which they themselves moved;
and one of the necessary consequences of this desire, added to their utter
ignorance of the world beyond their own small circle, was, that any one
who could lay claim to an acquaintance with people of rank and title, had
a sure passport to the table at Oak Lodge, Camberwell.

A young man with black whiskers, a white cravat, ingratiating
manners, and poetical conversation has just 'come out' at their local
assembly, and it has been generally concluded from appearances that
'he must be *somebody*'. Mr. Malderton is easily prevailed upon to
invite him to Oak Lodge, by Mrs. Malderton, who is looking for a
husband for her eldest daughter, twenty-eight and single. Mr.
Sparkins, the young man, accepts an invitation to Sunday dinner,
but the family's exultation at this *coup* is tempered by regret when
Mrs. Malderton's brother invites himself for the same meal. This
brother is one of those who speak out:

'Upon my word, my dear, it's a most annoying thing that that vulgar
brother of yours should have invited himself to dine here today,' said Mr.
Malderton to his wife. 'On account of Mr. Sparkins's coming down, I
purposely abstained from asking any one but Flamwell. [Flamwell is a
small-time tuft-hunter.] And then to think of your brother—a tradesman
—it's insufferable! I declare I wouldn't have him mention his shop, before
our new guest—no, not for a thousand pounds! I wouldn't care if he had
the good sense to conceal the disgrace he is to the family; but he's so
fond of his horrible business, that he *will* let people know what he is.'

The dinner takes place. There is an exchange in which the author
makes his point with a pun:

'Talking of business,' interposed Mr. Barton [the vulgar brother], from the centre of the table. 'A gentleman whom you knew very well, Malderton, before you made that first lucky spec of yours, called at our shop the other day, and——'

'Barton, may I trouble you for a potato?' interrupted the wretched master of the house, hoping to nip the story in the bud.

'Certainly,' returned the grocer, quite insensible of his brother-in-law's object—'and he said in a very plain manner——'

'*Floury*, if you please,' interrupted Malderton again.

The tale has a very simple peripety and discovery. Horatio Sparkins who 'seemed like the embodied idea of the young dukes and poetical exquisites' the Malderton girls dreamed about, and who had a very flowery utterance ('he talks just like an auctioneer' is the comment of the unenchanted younger Malderton son) is encountered unexpectedly by Mrs. Malderton and the girls, when they are on a shopping expedition:

At length, the vehicle stopped before a dirty-looking ticketed linen-draper's shop, with goods of all kinds, and labels of all sorts and sizes, in the window. There were dropsical figures of seven with a little three-farthings in the corner, 'perfectly invisible to the naked eye'; three hundred and fifty thousand ladies' boas, *from* one shilling and a penny halfpenny; real French kid shoes, at two and ninepence per pair; green parasols, at an equally cheap rate; and 'every description of goods', as the proprietors said—and they must know best—'fifty per cent. under cost price'.

'Lor! ma, what a place you have brought us to!' said Miss Teresa; 'what *would* Mr. Sparkins say if he could see us!'

'Ah! what, indeed!' said Miss Marianne, horrified at the idea.

'Pray be seated, ladies. What is the first article?' inquired the obsequious master of the ceremonies of the establishment, who, in his large white neck-cloth and formal tie, looked like a bad 'portrait of a gentleman' in the Somerset House exhibition.

'I want to see some silks,' answered Mrs. Malderton.

'Directly, ma'am.—Mr. Smith! Where *is* Mr. Smith?'

Mr. Horatio Sparkins answers the summons. English society being what it is, the Malderton family suffer the mortification of having sought the acquaintance of an assistant at a cut-price shop. Mr. Sparkins, like the chief salesman, is a bad portrait of a gentleman. As such, he is related to the riding-master of Astley's.

The same axiom, that snobbery is the comic flaw of the English, is illustrated by 'The Tuggses at Ramsgate' (Tales, IV). Mr. Tuggs, who keeps a grocer's shop on 'the Surrey side of the water, within three minutes' walk of the old London Bridge', unexpectedly inherits twenty thousand pounds. His family all agree that to leave town is 'an indispensable preliminary to being genteel'. And they decide where to go, in this fashion:

'Gravesend?' mildly suggested Mr. Joseph Tuggs. The idea was unanimously scouted. Gravesend was *low*.
'Margate?' insinuated Mrs. Tuggs. Worse and worse—nobody there, but tradespeople.

Ramsgate is their choice, and there they fall in with a dashing couple, Captain and Mrs. Waters. They keep company, and go one day to the Pegwell Bay Hotel for lunch. Dickens's description of this middle-class idyll is beautifully ironic:

Mr. and Mrs. Tuggs, and the captain, had ordered lunch in the little garden behind:— small saucers of large shrimps, dabs of butter, crusty loaves, and bottled ale. The sky was without a cloud; there were flowerpots and turf before them; the sea, from the foot of the cliff, stretching away as far as the eye could discern anything at all; vessels in the distance with sails as white, and as small, as nicely-got-up cambric handkerchiefs. The shrimps were delightful, the ale better, and the captain even more pleasant than either. Mrs. Captain Waters was in *such* spirits after lunch! —chasing, first the captain across the turf, and among the flower-pots; and then Mr. Cymon Tuggs; and then Miss Tuggs; and laughing, too, quite boisterously. But as the Captain said, it didn't matter; who knew what they were, there? For all the people of the house knew, they might be common people.

But Captain and Mrs. Waters are bad portraits of a gentleman and lady, and they 'bounce' the Tuggses for a large part of their inheritance. The situations are unforcedly comic, and the life of a Victorian watering-place is brilliantly evoked.

The best of the Tales is probably 'A Passage In The Life Of Mr. Watkins Tottle' (Tales, X). The characters are well diversified: Watkins Tottle, timid and formal; Gabriel Parsons, rude and facetious; the wayward Fanny Parsons, the simpering Miss Lillerton, the smoothly ingratiating Reverend Charles Timson; Ikey and the denizens of the Cursitor Street sponging-house. The construction is artfully episodic, so that the first chapter includes the contrasting narration of Gabriel Parsons's wooing of Fanny, and the second chapter includes the story of the young couple hounded by vindictive parents (a story that anticipates that of 'The Queer Client' in *Pickwick Papers*). It has the kind of multiple texture that is a feature of Dickens's later work.

Dickens is commonly good at dinner-table scenes, but in the whole of his work there is none better than that where Parsons is endeavouring to tell a story:

'When I was in Suffolk——' said Mr. Gabriel Parsons.

'Take off the fowls first, Martha,' said Mrs. Parsons. 'I beg your pardon, my dear.'

'When I was in Suffolk,' resumed Mr. Parsons, with an impatient glance at his wife, who pretended not to observe it, 'which is now some years ago, business led me to the town of Bury St. Edmund's. I had to stop at the principal places in my way, and therefore, for the sake of convenience, I travelled in a gig. I left Sudbury one dark night—it was winter time—about nine o'clock; the rain poured in torrents, the wind howled among the trees that skirted the roadside, and I was obliged to proceed at a foot-pace, for I could hardly see my hand before me, it was so dark——'

'John,' interrupted Mrs. Parsons, in a low, hollow voice, 'don't spill that gravy.'

'Fanny,' said Parsons impatiently, 'I wish you'd defer these domestic reproofs to some more suitable time. Really, my dear, these constant interruptions are very annoying.'

'My dear, I didn't interrupt you,' said Mrs. Parsons.

'But, my dear, you *did* interrupt me,' remonstrated Mr. Parsons.

'How very absurd you are, my love; I must give directions to the servants; I am quite sure that if I sat here and allowed John to spill the gravy over the new carpet, you'd be the first to find fault when you saw the stain to-morrow morning.'

'Well,' continued Gabriel, with a resigned air, as if he knew there was no getting over the point about the carpet, 'I was just saying, it was so dark that I could hardly see my hand before me. The road was very lonely, and I assure you, Tottle (this was a device to arrest the wandering attention of that individual, which was distracted by a confidential communication between Mrs. Parsons and Martha, accompanied by the delivery of a large bunch of keys), I assure you, Tottle, I became somehow impressed with a sense of the loneliness of my situation——'

'Pie to your master,' interrupted Mrs. Parsons, again directing the servant.

'Now, pray, my dear,' remonstrated Parsons once more, very pettishly. Mrs. P. turned up her hands and eyebrows, and appealed in dumb show to Miss Lillerton. 'As I turned a corner of the road,' resumed Gabriel, 'the horse stopped short, and reared tremendously. I pulled up, jumped out, ran to his head, and found a man lying on his back in the middle of the road, with his eyes fixed on the sky. I thought he was dead; but no, he was alive, and there appeared to be nothing the matter with him. He jumped up, and putting his hand to his chest, and fixing upon me the most earnest gaze you can imagine, exclaimed——'

'Pudding here,' said Mrs. Parsons.

'Oh! it's no use,' exclaimed the host, now rendered desperate. 'Here, Tottle; a glass of wine. It's useless to attempt relating anything when Mrs. Parsons is present.'

This attack was received in the usual way. Mrs. Parsons talked *to* Miss Lillerton and *at* her better half; expatiated on the impatience of men generally; hinted that her husband was peculiarly vicious in this respect, and wound up by insinuating that she must be one of the best tempers that ever existed, or she never could put up with it. Really what she had to endure sometimes, was more than any one who saw her in every-day life could by possibility suppose.

That exchange does not forward the (very simple) plot, and it is only incidentally a presentment of character. But the story is about a bachelor who is to be coaxed into marriage, and it is the artist's concern to exhibit married life in more than one aspect. But one feels, in any case, that Dickens could not help it: the prompting to set down what he had so often heard was too strong.

No account of Dickens's fictions that concerns itself solely with the plot or with the moral scheme, important as those are, can do them justice. There is an unhappy boyhood and an unhappy man-hood behind his life's writing, and the great novels are remarkable for the exploration of personality and the mechanism of society. But Dickens also felt the artist's primary need, to record. The *Sketches by Boz* give clear evidence of this. They are instinct with moral feeling, but they are, first and foremost, an artist's impressions of the life around him. For this reason, I suggest, he could not write for long in retirement.

PICKWICK: DICKENS AND THE ART OF FICTION

John Killham

'It is necessary to see him as a man in order to appreciate him as an artist.' Thus wrote Edmund Wilson in his now celebrated essay 'Dickens: the Two Scrooges'. He did not mean that we should study the biography (which of course becomes, as Lionel Trilling observes, more *interesting* as our admiration for the novels increases for other reasons), to see how he used his own experiences as material for his fiction, but rather that we should look in the novels for signs of those infant deprivations and shames, not to speak of adult infatuations, of which Dickens left abundant traces elsewhere. This approach is quite different from that of George Orwell's equally well known and only slightly earlier essay which, characteristically, seeks to construct the mind of Dickens from the novels themselves. Both essays see Dickens's fiction, however, not simply as creations, but rather as expressions of his personality. With Orwell it is the personality which confronts the world ('one has the impression of seeing a face somewhere behind the page'); in Wilson it is the 'animula vagula blandula' shut deep within that face, whose compulsive needs forced Dickens to write of prisons, murder, and rebellion, what Orwell called his 'Victorian morbidness and necrophilia'.

Both essays contain valuable insights, even if they neglect Mr. Eliot's admonition (equally applicable to novelists) that it is not in a poet's personal emotions—'the emotions provoked by particular events in his life'—that he is in any way remarkable or interesting. But it may surely be objected to Mr. Wilson's view that Dickens made considerable literary use of the painful experiences associated with Warren's Blacking Factory, the Marshalsea, and, if we are to believe Mr. Wilson himself, Ellen Ternan; whereas it is characteristic of the perilous stuff our minds brew from our humiliations and fears to appear to consciousness (and thus to literary expression) in a disguised state, the interpretation of which is, Freud insisted, only possible with the personal co-operation of the author. This being so, the argument that Dickens's art is to be appreciated for what it reveals of his obsessions and unconscious urges is not merely circular, but even misleading. For example, Mr. Wilson argues that the early interpolated stories in *Pickwick* (particularly that in Ch. 21, 'The Old Man's Tale about the Queer Client') show 'rising to the surface' the themes which were to dominate his later work, and in which 'Dickens's obsessions appear most plainly'. These tales are certainly horrible, and, as Mr. Wilson says, mostly bad, a fact which shows that obsession, if that it is, has no necessary connection with good art, and therefore might wisely be neglected in criticism. But it is to be observed that as *Pickwick* darkens, the interpolated tales brighten; which rather suggests that Dickens was working out the principle of contrast which is implicit in many features of his writing, and emerges in full force, not wholly satisfactorily perhaps, in *Oliver Twist*. 'There are dark shadows on the earth, but its lights are stronger in the contrast' is a sentence occurring in the last paragraph of *Pickwick* (before the 'few biographical words'). Again, it is *perhaps* true that *Pickwick*, 'from the moment it gets really under way, heads by instinct and, as it were, unconsciously, straight for the Fleet prison'; but it may well be truer to say that it went there because Dickens knew that debtors' prisons figured in Fielding and Smollett and Goldsmith, and he liked to write of scenes he knew about and cared about (compare Orwell: 'you can only create if you can *care*').

What is perhaps more interesting in Edmund Wilson's essay is the soft transition from the discussion of 'obsessive' subjects like prisons to the 'symbolism' of fog, the railway, Old Krook, and the caged birds of Miss Flite. He writes that 'the people who like to talk about the symbols of Kafka and Mann and Joyce have been discouraged from looking for anything of the kind in Dickens', though in fact one finds in him a 'symbolism of a more complicated reference' than fog, etc. Another remark of Mr. Eliot's comes to mind: 'what happens when a new work of art is created is something that happens simultaneously to all the works of art which preceded it'. We are now so accustomed to discovering symbols in poetry and fiction (not to speak of spatial form and cubist perspective) that we cannot help looking for them in Dickens; and although Mr. Trilling is right to observe that 'we cannot read Kafka or Lawrence or Faulkner without learning a little better how to read Dickens', it is perhaps salutary to be on one's guard against actually blunting distinctions which really ought to be kept sharp.

The 'symbolism of a more complicated reference' Wilson mentions is not made out very clearly—he seems to suggest that after *Dombey* all the *characters* in a novel by Dickens are symbols (compare Chesterton's 'Sam Weller is the great symbol . . . of the populace peculiar to England'—a remark which made Orwell choke). 'Thus it is not at first that we recognize all the meaning of the people that thrive or survive in the dense atmosphere of *Bleak House.*' The idea we are to grasp is that the name *Bleak House* is not merely to be taken as referring to Mr. Jarndyce's dwelling but also to the whole of England (permeated by fog), which is shadowed forth as a 'gloomy edifice' whose 'social structure' must buckle in the end by virtue of the failings of the middle class. Ranged on the floors of this symbolic Victorian dwelling-house are representatives of the classes, the characters who 'symbolize' contemporary society. Mr. Morton Dauwen Zabel sees the same novel not vertically, in elevation, but horizontally, in plan. For him a 'central ganglion' spreads a deadly contagion from the Court of Chancery in London to Lincolnshire, Hertfordshire, and so on. But he too points to the fog, the river, the prisons, the dust-heap, as examples of a new symbolic control in Dickens's novels from 1846, a control enabling Dickens 'to reinforce their plots even when the plots verge on the incredible'. The same idea is expressed too by Mr. Walter Allen, who sees the 'movement of the symbolism' to be the important thing, the movement of the plot being mechanical and inclined to distort the true shape of the book.

We can see, then, that the *cachet* enjoyed by symbolism in modern literature has taken off the edge of the older criticism of plot and 'caricature'. The later novels have come into their own. Mr. Allen writes that 'in the last analysis we respond to the later novels as to great poems': and Mr. Trilling tells us of a class of students capping each other in pointing out parallels between *Our Mutual Friend* and *The Waste Land* in terms of 'the dominating symbols of waste and decay', no account being taken of the presence of narrative in the former. It might seem that *Pickwick* could not fit into this sort of discussion; but, after all, Edmund Wilson saw in it the themes which were to dominate the later work. Moreover, it has no complicated narrative to distract a reader from the least sign of an emergent symbol.

We find clear anticipations in *Pickwick* of that so-called symbolism represented in later work by the railway (said by some to hint at the ruthlessness of Dombey, by others at the change from commerce to industry which was to oust Dombey); by the fog, the caged birds, the dust-heap, and perhaps the river in *Our Mutual Friend*. Dickens uses one of Tennyson's favourite words to refer to the railway train in *Dombey*—he calls it 'a *type* of the triumphant monster, Death'. Mr. Wilson, who saw a more complicated symbolism in Dickens's characters, refers to such things as this as 'metaphors that hang as emblems over the door'. 'Emblems' is an excellent word to use, for they are not really symbols acting as signs for the total insights of the novels in which they occur. A symbol does not *resemble* what it signifies, as does—in some significant respect—an image or emblem. So it is a pity to use the term symbol, perfectly suited to indicating the function of, say, the idea of 'the wings of the dove' in James's novel, in reference to something which is so different in kind. 'Emblem' justly indicates their traditional nature, and has, too, the additional merit of being Dickens's own word to describe, in *Pickwick*, a withered plant vainly watered by the wife of a prisoner in the Fleet—'too true an emblem, perhaps, of the office she had come there to discharge'. When Mr. Pickwick was greeted on his first arrival in the prison by the sight of a Dutch clock and a bird-cage, Sam Weller was quick to point out the meaning of these objects. 'Veels within Veels, a prison in a prison.' Sam does not owe his emblematical turn of mind, we may assume, to that form of education on which his father placed so much reliance; for it is clear from Ch. 51 that he had read, and well remembered, *A Sentimental Journey*; and despite his general distaste for Job Trotter's lachrymose display, no doubt recalled the poignant episode in which poor Yorick's sight of the caged starling made him tearfully reflect upon the fate of an imaginary prisoner in the Bastille.

Dickens does not of course allow his emblems to arrest his narrative as does Bunyan. The dust-heap in *Our Mutual Friend* plays its part in the narrative very well; but it is clear that it is to bear from time to time a pejorative construction as an analogue for filthy lucre. That it is an emblem rather than a symbol is shown by the fact that its meaning (over and above that required in the fiction) is to be taken at some times and not others. Dickens does not examine the merits of being allowed to inherit large unearned incomes, only the legality of so doing. Consequently the Harmon money comes in the end to the virtuous Rokesmith and Bella, its disagreeable origin, as emblematically represented, no longer felt to be disturbing. Obviously we cannot say, as we might say of the bullfight in *The Sun Also Rises*, for example, that it is a symbolic control enabling the author to reinforce the *plot*, for at times the analogue could, if remembered too long, actually oppose it.

Pickwick also throws some light on the nature of the image of fog at the beginning of *Bleak House*. First, it must really be insisted upon that it does *not* permeate the whole novel and give it consistency of tone. Atmospheric effects of various kinds are certainly admirably used. The thaw during the search for Lady Dedlock, the rains in Lincolnshire, and so on, are all most effective, but Ruskin defines their function justly in his phrase 'pathetic fallacy'. Robert Liddell puts his finger on it too when he writes: 'If, in *Bleak House*, it rains in Lincolnshire, it is because it is raining in the heart of Lady Dedlock.' We see the beginning of such effects in *Pickwick*. When in Ch. 2 Mr. Winkle goes forth (in mid-May) to meet Dr. Slammer at sunset, the weather takes a sudden turn for the worse: 'The evening grew more dull every moment, and a melancholy wind sounded through the deserted fields like a distant giant whistling for his house-dog. The sadness of the scene imparted a sombre tinge to the feelings of Mr. Winkle.' On the eve of Lady Dedlock's exposure (Ch. 40) the sky is likewise full of portents. The fog at the beginning of that novel is undeniably impressive; but we should see it for what it is, not a symbol of a blindness between top floor and basement preventing one class from seeing another, but rather as an emblem for the 'old miasmal mist' of Chancery (and nothing else), and, in addition, as a characteristically Dickensian piece of writing aiming at his sort of intensity—'the grace', as Henry James put it, 'to which the enlightened story-teller will at any time, for his interest, sacrifice if need be all other graces whatever'. Dickens always seeks to make *everything* visually vivid, and where possible pregnant with moral meaning. Pathetic fallacy and emblematic writing are his stock-in-trade.

Dickens's characters are not symbolic either, only representative of classes of persons for whom he felt pity or disgust. *Bleak House* does not anatomize society; Dickens's eye is much too much on quite personal faults of laziness and pride. Although he satirizes the Barbarians, as elsewhere he satirizes the Philistines, when the story shows Sir Leicester true to his class code in forgiving his lady, Dickens allows all the reader's sympathy to go out to him in a way that quite upsets any conception we may have formed of the wrongness of granting his kind the privileges they have by virtue of their station. Episodic intensification is Dickens's fatal Cleopatra, causing his story and the moral attitudes it is meant to illustrate to come into conflict. Lady Dedlock, for instance, belongs to the action of *Bleak House*. Unlike her husband, she has no representativeness. She is a woman who made a mistake and dies of shame. Her story, unlike that of *Anna Karenina*, demonstrates nothing. It is an intrigue of absorbing interest while it lasts, but one is almost inclined to agree with Mr. Forster and call it not so much a backbone as a tapeworm. Yet, of course, it is not always like that. Scenes of absorbing psychological interest can arise when Dickens's formulae for judging people are led by the story to cancel one another out. The Bradley Headstone-Eugene Wrayburn opposition can be read (in manners equally Dickensian) as either Hard Work *vs* Indolence or Soulless Education *vs* Unspoilt Development; leaving Dickens to explore the psychology of murderous feelings without a moral *parti pris*. (Unusual mental states were Dickens's *forte*; the description of hypnagogic imagery in *Oliver Twist* (Ch. 34) is remarkably fine.)

Pickwick foreshadows this too. Dickens allows Jingle, the keenest of blades, to lose all his wonderful skill at thrust and parry in order that the evils of the Fleet ('It's unekal, and that's the fault on it') should be impressed upon the reader. One can see too that *Pickwick* gravitates to elections and magistrates' courts (Sam Weller is the prototype of the Artful Dodger) more naturally than to Fielding's mistaken bedrooms. The impulse to expose abuses is strong and grows stronger. Dickens later wrote of *Pickwick*, 'I could perhaps wish now that these chapters were strung together on a stronger thread of general interest'; and one can be sure that what he had in mind was not so much that *Pickwick* lacked plot (for that he never achieved), but that it lacked topicality and range in its exposure of abuses.

To argue as I have done, that Dickens was not really a 'poet' juxtaposing symbols, but rather a writer of fiction who must be judged primarily in terms of skill in narrative, may seem to be reverting to the old ground of plot and 'character'. Admirers of Dickens often find this disagreeable, since they maintain that he was great despite his faults of melodrama and improbability. To analyse his plots for their power of creating situations productive of insight in the reader is, they argue, to bring to him a standard appropriate enough to Henry James, who wrote novels the first parts of which were 'theatres' for the second and whose talk of *ficelles* and 'reflectors' shows his paramount concern with focusing attention on an ever-diminishing but brightening 'centre'. Dickens's strength is often in his perimeter, in giving the impression of a large and free life, and of burning upon the imagination individual scenes and characters of such power that the critic is tempted to take up arms against the claims of Jamesians to have discovered the secret of the novel. The weapons he has found to hand have been those modern ones of Symbol and Myth.

It is a pity that the discussion takes the form of opposing Dickens to Henry James. There is, after all, Jane Austen, and particularly *Emma* (the Jamesian quality of which Dr. Leavis has observed), to stand for excellence of construction in the English novel; while in other departments of art Arnold (in his 1853 preface) cried up *architectoniké* and Ruskin (in *Modern Painters*) distinguished 'invention'—'an arrangement in which everything in the work is . . . consistent with all things else, and helpful to all else'. To oppose the kind of modernity attributed to Dickens by Mr. J. Hillis Miller (who virtually disregards the 'story' and the 'characters', and reads the novels as if they had been composed upon a psychiatrist's couch) is not to see them as indefensible to post-Jamesian criticism, that is, as incompetent in the field of fictional narrative. For even if one holds (again with Dr. Leavis) that Dickens was—in a Pickwickian, that is, a Shakespearian sense—more of a popular entertainer than a great novelist, it is still as a writer of fiction that he must be judged. For this to be done, a few important distinctions must be made, and here again *Pickwick* can help.

'Who has not felt sometimes,' wrote Orwell, 'that it was "a pity" that Dickens ever deserted the vein of *Pickwick* for things like *Little Dorrit* and *Hard Times*?' Orwell suggested that Dickens was obliged to produce his needless ramifications of 'awful Victorian plot' because he had no idea how to show his characters at *work*, of which he was profoundly ignorant. For him Dickens's greatest success was *Pickwick*, 'which is not a story at all, only a series of sketches; there is little attempt at development—the characters simply go on and on, behaving like idiots, in a kind of eternity. As soon as he brings his characters into action, the melodrama begins.' One may object to this that Dickens was *not* ignorant of work, by no means left it out of account in his fiction, that in any case he was no more ignorant than James. But more important, it is necessary to insist that *Pickwick* only *starts* as a series of sketches, and very soon exhibits a good deal of story. The events are quite well connected, and relate to the comedy of love, marriage, courtship, spinsters, old bachelors, affairs of honour, and the like. An elopement, a breach-of-promise action, an irate husband and papa—all the obvious ingredients are there, not omitting domestic squabbles. The amorous propensities of the Club provide the motive power for the story which grows out of the original plan; and as soon as there is a story the famous characters naturally swim into the happy orbit, where life is not taken *au grand sérieux*. Jingle starts it off in Mr. Winkle's coat at Rochester; Sam Weller joins in at a delicate point in Jingle's adventure, and his father is a warning of the hazards of marriage. Even the interpolated stories touch upon this theme by way of long-suffering wives and the like.

The important thing to note is that the characters are only made possible by the story. Jingle cannot exist independently of Dr. Slammer and the widow, of Rachael Wardle and the White Hart. Likewise the material for the existence of Tony Weller is provided by Mr. Stiggins's presence at the Marquis of Granby at Dorking. Although we may in fact forget the details of the action, they have done their work. Admittedly, as Orwell remarks, the characters do not develop, or if they do, they cease to interest, like Jingle in the Fleet. But to suggest that it would have been better if they *had* developed is to misunderstand the way fiction works. *Pickwick* is an example of *story*, a category to be distinguished from *plot*, with which it is often confused. It is not true to say, with· Mr. Forster, that plot shows causality, whereas story is just a succession of incidents. No one who read a succession of incidents lacking causality would call it a story, though it may be narrative of a rudimentary kind. Story is the protoplasm of all fiction including plot, which is to be distinguished from it by virtue of its focusing the reader's attention on a different object; though one must remember that like all critical terms, plot and story (as well as character) refer to 'objects' purely mental, called forward into consciousness (and memory) by the flow of words being 'read' by the brain. Although time passes while we read, and we are told that time passes at various rates between the passages of dialogue recorded in the novel itself, the imagination constructs static images which have the timeless quality of people (and relationships between them) recalled to memory from our actual past—more or less instantaneously. Orwell speaks of the Pickwickian 'characters' as existing in a kind of eternity. He is quite right. The feeling of successiveness drains away as the mind turns dialogue and action into an identity, or 'character'. (The timeless but completed quality of a fictional action is illustrated by the fact that *Bleak House* is in part written in the present tense. It makes no difference; the commoner past tense is virtually a convention. As one reads, everything becomes part of the moment one has arrived at in the story.) The static identities ('characters') summoned up by the words read have to be placed in some relationship with each other, and although there are probably variations in the ways people imagine them, it seems usual to keep them distinct by locating them (according to their relationship to one another) in a geometrical way (e.g., a *triangular* relationship). The difference between *story* and *plot* consists in whether the reader is required primarily to construct personal identities ('characters') or whether he is to go beyond that to constructing a 'relationship' between them, and keep his eye upon that.

The difference in possible *effects* resulting upon a writer's choice between story and plot is great. A story-teller, having no need to maintain interest in *relationship* as the important static image to be presented to his reader, can spend his effort upon inventing episodes in which his characters show their ability to shape events to their own way of thinking. Falstaff and Lady Wishfort, Tony Weller and Mrs. Nickleby are notable examples. Their memorability consists in their power to transform accident into essence, as it were. Provided the novelist can supply events within their capacity of adjustment, there is no need for him ever to stop. Edwin Muir's happy remark has point here. 'The task of the character novelist is more like the choreographer's than the dramatist's; he has to keep his characters moving rather than acting.' *Pickwick* is a perfect example of story. Incidents succeed one another ('a grand chain', says Mr. Forster) to produce an ever stronger concept of character until Jingle collapses (like Falstaff and Sir Roger before him) because we can no longer sustain the image we have built up of him in face of an event which Dickens thinks too important (because too painful for him personally) for Jingle to convert into his own nature. That we are dealing with story is shown, too, by the rebirth of Pickwick and the Wellers in *Master Humphrey's Clock*. Although he is there a lesser Pickwick than we knew, he brings us a Tony Weller who is like himself, and in the scenes with his amazing grandson has almost the note of Shakespeare's Nurse and even of the great Falstaff.

There are two other features of story to be noticed. It can be made to illustrate a theme, be *utile* as well as *dulce*. What it illustrates is probably well known to the reader already; the function of story (with its power of creating imaginary personages whose existence depends upon their highly individual interpretation of events) is to impress the reader with *demonstrations* of the effects of good and evil behaviour. Secondly, story has the weakness that it tends to slow down more and more, to become scenic to excess. The Falstaff scenes in Eastcheap and Gloucestershire show what can be done within limits that are very tight. To overcome this, a special variety of story which gives a simulacrum of onwardness may be used—this is *intrigue*. It can be accompanied by character-drawing on the same scale (one thinks of *Tom Jones*). Intrigue involves mystery and concealment of relationship from the reader to create suspensiveness; but the relationship is only of birth, or inheritance or something not really personal. Dickens resorts to this sort of story in his later novels, and Mr. Wilson attaches much importance to it as if it were an innovation.

The sort of relationship that plot concentrates upon is not that of intrigue. Intrigue tries to provide momentum for a method which centres on character, and Orwell's remark that Dickens's characters 'start off as magic-lantern slides and . . . end up by getting mixed up in a third-rate movie' is very apt. The difference between story and plot is well illustrated by comparing, say, the voyage to Lilliput with that to the Houyhnhnms. The first *illustrates* its theme that political life is corrupt; typically, as with Dickens in *Pickwick* and every other of his novels, there is satire. The second creates a relationship in which Gulliver is at one corner of a triangle. As the events succeed one another the attitudes and tensions in the relationship change as Gulliver recognizes that his role *vis-à-vis* his master and the Yahoos is not as he first took it to be. The reader sees the change in the relationship with the eyes of Gulliver, and in the end is forced to accept the new one as *more true*. The reader, in fact, in reflecting upon his new concept of relationship, is invited to intuit something that he had perhaps never entertained before, something which gives him a new conception of life in one of its major aspects, a conception which he feels to affect himself. ('Why is it,' asks Orwell, 'that [Tolstoy] seems able to tell you so much more about yourself?') Plot does not illustrate; it offers an insight. James, in *The Golden Bowl*, constructs between the Prince and Maggie, Adam Verver and Charlotte, a kind of parallelogram of forces, which is miraculously sustained despite the change in the 'identities' of these imagined people at each angle. This change, commonly called development, is absolutely essential to plot; but equally obviously it absolutely precludes strong character-drawing. To keep the reader's eye off the characters, and on the relationship between them, it is worthwhile telling the 'plot' through one of themselves, exactly as James recommends, though we see the same thing in *Emma* and *Gulliver's Travels*. Only thus is the peculiar metaphysical or moral insight procurable; for this intensity the grace of 'character' is sacrificed, at least in some degree. An incidental advantage with plot is the circumstance that the insight can genuinely be represented by a symbol, a sign holding the meaning poetically but not emblematically.

Dickens is a master of story, and what happens in *Pickwick* shows the nature of his genius. He is Victorian in making his art serve the ends of morality, and he is 'modernist', as Ruskin put it, in his suspicion of the claims of history and traditional expressions of faith and spirituality. The Christmas festival at Dingley Dell expresses, as does much else in *Pickwick*, his temperamental sympathy with the philosophy behind eighteenth-century sentimental writing, that benevolence and kindness are not exclusively Christian virtues, nor a product of high civilization, but rather are to be found in all levels of people not spoiled by false teaching and pride. The Fleet prison in *Pickwick* illustrates, as do the poor law institutions and so on in other novels, man's inhumanity to man, not merely abuses of the time. So strong is the urge in Dickens to treat transgressions against the laws of Nature (if not of Nations) that he is led to illustrate the wickedness of imprisonment for debt so powerfully that the comic tone preserved by a genuinely sentimental writer dealing with such a scene (like Goldsmith showing Dr. Primrose in prison for debt) is lost. Thereafter he continues to devise stories displaying characters illustrative of natural goodness (even if they come much closer to genuine idiocy in Mr. Toots and Mr. Dick than any in *Pickwick*) contrasted with others rendered corrupt by modern life. The intensification of contrast is achieved by placing his scene in cities, where, as Master Humphrey observes, things may occur which some would say were impossible and out of Nature—'as if all great towns were not'. His narrative method is always illustrative, even when in later work (*Dombey* and *Great Expectations*) the story is given more unity of action by showing an 'illustrative character' change from one moral category to another; and also when he resorts to intrigue to provide the reader with a string to guide him through the gallery. His 'story' has something in common with that of Spenser. It allows the introduction of innumerable characters who appear and reappear as the strands of story are interlaced. The principal ones, as many critics have testified, represent, at bottom, abstract vices like Pride (Dombey) and Avarice (Chuzzlewit)—one recalls '. . . I wish to show, in little Oliver, the principle of good surviving through every adverse circumstance, and triumphing at last'. And often it reveals Dickens's preoccupation with the fashioning of a gentleman, though 'many other adventures are intermeddled, but rather as accidents than intendments', as Spenser himself put it.

Story functions differently from plot, but its triumphs in creating characters are many. Pickwick and the Wellers may not develop, but they are remembered. 'So much more profitable and gracious is doctrine by example than by rule', to quote Spenser again, that we centre our moral worlds around characters like these. Mr. E. M. Forster's celebrated observation that 'at any moment we may look at Mr. Pickwick edgeways and find him no thicker than a gramophone record' is really a confusing remark springing naturally from an analysis which discounts narrative as tiresome. It is his being a 'caricature' that makes him 'flat' for Mr. Forster; but 'round' characters have no greater substantiality, being themselves purely mental creations from the dynamic inflow of narrative. Pickwick is to be distinguished from a personage in a plot by virtue of his being an end in himself; like Sam he embodies the qualities Dickens wants us to admire; lack of pride (we think of Sam's sarcasms at the 'swarry' in Bath, Mr. Pickwick at Bob Sawyer's lodgings), loyalty, unselfishness, friendliness; qualities independent of considerations of class and income. Such a character is not inferior, but different, and the art whereby he has been created is worth study.

Such a study is easier today than when G. H. Lewes wrote: 'Give a child a wooden horse, with hair for mane and tail, and wafer spots for colouring, he will never be disturbed by the fact that this horse does not move its legs but runs on wheels—the general suggestion suffices for his belief . . . It may be said of Dickens's human figures that they too are wooden, and run on wheels; but these are details which scarcely disturb the belief of admirers.' Modern visual art has brought expressive distortion into favour. But the term 'mythic' has come to be used of characters like Pickwick and the Wellers (Walter Allen), Mrs. Nickleby, Mr. Micawber, Mrs. Gamp, Bounderby and Gradgrind (E. A. Baker); Messrs. Wellek and Warren cite *Pickwick* as an example of 'mythic plot'; Mr. Zabel observes that by 1851 Dickens's work had become part of the 'folklore and familiar mythology' of his contemporaries' lives; and Mr. Hillis Miller maintains that all that happens in *Pickwick* repeats over and over again a single, significant adventure. Thus does the eye see what it seeks. Surely the world of Dickens is far from true mythology, which is connected with religion. Like all story-tellers 'illustrating' a moral view, he wishes his readers to 'see' his personages, and consequently 'draws' them in highly characteristic utterances so that they dominate our imaginative field, and draw towards themselves the maximum of our stored-up associations. They are not conceived in terms of reflecting what we perceive with our eyes, as in a mirror. They really are, very often, literary analogues of nursery toys; not like real people, but composed of hair and wafer spots, so arranged as to present a mask highly expressive of friendliness or of hostility. The witch-like Miss Havisham and the cat-like Mr. Carker are not symbols or 'myths'; they constitute, like Mr. Pickwick, a focus for our fantasies of good and evil. Manipulation of our response to them is a major part of Dickens's art, and we have no need to be ashamed of a concern with them, and with the stories that produce them, simply because such a concern is old-fashioned. Dickens is not an inferior or 'primitive' artist because he eschews plot and invents characters 'impossible and out of Nature'; his 'hobby-horses' are more compelling than other men's horses. Why they prove to be so has become more intelligible as art has been considered more in terms of invention than of imitation.[1]

[1] See E. H. Gombrich, 'Meditations on a Hobby Horse or the Roots of Artistic Form', in *Aspects of Form*, ed. Lancelot L. Whyte (1951), p. 209. The passage from G. H. Lewes is quoted from George H. Ford, *Dickens and his Readers* (Princeton, 1955), p. 153.

OLIVER TWIST: 'THINGS AS THEY REALLY ARE'

John Bayley

Oliver Twist is a modern novel. It has the perennially modern pretension of rejecting the unreality of a previous mode, of setting out to show us 'things as they really are'. But its modernity is more radical and more unsettling than this pretension implies; it can still touch us—as few novels out of the past can—on a raw nerve; it can still upset and discountenance us. *Pickwick* is not modern. It is a brilliant and successful recreation of the English novel's atmospheres and personalities; but Dickens, like Kipling, had a bargain with his daemon not to repeat a success. It was not *Pickwick* that made Thackeray ruefully praise Dickens's perpetual modernity, or Chesterton announce that Dickens had remained modern while Thackeray had become a classic.

Oliver Twist lacks only one attribute of the modern novel—complete self-consciousness. No novelist has profited more richly than Dickens from not examining what went on in his own mind. His genius avoids itself like a sleep-walker avoiding an open window. Chesterton says what a good thing it is we are not shown Pecksniff's thoughts—they would be too horrible—but the point about Pecksniff is that he has no thoughts: he is as much of a sleep-walker as Dickens: he is the perfect hypocrite because he does not know what he is like. Dickens recoiled from what he called 'dissective' art, and if he had been able and willing to analyse the relation between our inner and outer selves he could never have created the rhetoric that so marvellously ignores the distinction between them. Unlike us, he had no diagrammatic view of mind, no constricting terminology for the psyche. The being of Bumble, Pecksniff, Mrs. Gamp is not com-

49

partmented: their inner being *is* their outer self. When Mrs. Gamp says: 'We never know what's hidden in each other's hearts; and if we had glass windows there, we'd need to keep the shutters up, some of us, I do assure you'—she is saying something that will be true of John Jasper and Bradley Headstone, but the great early characters are in fact windowed and shutterless. Noah Claypole carousing with Charlotte over the oysters, a *mass* of bread and butter in his hand; Bumble announcing the cause of Oliver's rebellion to Mrs. Sowerberry—' "It's not madness, Ma'am, it's meat", said the beadle after a few moments of deep meditation'—their monstrosity luxuriates without depth or concealment. When Proust sets out to 'overgo' the Dickensian monster with his Charlus and Françoise, the ebullience and energy are seen to proceed from a creative centre which is meticulous, reflective, and the reverse of energetic: the peculiar Victorian harmony of created and creating energy is lost.

Their wholeness and harmony have a curious effect on the evil of Dickens's monsters: it sterilizes it in performance but increases it in idea. The energy of Fagin or Quilp seems neutral; there is not enough gap between calculation and action for it to proceed to convincingly evil works. By contrast, Iago and Verhovensky are monsters because they know what they are doing; their actions let us loathe them and recoil from them into freedom, but we cannot recoil from Dickens's villains: they are the more frightening and haunting because we cannot expel them for what they do; they have the unexpungable nature of our own nightmares and our own consciousness.

We cannot recoil—that is the point. For in spite of the apparent openness of its energy and indignation *Oliver Twist* is in fact the kind of novel in which we are continually oppressed by the disingenuousness of our own impulses and fantasies, the kind of novel in which the heroine. say, is immured in a brothel, and in which we, like her, both shrink from the fate and desire it. *Clarissa* is in the background. 'Richardson', says Diderot in a famous passage, 'first carried the lantern into the depths of that cavern . . . he breathes on the agreeable form at the entrance and the hideous Moor behind it is revealed.' The lantern has been carried pretty often into the cave since then, and the hideous Moor has become a familiar enough figure: we are introduced in many a modern fiction to our hypothetical sado-masochistic interiors. But whereas a novel like *Death in Venice*, or *Les Caves du Vatican*, divides one aspect of the self from another with all the dramatic cunning and the nice impassivity of art—the author being perfectly aware what he is up to—Dickens presents the nightmare of what we are and what we want in its most elemental and undifferentiated form. All unknowing, he does not let us escape from the ignominy of our fascinations, because he does not try to escape from them himself.

Oliver Twist is not a satisfying novel—it does not liberate us. In achieving what might be called the honesty of the dream world it has to stay in prison. The sense of complete reality in fiction can perhaps only be achieved by the author's possessing, and persuading his reader to share, a sense of different worlds, different and indeed almost incompatible modes of feeling and being. The awareness of difference is the awareness of freedom, and it is, moreover, the knowledge of reality we normally experience in life. But in *Oliver Twist* there are no such contrasts, no such different worlds. Even the apparent contrast between Fagin's world and that of Rose Maylie and Mr. Brownlow is not a real one, and this is not because the happy Brownlow world is rendered sentimentally and unconvincingly by Dickens, but because the two do in fact co-exist in consciousness: they are twin sides of the same coin of fantasy, not two real places that exist separately in life. And there is no true activity in the two worlds, only the guilty or desperately innocent daydreams of our double nature.

The superior power and terror of the unreal is continually harped on. Nancy tells Mr. Brownlow that she can think of nothing but coffins and had just seen one carried past her in the street.

'There is nothing unusual in that. They have passed me often.'
'*Real ones*,' rejoined the girl. 'This was not.' (Ch. 46.)

Where the reality of action is concerned, Fagin's world has the technical advantage over the Maylie one of *reporting*—as in the dialogue of the thieves' kitchen and the boys going out with Oliver to pick pockets—but it is significant that the long burglary sequence, when Sikes takes Oliver down to Chertsey to crack the Maylie house and the two worlds collide at last, is one of the most dreamlike in the novel. Dreamlike too is a later collision, the meeting of Nancy and Rose Maylie in the hotel bedroom: another novelist would make such a confrontation of worlds the most reality-enhancing note in his tale, but in *Oliver Twist* they only confirm the dream atmosphere. Even when he is firmly inside the Maylie world, Oliver can, so to speak, deprive another character of reality by compelling him to act out Oliver's fantasy of what life in such a world is like. Oliver goes out to gather flowers every morning, and when Henry Maylie returns home 'he was seized with such a passion for flowers, and displayed such a taste in their arrangement, as left his young companion far behind'.

As we shall see, Dickens frequently defends himself against the charge of using literary devices and conventions by pointing out their similarity to real life, and he seems to imply that he is using the dream atmosphere as a kind of convention in this spirit. He gives two accounts of the nature of waking dreams, the first at Fagin's, and the second when just after the flower episode Oliver sees Fagin and Monks at the window of the Maylie's parlour and their eyes meet. 'There is a kind of sleep that steals upon us sometimes which, while it holds the body prisoner, does not free the mind from a sense of things about it, and enable it to ramble at its pleasure.' (Ch. 34.) So similar are the two accounts of this state that it seems likely Dickens repeated himself accidentally in the hurry of composition (for the second half of the novel was written under great pressure), but the effect is none the less potent for that. It is a dream from which Oliver awakes to find it true, even though no footprints of the pair can be found. It recalls the earlier waking dream, when he lay watching Fagin sorting his stolen goods, and we realize it is not physical distance that keeps him from Fagin's house, a house which had once belonged to respectable people like the Maylies, and in which the mirrors of the unused rooms where Fagin and Monks confer now only reflect the dusty floor and the slimy track of the snail.

That the two worlds are one in the mind appears even in Cruick-shank's drawings, where Oliver often has a distinct look of Fagin. Henry James remarked that as a child the pictures of the good places and people frightened him more than the bad! It is often said, and with some justice, that Dickens muddles the message of his novel by making Oliver immune to an environment which is denounced as necessarily corrupting. But Oliver is not psychologically immune, nor is Dickens, nor are we. It is true that Dickens cheerfully adopts a vaguely Rousseauesque notion of the innocent warped and made evil by institutions—('what human nature may be made to be') and also seems to adopt with equal readiness the tory doctrine that birth and breeding will win through in the end. But however muddled as propaganda—indeed perhaps because they are muddled—these contradictions are entirely resolved in the imaginative certainty of the novel. Dickens might well proclaim, as he did to critics who found Nancy's love for Sikes implausible—that IT IS TRUE! His imagination makes nonsense, just as life does, of theories of how human beings will or will not behave in a given environment. Notwithstanding the claustrophobic nature of the book, and its heavy dream atmosphere, Dickens's triumph is to have made Oliver—and Charley Bates and Nancy too—free of all human possibility, free in spirit and impulse against all physical and factual likelihood. The world of the novel may be a prison but they are not finally enclosed in it. And he has made this ultimate freedom seem true.

Still, Fagin's wish to incriminate Oliver, and hence confine him for ever in the evil world, is an objective and social terror as well as a psychological one. There remains the plain and sickening fact that Fagin's school and all it stands for extinguishes the hope and chance of better things, though not necessarily the capacity for them: of his pupils, Oliver escapes by the needs of the plot, Charley Bates by the death of Sikes and Fagin, and Nancy not at all. Dickens himself had been at Fagin's school—the blacking factory—and the boy who chiefly befriended him there was actually called Fagin. No wonder Fagin the criminal is such an ambivalent figure when the real Fagin's kindness had, so to speak, threatened to inure Dickens to the hopeless routine of the wage-slave. So passionate was the young Dickens's desire for the station in life to which he felt entitled, and so terrifying his sense that it was being denied him, that he must have hated the real Fagin for the virtue which he could not bear to accept or recognize in that nightmare world, because it might help to subdue him into it. The real Fagin's kindness becomes the criminal Fagin's villainy.

Like Oliver reading the tales of crime in Fagin's den, Dickens 'prayed heaven to spare him from such deeds'. He came later, at the time of his readings from *Oliver Twist*, to have a clear and horrifying awareness of his split personality: he dreaded himself, and the possibility that he might be exiled by his own doing into the world of the murderer and the social outcast. The premise of *Oliver Twist* is the gnostic one of Melville's poem:

> Indolence is heaven's ally here
> And energy the child of hell . . .

Dickens feared the surrender to the demon of energy which his nature continually imposed on him. One of the many biographical glosses on the novel is the idyll which in the summer of 1849 he claimed to be enjoying with his family in the Isle of Wight, an idyll rudely interrupted when Dickens could stand it no longer and hurried them all away again from the picnics, the charades, and the flower gathering.

The power of *Oliver Twist* depends more than any other of Dickens's novels on his personality and background—that is why one has to insist on them so much. Everything in the novel means something else; it is shot through and through with involuntary symbolism, with that peculiar egocentric modernity which Edmund Wilson tells us to be fiction's discovery of its true self. Except possibly for Giles the butler, nobody and nothing exists merely in itself. Even the famous 'household' passages, like Oliver asking for more, do not have the legendary authority of an epic moment but make a piercing appeal to something private and vulnerable in the memory of the reader. 'Things as they really are' turn out to be things as the fantasy fears, and feared in childhood, that they may be. In *David Copperfield* childhood fantasy is also dominant, but in the objective setting of true existences, David's mother, Peggotty, Betsy Trotwood, and Barkis—there is the breadth and solidity of epic. In *Oliver Twist* the child is *right*: there is no suggestion that his vision of monsters is illusory or incomplete, and the social shock to us is that the child here is right to see things thus—the system is monstrous because he finds it to be so. His vision is the lens to focus Dickens's *saeva indignatio*. The grotesque conversation between Noah, Bumble, and the gentleman in the white waistcoat, about what is to be done with Oliver, is true because it is just how Oliver would imagine it. But in *Copperfield* the child may be wrong; he only partially apprehends the existences around him, and Murdstone, for instance, is more arresting and intriguing than anyone in *Oliver Twist* because there is no assumption that David really knows what he is like.

Dickens's crusading purpose underwrites Oliver's view of things and creates a powerful satiric method at the cost of losing the actual child's involuntary existence. Indeed it is the loss of the mere condition of childishness, as an abused animal or bird loses its natural status, which is so heart-rending—Oliver is never allowed to *be* what he is, and when liberated he has to act the part, a fact uncon-

sciously recognized by Cruickshank in drawings which have the
look of a twenty-year old actor playing a schoolboy. Oliver has been
cheated of childhood like his friend Dick, whose limbs are 'like those
of an old man'. Acting, indeed, as Dickens implies in his facetious
but revealing preamble to Chapter 17, is the clue to the mode by
which we are to be moved by the persona and events of the story.
We must put ourselves in their place and act as they are acting. We
must be like the crazy old woman for whom her daughter's death
was 'as good as a play'.

It is the custom on the stage, in all good murderous melodramas, to
present the tragic and comic scenes in . . . regular alternation. . . . We
behold, with throbbing bosoms, the heroine in the grasp of a proud and
ruthless baron: her virtue and her life alike in danger, drawing forth
her dagger to preserve the one at the cost of the other; and just as our
expectations are wrought up to the highest pitch, a whistle is heard, and
we are straightway transported to the great hall of the castle: where a
grey-headed seneschal sings a funny chorus.

  Such changes appear absurd: but they are not so unnatural as they
would seem at first sight. The transitions in real life from well-spread
boards to death-beds, and from mourning weeds to holiday garments,
are not a whit less startling; only, there, we are busy actors, instead of
passive lookers-on, which makes a vast difference. The actors in the
mimic life of the theatre, are blind to violent transitions and abrupt impulses of passion or feeling, which, presented before the eyes of mere
spectators, are at once condemned as outrageous and preposterous.

It is a brilliant apologia for his whole creative method. He implies
that it is *because* Oliver is an actor that the spectator should not withhold sympathy if the tale seems artificial and implausible, thus ingeniously confounding the stage actor with the actor in real life
and claiming that in both cases the only true view is the participant's:
we must ourselves participate in order to feel the truth of the thing,
and not merely appraise it from outside.

  In seeking to disarm criticism by drawing his readers into a
hypnotic unity with the tale and the author, Dickens relies heavily
on convention to increase both the shared hypnosis and the emotion
of truth. As Forster tells us, he delighted in coincidence and in
pointing out how common it was in life. And in *Oliver Twist* he
positively takes refuge in melodramatic ceremonial: it would be a
disaster if the taste of the age had allowed him to describe what must

have been the continual and brutish sexual activity in Fagin's hole—
(*Jonathan Wild*, and *The Beggar's Opera*, which Dickens protests
is unrealistic, are much franker about this)—or to have rendered the
actual oaths of Sikes instead of giving him grotesquely and perhaps
deliberately exaggerated euphemisms like 'Wolves tear your
throats!' . . . Though he may not have been conscious of it, Dickens
knew that such disguises and prevarications are indeed the truth of
the fantasy. And he enhances their effect by putting them beside facts
of a neutral and professional kind, like his catalogue of the districts
—Exmouth Street, Hockley in the Hole, Little Saffron Hill, etc.—
through which Oliver is led by the Artful Dodger, and through
which Sikes wanders after the murder. The setting in which Noah
eavesdrops on the meeting between Nancy and the Maylies is detailed
with the offhand expertise of Kipling:

These stairs are a part of the bridge; they consist of three flights. Just below
the end of the second, going down, the stone wall on the left terminates
in an ornamental pilaster facing towards the Thames. At this point the
lower steps widen: so that a person turning that angle of the wall, is
necessarily unseen by any others on the stairs who chance to be above
him, if only a step. (Ch. 46.)

The old device of the eavesdropper has never been more effectively
localized. But reality depends on the convention. Dickens was the
first to protest against the new French 'realism', because he felt it
might discredit his mystery. He has often been blamed for giving the
happy ending to *Great Expectations*, in deference to Bulwer Lytton,
but he has there a sure sense, as in *Oliver Twist*, not of what the
donnée demanded, but of upholding the kinds of agreement he had
made with the reader. The artistic rigour of a Flaubert alienates, and
Dickens is faithful only to what he and his audience can make of the
thing together.

Yet in his last novels he is beginning to hold the reader off. It is
extremely illuminating to compare *Oliver Twist* with *Edwin Drood*,
because we are not required to participate in the exquisitely murderous atmosphere of the last novel. We can stand back, and watch
the familiar two worlds—the world of goodness and innocence and
the world of murder and hallucination—conjured into a real and
objective existence. Canon Crisparkle and his mother, the Virginia
creeper, and the home-made wines and jellies, are solid and reassur-

ing presences: they have strength as well as gentleness. Rosa Budd and Helena Landless, 'a beautiful barbaric captive brought from some wild tropical dominion', are as meticulously alive as Jasper, raising his high voice in the shadowy choir and hating the rôle he has made for himself. Dickens has adopted the principle of depth; hypocrisy is real at last. Instead of the divided nature being flat and two-dimensional as a Rorschach ink-blot, spreading over the whole of life, it now exists in and perceives an upper and lower world. At the cost of transforming his social earnestness into an earnestness of craftsmanship Dickens keeps his imagination working at full pressure, but in a new sphere of complication and plurality. His vision proves to be as fecund as Shakespeare's, and to have the same power of continued transformation. It was transforming itself afresh when he died.

So far I have stressed the waking nightmare which is the imaginative principle of *Oliver Twist*, and the way it dispels any true distinction between the world of darkness which Oliver is in, and the world of light which he longs for. None the less the impressive power of the novel does depend upon a most effective distinction, of quite another kind, and of the force of which Dickens seems equally unaware. It is the distinction between crime and murder.

We are apt to forget how early-Victorian society, the society of laissez-faire, took for granted individual conditions of privacy and isolation. It was a society where each unit, each family and household, led their secret lives with an almost neurotic antipathy to external interference. It was the age of the private gentleman who wanted nothing but to be left alone. He could ignore politics, the Press, the beggar who happened to be dying of hunger in the coach-house; he need feel no pressure of social or national existence. Noah Claypole provides an ironic gloss when he says about Oliver: 'let him alone! Why, everyone lets him pretty much alone!' And the poor had the same instincts as their betters. At the time of the Crimea, when a suggestion of conscription was raised, labourers and miners said they would take to the woods or go underground rather than be caught for it. There has probably never been a time when England was—in the sociological phrase—less integrated.

Dickens has a most disturbing feeling for this. Like most Victorians his sense of other things, other places and people, was founded on fear and distrust. The Boz of the Sketches seems to hate and fear almost everything, even though it fascinates him. For unlike other people he had no home to go to, no hole in which he could feel secure. Normal living and the life of crime are almost indistinguishable in *Oliver Twist*, for both are based on the burrow. Both Jacob's Island and the town where Oliver is born consist largely of derelict houses which are not owned or occupied in the normal way but taken possession of as burrows, or 'kens', with an 'aperture made into them wide enough for the passage of a human body'. Fagin, who when out of doors is compared to a reptile 'looking for a meal of some rich offal', has his den on Saffron Hill; when he first enters the district Oliver sees that from several of these holes 'great ill-looking fellows were cautiously emerging, bound, to all appearance, on no very well-disposed or harmless errands'. The stiltedness of the writing here somehow emphasizes the effect of evening beasts coming out on their normal business. Mr. Brownlow (whose name oddly suggests a fox) and Mr. Grimwig are holed up in Clerkenwell; Mrs. Corney has her snug corner in the workhouse; the Maylies live behind the walls of their Chertsey house as if it were in the Congo. The house to which Oliver is taken before the abortive 'crack', and which he afterwards identifies, is found then to have some quite different tenant, an evil creature who is hastily left to his own devices. A man on the run makes the round of the kens and finds them already full, as if they were shells tenanted by crabs.

All these people have the same outlook and the same philosophy of life, a philosophy which that private gentleman, Fagin, sums up as 'looking after No. 1'. As one would expect, Dickens can see nothing in the idea of 'private vices, public virtues' except a degradingly mutual kind of blackmail. In presenting his characters as animals, purposeful, amoral, and solitary in their separate colonies, with no true gregariousness or power of cohesion, he draws a terrifying imaginative indictment of what private life may be like in an open society, in his age or in our own.

Murder transforms all this. Like a magic wand it changes the animals back into men again: what we think of as 'human nature' returns with a rush. And it is an extraordinary and sinister irony that makes murder the only imaginative vindication in the book of human stature and human meaningfulness. Though Dickens may not have bargained for the effect it is the crowning stroke in the satirical violence of his novel. Just as murder, in the Victorian literary mythology, was cleaner than sex, so in Dickens's vision is it more human than crime and the inhumanity of social institutions, for crime is the most characteristic aspect of the social order. Bumble, Fagin and the rest are evil beings because they are not human beings; they are doing the best they can for themselves in their business, and Sikes was similarly an animal in the business—'the mere hound of a day' as Fagin says—until murder turns him into a kind of man. Thereupon, too, society develops the cohesion and point that it had lacked before—indeed this, like so much else in the book, is grotesquely though effectively overdone. Nancy's murder assumes the proportions of a national crisis, 'Spies', we hear, 'are hovering about in every direction'. Significantly, until the murder no one seems to take notice of Fagin—he is engrossed in his repellent business like any other citizen—but after it he is nearly lynched. Crime is like animal or mechanical society, cold, separated, and professional, but murder is like the warmth and conviviality which Dickens always praises—a great uniter.

Undoubtedly Dickens is saying something here about society which has lost none of its potency. With a shudder we realize what we are still like. Of course, Dickens had a perfectly 'healthy' interest in murder and hanging, just as he took a normal English pleasure in illness, funerals, and ballads like 'the blood-drinker's burial'; but murder in *Oliver Twist* has a more metaphysical status, is less literary and less purely morbid and professional, than any other in Dickens. His later murders, beautifully done as they are, have by comparison a dilettante flavour. In *Our Mutual Friend* and *Drood* other characters mime the murderous atmosphere in proleptic touches that are almost Shakespearian. Lammle wrenches the stopper off a siphon 'as if he wanted to pour its blood down his throat'. At the end of term celebrations in the dormitory of Miss Twinkleton's seminary, one of the young ladies 'gives a sprightly solo on the comb and curl-paper until suffocated in her own pillow by two flowing-haired executioners'. But murder in *Oliver Twist* is definitely not considered as one of the fine arts. It is not an aesthetic matter sealed off in its artifice and our satisfaction, but a moral act which for that reason penetrates not only the life of the novel but our own lives as well.

Dostoevsky, a great admirer of *Oliver Twist*, also makes murder a kind of social revelation. Writers who learn from Dickens usually develop explicitly an effect which is implicit in their source, and Dostoevsky makes Roskolnikov a rebel who murders the old money-lender out of frustration, as a kind of thwarted substitute for idealist terrorism. We know from his diary that Dostoevsky was bothered by Roskolnikov's lack of an obvious motive—he realized that the significance with which the author endowed the crime was showing too clearly through the story. But Sikes's motive is brutally simple and straightforward. Nancy must be got rid of because she has betrayed the gang: the whole burrow principle of looking after No. 1 demands her instant elimination. None the less, it is a duty, and duty is a human and not an animal concept.

Without once turning his head to the right or left, or raising his eyes to the sky, or lowering them to the ground, but looking straight before him with savage resolution: his teeth so tightly compressed that the strained jaw seemed starting through his skin; the robber held on his headlong course, nor uttered a word, nor relaxed a muscle, until he reached his own door. (Ch. 47.)

Like Macbeth, Sikes 'bends up each corporal agent to this terrible feat'. An animal kills naturally, like a cat killing a bird; and in Dickens's other murders the murderer's animality is increased by the deed. Jonas Chuzzlewit skulks like a beast out of the wood where his victim lies; Rogue Riderhood lives by furtive killing, and Dickens suggests his nature in two brilliant images—the fur cap, 'like some small drowned animal', which he always wears, and the shapeless holes he leaves in the snow, 'as if the very fashion of humanity had departed from his feet'. Headstone's course is the exact opposite of Sikes's: the lust to kill strips the veneer of decency and laboriously acquired culture from him, and turns him into the terrifying creature who grinds his fist against the church wall until the blood comes. Like Chuzzlewit he feels no remorse, only the murderer's *esprit de l'escalier*—he cannot stop thinking how much more ingeniously the deed might have been done. Reduced to the animal status of Riderhood, he loses even his own name, his last link with humanity, when at Riderhood's bidding he writes it on the school blackboard and then rubs it out.

But Sikes finds his name. It is on every tongue in the metropolis. Other murderers become conscienceless animals, but he acquires the form and conscience of a man, almost indeed of a spirit. 'Blanched face, sunken eyes, hollow cheeks . . . it was the very ghost of Sikes.' And as his killing of Nancy makes him a man, so her love for him transforms her into a woman. 'Pity us', she says to Rose Maylie, 'for

60

setting our rotten hearts on a man. Pity us for having only one feeling of the woman left, and that turned into a new means of violence and suffering.' The act she puts on when she enquires for Oliver at the police station, and helps to recapture him in the street, is a nightmare parody of social pretences and what they conceal, a sort of analogue to the pomposities of Bumble and the realities of the workhouse. Her revulsion when Oliver is brought back to Fagin's den is one of the most moving things in the book, but its denizens suppose she is still keeping up the part ('You're acting beautiful,' says Fagin) and they eye her ensuing rage and despair with bestial incomprehension. 'Burn my body,' growls Sikes, 'do you know what you are?', and Fagin tells her 'It's your living.'

'Aye, it is!' returned the girl; not speaking, but pouring out the words in one continuous and vehement scream. 'It is my living and the cold wet dirty streets are my home; and you're the wretch that drove me to them long ago, and that'll keep me there, day and night, night and day, till I die!' (Ch. 16.)

Nancy's living is the living of England, a nightmare society in which drudgery is endless and stupefying, in which the natural affections are warped, and the dignity of man appears only in resolution and violence. It is a more disquieting picture than the carefully and methodically symbolized social panoramas of *Bleak House*, *Little Dorrit*, and *Our Mutual Friend*. It is as raw and extemporized as Nancy's outburst. *Oliver Twist* quite lacks the overbearing pretension of the later novels, a pretension which Edmund Wilson defers to rather too solemnly when he tells us that Dickens in *Our Mutual Friend* 'had come to despair utterly of the prospering middle class'. It is the same pretension which G. K. Chesterton notes a-propos of Riah, the good Jewish money-lender introduced because of complaints from Jewish correspondents about Fagin: 'It pleased Dickens to be mistaken for a public arbiter: it pleased him to be asked (in a double sense) to judge Israel'.

Oliver is not in a position to despair of the middle class, or anything else, and the humility of this is communicated in some way to the author and moves us more than all his later stridency. Oliver is a true everyman: he does not, like David Copperfield or D. H. Lawrence, shriek at us incredulously—'They did this to *me*!' It is logical that he has no character, because he has no physical individuality—he is the child element in a nightmare which is otherwise peopled by animals, and precariously by men. Child, beast, and man indeed merge and change places phantasmagorically throughout the book. Oliver is sometimes adult, almost middle-aged, and sometimes like an animal himself, as when his eyes glisten at the sight of the scraps of meat in Mrs. Sowerberry's kitchen—one of the few really physical intimations of him we have. After the murder the lesser criminals are as lost and bewildered as children, and the hardened Kags begs for a candle, saying 'Don't leave me in the dark'. Sikes and Nancy, as hero and heroine, have their transformation from beast to man: only Fagin remains a reptile throughout and to the end, losing at last even his human powers of speech and intellect and crouching in the dock like something snared, his glittering eyes 'looking on when an artist broke his pencil point and made another with his knife, as any idle spectator might have done.' He has the animal victim's unnerving air of detachment from his own predicament, and the butchery of one kind of beast by another is the final horror of his execution. 'Are you a man, Fagin?' asks the gaoler.

'I shan't be one long,' he replied, looking up with a face containing no human expression but rage and terror. 'Strike them all dead! What right have they to butcher me?'

It is a horribly penetrating appeal, when we think of society as *Oliver Twist* presents it. And in contrast to the almost heroic death of Sikes, Fagin will lose even his animal identity at the very end, and revert to a dreadful human simulacrum, 'a dangling heap of clothes'.

'To be thoroughly earnest is everything, and to be anything short of it is nothing.' Dickens's credo about novel-writing is certainly true of *Oliver Twist*, but whereas in the later novels this seriousness extends to the technique which fashions symbols and symbolic atmospheres— the famous fogs, prison, dust, etc.—he does not insist on, or even seem aware of, the animal symbolism here: it hits the reader like a sleepwalker's blow, involuntarily administered. It seems a natural product of the imagination, like that of Shakespeare and Hardy; though Dickens's later symbolic technique is closer to Lawrence's, purposeful and claustrophobic, the meaning too unified to expand into an ordinary human range of possibility. Character remains imprisoned in the author's will and we are uneasily aware of the life that has been left out. The Dickens of *Hard Times*, whom Dr. Leavis admires, manipulates symbolic meaning in a manner that reaches its apotheosis with Clifford Chatterley sitting in his motor-chair. Nor do his 'straight' characters always escape the same fate. It is with some complacency that he reports how his mother, his model for Mrs. Nickleby, protested that there could not be such a woman. One sympathizes with her, and one is inclined to think she was right. Her son was rather too confident that his imagination could give another being its real life, and that what Mrs. Nickleby (or Mrs. Dickens) felt themselves to be was nothing in comparison with what Dickens saw them to be.

It is the more remarkable, therefore, that Sikes and Nancy have such a range. His intentions about them are overt enough. He says he is not going to abate one growl of Sikes or 'one scrap of curl-paper in Nancy's dishevelled hair'. This confidence of the realist is hardly very encouraging. The description of the Bow Street officers, based on a 'Wanted' notice, 'reveals them', says Dickens, 'for what they are'; and we are not allowed to forget Cratchit's shawl-pattern waistcoat or the humorous overcoat sported by the Dodger. Sikes himself

was a stoutly-built fellow of about five and thirty, in a black velveteen coat, very soiled drab breeches, lace-up half boots, and grey cotton stockings, which enclosed a bulky pair of legs, with large swelling calves—the kind of legs, which in such costume, always look in an unfinished and incomplete state without a set of fetters to garnish them. (Ch. 13.)

The bit about fetters gives the game away, and shows that for all his protestations of realism Dickens is really drawing on Gay and Hogarth. But what brings Sikes and Nancy to life is the gap between what they look like and what they are like, between their appearance as Dickens insists we shall have it, and the speech and manner with which another convention requires him to endow them. They rise, as it were, between two stools; they achieve their real selves by being divided between two modes of artifice. Nancy looks like the slattern in curl-papers lifting the gin bottle and exclaiming 'Never say die'! but inside there is the desperate being who confronts Fagin and bitterly describes herself to Rose Maylie. The Sikes in grey cotton stockings is the same man who goes to murder like Macbeth.

In asserting an apparent realism, Dickens actually achieves a striking balance—very rare in his characterization—between the outward and inward selves that make up a whole person. The nonsense talked by Bumble, Pecksniff, or Squeers, their total lack of the responsibilities of intercourse, mark Dickens's most contemptuous, though most inspired, refusal to recognize an inner self in such persons. But Sikes and Nancy have an eloquence, a brutal and urgent power of communication, that shows how seriously Dickens takes them, and how seriously they are compelled to take themselves. The dimension of these two is the triumph of the novel, and it closely corresponds to the main feat—surely unique in the history of the novel—which Dickens has achieved in combining the genre of Gothic nightmare with that of social denunciation, so that each enhances the other.

NICHOLAS NICKLEBY

Bernard Bergonzi

THE EMPHASIS that recent criticism has placed on Dickens's late novels, though certainly justified, has meant that the earliest works, traditionally so beloved, have come to seem a little remote. And this is particularly true of *Nicholas Nickleby*. Of the novels written before 1840, *Pickwick*, however little it may have to offer the seeker after high moral seriousness, preserves its early morning freshness, and its place in the popular imagination is likely to remain inviolable. Mr. Pickwick is one of the great mythical figures of the English consciousness. *Oliver Twist*, though a less interesting work, has its own considerable appeal as a book about childhood, and wears exceedingly well; its survival has certainly been helped by its comparative brevity. Compared with these, Dickens's third novel, *Nicholas Nickleby*, has a decidedly insecure place; it is clearly inferior to *Pickwick*, but it does not possess the qualities we have come to expect from the later Dickens. Yet there is a sense in which *Nickleby* is of crucial importance in Dickens's development. As Chesterton noted, it was Dickens's first attempt at a large-scale novel, with a sustained and varied range of moods and emotional attitudes. *Pickwick*, as we know, was not planned as a novel at all; it was pre-eminently a work by the author of *Sketches by Boz*, and might have been an extension of one of the bright sketches, just as *Oliver Twist* might have been an extension of one of the darker sketches. But, Chesterton observes, *Nicholas Nickleby* 'coincided with his resolution to be a great novelist and his final belief that he could be one.' [1] This gives the novel some claim to closer attention than it has so far received, and without implying that it is a neglected masterpiece I shall try to show that it does

[1] *Criticisms and Appreciations of Charles Dickens*, 1911, p. 31.

offer a number of valuable insights into the Dickensian imagination at a formative stage.

Some of the positive qualities in *Nickleby* are of a kind greatly relished by the Victorians, and still readily appreciated by unsophisticated readers; in particular, the richness of characterization. Here, however, the alert modern critic has nothing to say: he may secretly enjoy the exuberance of Squeers, of Mrs. Nickleby, the Kenwigs, Mr. Lillyvick, Mr. Mantalini, and Crummles and his associates; or he may, if he is sufficiently fastidious, find them something of an embarrassment. In many ways our critical inability to share the simple Victorian interest in character as such is a considerable loss, since it makes us unable to grasp one of the fundamentals of Dickens's art. There is, in fact, something essentially puzzling about Dickens's larger-than-life characters, such as those I have just named. They are not, of course, realistic figures as we are used to finding them in, say, Jane Austen or George Eliot; but on the other hand, the comparison with Jonson's comedy of humours which is sometimes made is only of limited value. There is a solidity and vitality about these characters which one would not expect to find in mere stage types; still less are they simply 'caricatures' as is sometimes alleged. Even within the confines of *Nickleby* itself there is an obvious difference between these memorable characters, the amiable stock figures such as Nicholas and Kate, and the obviously melodramatic types such as Ralph, Sir Mulberry Hawk, Lord Frederick, and Gride (though even within this last group further distinctions can be drawn). Dickens, in creating these characters, seems to have had access to certain deep springs of unconscious life of a kind which are not available to more sophisticated novelists.

The serious modern reader, however, might feel on safer ground in asserting that, lively and remarkable though the characters in *Nickleby* might be, they exist in complete isolation from each other; they do not form part of a significant moral pattern. And this is certainly true. More than any other of Dickens's novels, *Nickleby* displays an atomistic world. *Pickwick* was picaresque both in form and spirit; its one unifying principle was the desirability of constant motion, and it was infused with a sense of the infinite and delightful possibilities of life. *Nickleby* is also in the picaresque mode, but much less wholeheartedly so. Incidents do not follow one another with quite the same breathless rapidity as in *Pickwick*, where they blur together to form an acceptable substitute for the lack of extended fictional pattern. In *Nickleby* the progression of events is slower, and one has time to be aware of them—and the characters involved—as separate and isolated. We are still a very long way from the great ramifying symbols that unify the major works of Dickens's maturity: the fog and the Court of Chancery in *Bleak House*, the prison in *Little Dorrit*, the river and the dust-heaps in *Our Mutual Friend*. *Nickleby* suffers by offering neither the carefree linear progression through the world of *Pickwick*, nor the intricate movements round a central point of the later fiction.

Nicholas is not a very robust picaresque hero when compared with Tom Jones or Roderick Random; nevertheless, he is their genteel descendant, and at the beginning of the novel we see him footloose and with his way to make in the world. Yet even here, his freedom is far from total. It is significant that the start of his first adventure, the episode in the Yorkshire school, is dominated by an anticipation of one of the great fixed symbols of Dickens's later fiction: the prison. The Saracen's Head Inn, Squeers's headquarters when he is in London, is overshadowed by Newgate:

There, at the very core of London, in the heart of its business and anima-tion, in the midst of a whirl of noise and motion: stemming as it were the giant currents of life that flow ceaselessly on from different quarters and meet beneath its walls: stands Newgate; and in that crowded street on which it frowns so darkly—within a few feet of the squalid tottering houses—upon the very spot on which the venders of soup and fish and damaged fruit are now plying their trades—scores of human beings, amidst a roar of sounds to which even the tumult of a great city is as nothing, four, six, or eight strong men at a time, have been hurried violently and swiftly from the world, when the scene has been rendered frightful with excess of human life; when curious eyes have glared from casement, and house-top, and wall and pillar; and when, in the mass of white and upturned faces, the dying wretch, in his all-comprehensive look of agony, has met not one—not one—that bore the impress of pity or compassion. (Ch. 4.)

Here, in this image of the prison 'stemming as it were the giant currents of life' we are in touch, for a moment, with a major Dicken-sian preoccupation. In its context it prepares us for Nicholas's, and our, encounter with the nearest equivalent to a prison in *Nicholas Nickleby*, Dotheboys Hall, and for Squeers's cruel and pitiless regime.

The picaresque hero traditionally had the right to get up and leave when he found himself in an insupportable position; and Nicholas prepares to exercise this right when he can take no more of the horrors of Dotheboys Hall. The world is, indeed, all before him where to choose. But, as the following exchange with his pitiful *Döppelganger* (and, as we are to discover, cousin), Smike, suggests, his faith in the infinite possibilities of the world is not very great. The best he can say is that it is a better place than Dotheboys Hall:

'Tell me,' said the boy imploringly, 'Oh do tell me, *will* you go—*will* you?'

'I shall be driven to that at last!' said Nicholas. 'The world is before me, after all.'

'Tell me,' urged Smike, 'is the world as bad and dismal as this place?'

'Heaven forbid,' replied Nicholas, pursuing the train of his own thoughts, 'its hardest, coarsest toil, were happiness to this.' (Ch. 12.)

Nicholas, it is true, is still able to exercise his freedom in a direct and physical way—by beating Squeers, and then making off with Smike.

After his return to London, Nicholas sets off with Smike in traditional picaresque fashion to see what the world has to offer him. But immediately before starting out, and before he knows that Smike is to accompany him, Nicholas is oppressed by the separation from his family and the sense of his own isolation:

To have committed no fault, and yet to be so entirely alone in the world; to be separated from the only persons he loved, and to be proscribed like a criminal, when six months ago he had been surrounded by every comfort, and looked up to, as the chief hope of his family—this was hard to bear. He had not deserved it either. (Ch. 20.)

The atomization to which I have referred is very apparent here; it had already been exemplified—as J. Hillis Miller has noted—in Dickens's account of Miss La Creevy, who 'existed entirely within herself, talked to herself, made a confidant of herself, was as sarcastic as she could be, on people who offended her, by herself; pleased herself, and did no harm.' (Ch. 20.)

After Smike and Nicholas have left London to make their way to Portsmouth the picaresque mode is, as it were, swallowed up by the other element which literary historians would indicate as a dominant influence on *Nicholas Nickleby*, namely the theatre. The two wayfarers are absorbed into the larger entity of Mr. Vincent Crummles's travelling theatre. Crummles and his troupe provide a good many entertaining passages, and on any level the scenes in which they feature must be reckoned as among the most successful in the book. Beyond this, however, the theatre represents the nearest equivalent to a central unifying metaphor that *Nickleby* has to offer. Its significance has been well stated by Hillis Miller:

Nicholas Nickleby's experience among the provincial actors of Crummles's company is of great importance as a critique of the way of life of all the characters here . . . we come to recognize that the other characters in the novel have the same kind of existence, make the same theatrical gestures and speeches, and that the central action of *Nicholas Nickleby* is the elaborate performance of a cheap melodrama, complete with sneering villains, insulted virginity, and a courageous young hero who appears in the nick of time. . . . The scenes of the provincial theatre thus act as a parody of the main plot, and of the life of the chief characters in the main story.[2]

This is substantially accurate, though I think Mr. Miller has underestimated the amount of sheer vitality that the theatricality conceals, and that his fixing of the epithet 'cheap' to 'melodrama' is something of a stock response. We are in need of a critical theory of melodrama; if we had one, it might shed light on a number of obscure places in Dickens. Nevertheless, there can be no doubt that the whole novel is pervaded with theatricality. This is true not only of Crummles and the other players, but of such obvious stage villains as Ralph, Sir Mulberry Hawk, and the miser Gride, not to mention the stock heroines, Kate and Madeline Bray. Nicholas himself, for that matter, is more at home in the rôle of juvenile lead than of wandering hero. Mr. Crummles recognizes his essential theatricality at their first meeting: ' "There's genteel comedy in your walk and manner, juvenile tragedy in your eye, and touch-and-go farce in your laugh," said Mr. Vincent Crummles.' (Ch. 22.) And when Nicholas finally takes his hurried departure from the company, Mr. Crummles ruefully observes that Nicholas is a better actor off the stage than on it: 'if he only acted like that, what a deal of money he'd draw!'

Yet granted this dominant note of theatricality one can go on to make certain distinctions. Although it is in one sense a crude result of the fact that the young Dickens was still learning the art of writing novels, it does have its function in *Nickleby*. In a novel where the mode of presentation is atomistic and fragmentary, theatricality plays a certain part in uniting the various elements. Thus, whilst Nicholas

---

[2] *Charles Dickens: the World of His Novels*, 1958, pp. 89–90.

is working as an actor, his sister and mother in London are becoming increasingly involved in a world where life itself is theatrical to a high degree. The centre of this world is Sir Mulberry Hawk. Hawk and his aristocratic hangers-on are usually dismissed as being feeble attempts by Dickens at the sort of thing that Thackeray did infinitely better in *Vanity Fair*. Certainly they show that the young middle-class radical had a decidedly external view of upper-class debauchery. Yet Hawk does have his own kind of vigour if we consider him not as a ludicrous imitation of a real-life baronet, but rather as a splendid example of the demon king of traditional pantomime (he can also be seen as a debased version of Richardson's Lovelace). Hawk's acolytes are also very stagy creatures, as we see when Mr. Pyke and Mr. Pluck visit Mrs. Nickleby on Sir Mulberry's behalf. ' "Ha!" cried Mr. Pyke, at this juncture, snatching something from the chimney-piece with a theatrical air. "What is this! what do I behold!" ' (Ch. 27.) Hawk and Lord Frederick invite Mrs. Nickleby to the theatre, and whilst there they meet Kate and Kate's employer, Mrs. Wititterly: ' "I take an interest, my lord," said Mrs. Wititterly, "such an interest in the drama." ' (Ch. 27.) Mrs. Wititterly is as theatrical in her own way as the rest; we are told in the next chapter, that after lying on the same sofa for three and a half years she had 'got up a little pantomime of graceful attitudes, and now threw herself into the most striking of the series, to astonish the visitors.'

Theatricality extends beyond Crummles and Nicholas, and Hawk and Mrs. Wititterly (and here one would include Mr. Mantalini also); Newman Noggs, Nicholas's faithful ally in his uncle's camp, is also affected by it:

As the usurer turned for consolation to his books and papers, a performance was going on outside his office-door, which would have occasioned him no small surprise, if he could by any means have become acquainted with it.

Newman Noggs was the sole actor. He stood at a little distance from the door, with his face towards it; and with the sleeves of his coat turned back at the wrists, was occupied in bestowing the most vigorous, scientific, and straightforward blows upon the empty air. (Ch. 28.)

Even the Kenwigs family, who have little to do with the central figures, have their actress friend Miss Petowker, and are inordinately proud of their daughter, the dancing Morleena: ' "If I was blessed with a—a—child——" said Miss Petowker, blushing, "of such genius as that, I would have her out at the Opera instantly." ' (Ch. 14.)

Yet though the prevailing theatrical images and behaviour give us an indication of how the novel should be read, and though they provide a certain unifying element, their value is manifestly limited. The limitation is evident from the two possible senses of the word 'theatrical' itself; it can either mean pertaining to the theatre, or showy and affected, with the further implication of being deficient in reality. The element of theatricality in *Nicholas Nickleby* cannot, by its very nature, make up for the absence of true relationships between the characters; it can partially conceal the fundamental atomism of the work, but does not abolish it. What remains, quite vividly in many places, is the vitality of the isolated individuals; but there is no meaningful relation between them. *Nicholas Nickleby*, one might say, is theatrical without being dramatic. And nowhere is this lack of relationships more apparent than in the absence of the most extensive of all: society itself. Lionel Trilling, in his essay on *Little Dorrit*, writes, '*Little Dorrit* is about society, which certainly does not distinguish it from the rest of Dickens's novels . . .'.[3] This, I think, needs some qualification; it is hard to see that *Pickwick* is about society in a very central way, though the absence is not felt there; in fact, much of its charm stems from the fact that its characters are not crushed by a burden of social consciousness. The eighteenth-century picaresque novel, from which *Pickwick* and *Nickleby* were descended, was certainly not concerned with society in the manner of the later Dickens and other Victorian novelists; rather, it took it for granted, and was much more concerned with the assertion of the hero's individuality. Nicholas, as we have seen, is much less fitted for this assertiveness than the heroes of Smollett or Fielding; but at the same time, the social dimension, so exigent in the later Dickens, is conspicuously lacking. And its absence is felt far more than in *Pickwick*, since Dickens is quite clearly concerned with concrete manifestations of society. Thus, we have in the second chapter the satirical account of the United Metropolitan Improved Hot Muffin and Crumpet Baking and Punctual Delivery Company, which Humphry House has related to a feverish wave of company promoting in the mid-1820's.[4] And of course in his picture of Squeers and Dotheboys Hall, Dickens was prompted by his passionate moral fervour about the actual Yorkshire schools of the 'twenties and 'thirties. Neverthe-

[3] *The Opposing Self*, 1955, p. 51.   [4] *The Dickens World*, 1950, p. 58.

less, we see from the list of negatives by which Ralph Nickleby is presented at the beginning of Chapter 2, that Dickens wishes to avoid giving him any precise social identity:

Mr. Ralph Nickleby was not, strictly speaking, what you would call a merchant, neither was he a banker, nor an attorney, nor a special pleader, nor a notary. He was certainly not a tradesman, and still less could he lay any claim to the title of a professional gentleman; for it would have been impossible to mention any recognized profession to which he belonged.

Ralph is sometimes referred to by the pre-capitalist term, 'usurer', which has powerful associations, and tells one a good deal about Dickens's attitude. But Ralph is, in essentials, the evil fairy who malignly intervenes in the action whenever he can. And Ralph, the bad fairy disguised as a man of business, has to be balanced by the Cheerybles, who are good fairies in similar disguise (despite their origin in the Brothers Grant). At the end of the novel, Ralph is hanged and Squeers is transported, and Nicholas triumphantly breaks open the hated prison of Dotheboys Hall and releases the wretched inmates. It is a stirring example of the ultimate triumph of right over wrong; but it could only have been presented as a solution by a writer who was not yet thinking in social terms. What, in fact, does the overthrow of Dotheboys Hall accomplish, and what becomes of the boys? Earlier on, Squeers himself had ironically hinted at this very possibility:

'Hold your noise, sir, in a gentleman's office, or I'll run away from my family and never come back any more; and then what would become of all them precious and forlorn lads as would be let loose on the world, without their best friend at their elbers!' (Ch. 34.)

In all of Dickens's later fiction, certainly from the mid-forties onwards, society is inescapably present: one need only consider the vast intricate image of *Bleak House* where all levels of society, from the Dedlocks to poor Jo, are seen as inextricably related. Often, it is true, Dickens tries to adopt an attitude of rejection to society; Raymond Williams has remarked that *Hard Times*, for example, 'is the work of a man who has "seen through" society, who has found them all out.' [5] Yet he has first to experience its reality. The idyllic, presocial world of *Pickwick*, one might say, represented an Eden to which the imagination of the mature Dickens constantly strove, though unsuccessfully, to return. *Nickleby* is far less idyllic, but it is

---

[5] *Culture and Society*, 1958, p. 96.

certainly pre-social: it merely shows us groups of isolated individuals gesticulating in front of a painted backcloth. The theatricality of *Nickleby* is a substitute for actual social relationships.

Yet though *Nickleby* differs in this important respect from the later Dickens, it nevertheless embodies a theme which is constantly reflected in the mature novels, and which is, in fact, central to his work and rooted in his own most profound experience: the oppressed child. The almost contemporary novel, *Oliver Twist*, presents this theme in a clear-cut and unmistakable fashion; in *Nickleby* the treatment is less explicit, but much wider in its implications. The horrifying account of 'the young noblemen of Dotheboys Hall' in Ch. 8 makes very apparent Dickens's fascinated interest in cruelty to children, and the passionate response it aroused in him:

But the pupils—the young noblemen! How the last faint traces of hope, the remotest glimmering of any good to be derived from his efforts in this den, faded from the mind of Nicholas as he looked in dismay around! Pale and haggard faces, lank and bony figures, children with the countenances of old men, deformities with irons upon their limbs, boys of stunted growth, and others whose long meagre legs would hardly bear their stooping bodies, all crowded on the view together; there were the bleared eye, the hare-lip, the crooked foot, and every ugliness or distortion that told of unnatural aversion conceived by parents for their offspring, or of young lives which, from the earliest dawn of infancy, had been one horrible endurance of cruelty and neglect. There were little faces which should have been handsome, darkened with the scowl of sullen, dogged suffering; there was childhood with the light of its eye quenched, its beauty gone, and its helplessness alone remaining; there were vicious-faced boys, brooding, with leaden eyes, like malefactors in a jail; and there were young creatures on whom the sins of their frail parents had descended, weeping even for the mercenary nurses they had known, and lonesome even in their loneliness. With every kindly sympathy and affection blasted in its birth, with every young and healthy feeling flogged and starved down, with every revengeful passion that can fester in swollen hearts, eating its evil way to their core in silence, what an incipient Hell was breeding here!

This, indeed, is an Inferno of the Infants. Against it we may set, as a contrasting vision, Dickens's glimpse of what he conceives of as the paradisal lives of the gipsy children described at the beginning of Ch. 50. It is a primitivistic account, which has obvious affinities with the presentation of the circus in *Hard Times*:

Even the sunburnt faces of gipsy children, half naked though they be, suggest a drop of comfort. It is a pleasant thing to see that the sun has been there; to know that the air and light are on them every day; to feel that they *are* children, and lead children's lives; and if their pillows be damp, it is with the dews of Heaven, and not with tears: that the limbs of their girls are free, and that they are not crippled by distortions, imposing an unnatural and horrible penance upon their sex; and their lives are spent, from day to day, at least among the waving trees, and not in the midst of dreadful engines which make young children old before they know what childhood is, and give them the exhaustion and infirmity of age without, like age, the privilege to die. God send that old nursery tales were true, and that gipsies stole such children by the score!

The figure of Smike, in becoming Nicholas's faithful companion, connects the hell of Dotheboys Hall with the young people at the centre of the story: Nicholas and Kate, and, later, Madeline. For it is not only children who are victims; by extension of the fundamental theme, we see the four young people, scarcely yet entered upon adult life, surrounded by a menacing circle of oppressors, whose names betray their rôles to an extent unusual even in Dickens: Ralph Nickleby (=knuckle-boy; in Ch. 9, Fanny Squeers, appropriately enough in view of her environment, applies this term to Nicholas before she has met him, but it clearly belongs to Ralph); Squeers (=queer + squeeze); Hawk; and Gride (=grind + greed). It is in keeping with the general absence of meaningful relationships in *Nickleby* that the relationship which most vitally concerns children—that between child and parent—should be, for the most part, perverted or lacking. (The only relationships that cohere at all are those between the young people themselves; between Smike and Nicholas, and between Nicholas and his sister.) And here we have another link with the mature fiction; Trilling has pointed out the large number of false or inadequate parents in *Little Dorrit*. Dotheboys Hall itself is one huge indictment of the failure of parental responsibility, and Smike, its representative inmate, is revealed as trebly a victim; first, of Squeers, as the wicked foster father; then, of Snawley, Squeers's agent, who appears as his perjured would-be father; and finally it is revealed that his actual father, and the author of all his miseries, was Ralph himself, the arch-oppressor of youth. Nicholas and Kate are the victims of weak rather than of vicious parents; no one was less fitted for a rôle of maternal responsibility than Mrs. Nickleby, of whom Gissing remarked, 'it would be a delicate question of psychology to distinguish her from the harmless smiling idiot whom we think it unnecessary and cruel to put under restraint': [6] Madeline Bray is wholly subject to her ailing but tyrannical father, who prepares to offer her as a sexual victim to the miser Gride. It seems to me, incidentally, that Dickens was unwilling to face the full imaginative implications of the Madeline-Gride situation, which would have been extremely disagreeable, and that this is why Madeline is such a cypher, compared even with Kate, and why all the chapters centred on her are so inadequately realized and, indeed, so badly written (as so often in Dickens, a sense of emotional falsity is readily apparent from the large proportion of unconscious blank verse they contain).

Even if we turn to young Wackford Squeers, who is pampered by his father while the boys in the school starve, we have a picture of exploited youth of another kind, since the boy is made to gorge himself, not for his own good, but so that he will be a fitting advertisement for the school. Mr. Crummles, too, though in some sense a representative of the positive values of the novel, seems to exploit his several children; in particular, the suggestion that the Infant Phenomenon had had her growth stunted by gin and late nights, though only lightly made, has unpleasant implications. The nearest approximation to normal parenthood and family life is to be found in the mercenary Kenwigs, who are not very satisfactory representatives, one would have thought. It is against this background of false or inadequate parenthood that we must set the compensating factor of the oppressive paternalism of the Cheerybles, 'the good spirits of a fairy-tale', as Gissing described them.

And indeed, it is as a fairy-tale, the embodiment of a child-like vision of the world, that *Nicholas Nickleby* must ultimately be read. Nicholas and Kate remain children at heart, almost to the very end unwilling to take on the responsibilities of adult life. The overthrow of Dotheboys Hall is the oppressed child's vision of the tables finally being turned, rather than the genuine eradication of a social evil. Nicholas persuades himself that he cannot, or must not, see any more of Madeline, and he persuades his sister that of course she cannot consider marrying Frank Cheeryble. He looks forward to their unmarried old age together in a way that deliberately omits the intervening years of adult life:

[6] *Charles Dickens*, 1902, pp. 169-70.

It seems but yesterday that we were playfellows, Kate, and it will seem but tomorrow when we are staid old people, looking back to these cares as we look back, now, to those of our childish days: and recollecting with a melancholy pleasure that the time was, when they could move us. Perhaps, then, when we are quaint old folks and talk of the times when our step was lighter and our hair not grey, we may be even thankful for the trials that so endeared us to each other and turned our lives into that current, down which we shall have glided so peacefully and calmly. (Ch. 61.)

Passages like this suggest that *Nicholas Nickleby* is an embodiment of the Babes in the Wood myth, with its central image of the young people, lost and friendless in a menacing world, hugging each other for support. It is only by the direct intervention of the good fairies, the Cheerybles, that Kate and Nicholas are released from the spell and are enabled to marry and have families of their own.

To say that *Nicholas Nickleby*, with its pervading theatricality, its lack of social orientation, and its primitivistic longings to return to a child-like condition, is a fairy-tale, may be, in a sense, to account for it, but I am aware that this description is not likely to endear it to the tough modern reader, for whom 'adult' and 'mature' are basic critical touchstones. And yet to describe the novel as 'immature' seems somehow grotesquely inappropriate. Immaturity is a characteristic of adolescence rather than of childhood, and much that is positive in *Nicholas Nickleby* stems directly from Dickens's own involvement with the life of children. To understand it is to grasp a little more fully the varied and mysterious world of his imagination.

THE OLD CURIOSITY SHOP

Gabriel Pearson

'Let us go ring fancy's knell.'—DICK SWIVELLER

OF COURSE, the novel is seriously flawed: but is it beyond redemption? Terms like 'episodic intensification' are only an hieratic way of saying it has good bits which stop its being downright awful. For Oscar Wilde and Aldous Huxley, who danced with such glee on Little Nell's coffin, the book was dead, buried, and damned, slain by a slow poison of mawkish tears. Jeffrey, Hood and Poe thought their tears evidenced Shakespearian pathos, that they were guilty of justified bardolatry, not premeditated necrophilia. At least both parties knew where they stood. But recent commentators shift anxiously. Nell, they know, won't do. But, they explain, children did after all die more frequently then. And maybe, the argument runs, the Victorians were tuned in to a different emotional frequency. Tears once had a sanctioned place in the male repertoire: Homer's heroes wept. But in case Nell is impossible, there is always Quilp, 'crackling with vitality', as Edgar Johnson has it. Everyone today is of the devil's party, and knows it. Quilp is immensely respectable (resembling his creator in his ferocious practical joking, sadistic manipulation of character and omnivorous appetite for the indigestible jaggedness of things). And so, against Fitzgerald's 'Nelly-ad', we retort with a Quilpiad.

But one energetically sustained monologue hardly rescues the work. Nor does a discrete marking system—ticks for Quilp, waxworks, and the Brasses; crosses for Nell, Kit, and the Garlands—take one beyond, with luck, a bare pass. And so the documentary plea is entered once more: the novel is valued for the quality of its social outrage or its psychological revelation. There is ample material for

77

both approaches; though the first seems to me overplayed. The 'bands of unemployed . . . maddened men, armed with sword and firebrand . . .' remain a background to Nell's very personal suffering. Undoubtedly, Dickens wanted to force a connection; but the asocial, fairy-tale setting of Quilp and Nell, though inwardly consistent (so that Quilp living on Tower Hill gives the impression of actually living in the Tower, while Nell from the lumber of the shop through the punches, giants, dwarves, and wax-works to the village where she dies is wrapt in mock-Gothic gloom), effectively disables any social actuality. The biographical relevance is obvious and well-documented. Through Quilp, Dickens savages feeble wife and hostile mother-in-law. Little Nell represents the apotheosis of Mary Hogarth. And the whole novel can be read as an immense, unruly wreath laid on the clammy marble of Kensal Green Cemetery.

These approaches make the novel sound interesting, but do not justify it artistically. Even the discovery, beneath wreath and mortuary slab, of the bones of an early-Victorian Lolita, does no more than testify to the complexity of Dickens's emotional life. But primary concern must lie with the life of the novel. An initial survey is hardly reassuring. The Quilp-Nell disjunction seems entirely explained by the novel's forced expansion out of a short story hastily composed to rescue the dismal performance of Master Humphrey. All bears the sign of last-minute improvisation and consequent awkward backings out of blind-alleys. Master Humphrey's first-person narration hurriedly scrambles to a stop at the end of Ch. 3. Nell's promisingly nasty brother, Fred, simply disappears a third of the way through to turn up in the last chapter in a Paris morgue and make a blunt point about gambling and heredity. It is hard to say why the Garlands are there at all. In so short a novel, given that they neither act nor manifest themselves except through a communal club-foot, they hardly illustrate a Shakesperian foison. At first sight, there is nothing that can be dignified as plot; only a sketchy and, for Dickens, unusually skeletal intrigue. Garland's brother, the Bachelor, works as a hastily rigged-up line to communicate Nell's whereabouts. The Schoolmaster catches Nell in her death-swoon like a too artfully placed safety-net. A surfeit of improvised old men are retained to lend a hand with a commentary or coincidence. Dickens clearly did not know where he was going when in Ch. 1 in the manuscript Nell informs Master Humphrey that she is pawning diamonds. Altogether, the evidence points to a rush-job, executed with verve and journalistic insolence (Dickens virtually patented the scoop). But where is the artistic shaping, let alone intelligence or integrity?

But the figure of Nell remains the basic objection. Though the death-scenes are usually singled out for offensive exploitation of emotion, it is not so much these (they occupy little space) but the total conception of the child as heroine, martyr, angel, and child-bride of the underworld that repels. The reason why Nell offends more notoriously than Oliver is that so much significance is being read into her, and all so unsupported by anything she does or suffers. Ultimately, like Oliver, she remains a blank. Like Oliver she is crowded out of the centre by the peripheral life of the novel. But unlike Oliver, a great deal is being claimed for her, by lyrical commentary, by other characters, and by a structure that treats her death as climax. This crowding out of centre by periphery is characteristic of the early novels in general. Dickens must have realized this. So there seems to be a deliberate effort to build Nell up—to put behind her all the resources of 'style' and, at the same time, to allegorize her, to essentialize in her as far as possible one aspect of Dickens's diffused yet tenaciously held religion of Christian good cheer. Into this religion, the brutal blankness of death obstinately refuses to fit. Yet death was something that Dickens, unlike William Empson, was not prepared 'to be blank upon'. Undoubtedly, the death of Mary Hogarth was something like a religious crisis. Nell was an unsuccessful attempt to grope and feel a way through this crisis, to locate death as a human event. Dickens probes and rummages around the grave. He attempts to feel what it is like being dead. But this exploration yields only two sorts of imagery: the shadowy remembrance of pre-London Rochester and Victorian funereal decoration. Blank verse and pathetic fallacy meanwhile secretly give the game away. Dickens could not after all feel what death is like. He could only feel what it was like to try to feel it.

This is surely how his blank verse should be understood. But also, as an attempt to compensate for Quilp's rich riot of life in London. Dickens's use of blank verse has always been automatically censured, as though its occurrence in a prose work must be wrong. Yet there is no reason, on principle, why it should be. The query as to its quality, which is really a query about function, does not get raised. When Miss Monflathers brutally dismisses Miss Edwards for being nice to 'a wax-works child', Dickens, through contrast of class-inhumanity with quiet sympathy, has made his point. His blank verse line: '. . . the great gate closed upon a bursting heart' (Ch. 31) merely drowns the scene in irrelevant declamation. Yet this is not quite indefensible: 'Miss Monflathers, although she had long been known as a politician, had never appeared before as an original poet' (i.e. when she improvises on Dr. Watts at Nell's expense). Dickens then, however ineptly, tries to explode Monflathian pseudo-poetics with true Dickensian 'chords' rung from 'the human heart'. (Ch. 55.) These same chords he was later, with perhaps unconscious self-satire, to put in the mouth of Guppy in *Bleak House*.

Often, a blank verse line will act as a kind of charged formula which Dickens hopes will gather resonance and elevate wish-fulfilment and elegaic self-pity into significant statement. 'Death does not change us more than life, my dear' (Ch. 19) is a good example. Well, it is a thought; but a pretty blank one which conducts little meaning from what goes on in the novel, while having an air of asking to be taken seriously as valid consolation, which it isn't. Nell's flight from London can be read as Dickens's attempt to explore death. But it is, more than this, an effort to recover a pre-urban innocence, to redeem the waste land of the city where men live 'solitary . . . as in the bucket of a human well'. There is something mythic, if not heroic, as well as regressive in this search; and in one aspect Nell comes close to being a sort of folk-hero. When Dickens has this mythic intention firmly in mind, we get blank verse descriptions of her death-place like:

It was another world, where sin and sorrow never came; a tranquil place of rest, where nothing evil entered. (Ch. 54.)

This is the land of Cockayne, the pre-industrial paradise, the feeling for which is justified by the furnaces and blighting misery of the Black Country Nell has traversed. 'The primitive quality of the feeling is breath-taking: yet there is a corresponding mythic strength which is appropriately rendered in metre. Again, the symbolism of well and church-tower in the death-village, however blatant and forced, is not entirely external. If we bear in mind 'the bucket of a human well' and 'dead mankind a million fathoms deep', a texture of internal reference—or perhaps echo—does tentatively emerge. Metre catches these echoes and holds them in suspense so that they add up to an effect. However damaging the admission, this reader has to confess to an active resistance to the funereal blandishments of Nell's dissolution.

Yet in the end Dickens's manipulation and exploitation of 'poetical' language to evade insight and instigate excited reverie around the blank fact of death must be acknowledged. But before the point is relinquished, some genuine insight should be granted. Dickens has clearly caught hold of one aspect of death. In the scene of Nell's first mortuary meditation, she converses with an old woman visiting the grave of her long dead husband. This scene does expose one simple and richly disturbing insight: that the dead are static, embalmed in memory, while life plays havoc with the persistent identity men would like to rest securely in:

She spoke of the dead man as if he had been her son or grandson, with a kind of pity for his youth, growing out of her own old age, and an exalting of his strength and manly beauty as compared with her own weakness and decay; and yet she spoke about him as her husband too, and thinking of herself in connection with him, as she used to be and not as she was now, talked . . . as if he were but dead yesterday, and she, separated from her former self, were thinking of the happiness of that comely girl who seemed to have died with him. (Ch. 17.)

Here, in Dickens's noble *oratio obliqua* (generally one of his stylistic strengths), purity of diction fuses with an almost ballad-like singleness of insight ('he's young, but he's agrowing') to expose a central paradox that justifies itself in the serious pun on 'growing out of her own old age'. But this is admittedly exceptional. Normally, there is the frantic forcing into maxim and emblem which results in such limp reflections as '. . . how much charity, mercy, and purified affection, would seem to have their growth in dusty graves'. Here Dickens's own uncertainty, betrayed in abstraction and evasive syntax, neutralizes the possibilities of 'growth'. Clearly, the lyrical blank verse of the Nell sequences cannot balance the theatrical vitality of Quilp's cackling monologues and ferocious practical jokes. (His 'resurrection' scene almost parodies Nell's apotheosis.) Dickens does better when he abandons lyrical commentary for exploration of the relationship between Nell and her grandfather. This relationship turns upon reversal of rôles—Nell as mother, Grandfather as sometimes naughty child—determined by wish-fulment and fantasy (of the kinds which say: Really I am superior to my parents and my death will teach them my value). Hence the relationship is fore-

ordained, the rôles drearily static, written into the novel from without, not sustained and developed from within. Yet a surprising
tension sometimes develops, particularly in the scenes of Nell's tor-
mented vigils, when she waits for old Trent's return. One such scene,
early on, brilliantly renders her night-terrors and slightly hysterical
solitude. (One observes Dickens's ability to create a state of mind
even when he fails to create a person to suffer it. Indeed, in the early
novels mental states and concretely sustained presences both exist,
but separately.) Here, the crisis of Nell's terror is that her Grandfather 'should kill himself and his blood come creeping, creeping to
her own bedroom door'. Childhood emotion is not the less accurately
for being generally rendered, the visual detail blurring into sub-
jectivity:

> Still there was one late shop . . . which sent forth a ruddy glare upon
> the pavement even yet, and looked bright and companionable. (Ch. 9.)

This generalized zone of childhood consciousness is quite different
from the sharply recollected childhood of *David Copperfield* or
Great Expectations where the tension between the recollected child
and the remembering adult is a function of a more solid and integrated sense of identity existing through time. In those novels, the
child is morally situated, his emotions qualified and distanced by
comedy, not engulfed by raw emotion and haunted by humours as in
the early novels. In these, Dickens seems able to resuscitate childhood as a baffled, protean and fluid psychic economy in which people
change value, impulse and action are substitutes for each other and
absolutes clash and dissolve within the same personality. This state is
closer to actually lived childhood life than Pip's recollections of
himself, whose very vividness and clarity are slightly illusory
products of retrospect. Pip achieves himself as a man to find himself
neither very good nor very bad, but principally deceived and self-
deceived. What he could not have been, short of conversion, is very
good or evil. Yet impulses of love or aggression are, to the young
child, precisely very good or very evil. But the grown Pip, in order
to tell Pip's story at all, has to limit his childhood experience to what
made him grow up. His retrospect is bound to be both analytic and
exclusive if it is not to be discontinuous. Hence, his deep subjective
sense of guilt and evil has to be embodied separately—in Orlick.
Dickens failed to solve this problem in *Dombey and Son* and *David
Copperfield*. Consequently, Florence remains an adult child while

David's life falls into two ill-related segments. There is no such problem with Oliver and Nell, who do not attempt to mature. And so Nell remains a zone of consciousness in which the grandfather's imagined blood comes 'creeping, creeping along the floor' as though it were the murdered and, by primitive laws of guilt-transference, potentially murderous grandfather himself.

The force of this suggestion is substantiated by the chilling scene in 'The Valiant Soldier' where old Trent crawls into Nell's room to rob her: 'How slowly it (Trent's shape) seemed to move, now that she could hear but not see it, *creeping* along the floor'. (Ch. 30. My italics.) 'It', of course, brilliantly suggests one fragment of the old man's split personality:

She had no fear of the dear old grandfather . . . but (he) seemed like another creature in his shape, a monstrous distortion of his image, a something to recoil from and be more afraid of, because it bore a likeness to him . . . (Ch. 31.)

Dickens is certainly no novice in the underworld of consciousness. In his fundamentally impossible attempt to relate Nell to Quilp, he seizes on the gambling mania to show the grandfather as, in one aspect, Quilpine himself. This has the advantage of naturalizing Quilp's demonism by tethering it to psychic actuality. 'Monstrous distortion of his image, a something to recoil from' links the grandfather's obsession firmly to demonic possession by Quilpine malignity. Nell earlier 'shrank timidly from the dwarf's advances' (Ch. 11) while during the near encounter in the gateway 'Quilp showed in the moonlight like some monstrous image'. (Ch. 27.) Some paragraphs later, a tribute to his psychic pervasiveness, Nell feels 'as if she were hemmed in by a legion of Quilps, and the very air were filled with them'. The old man's evil takes the basic form of illegitimate dreams of wealth. Here sounds, however mutedly, the first criticism of the Great Expectations theme so complacently approved in *Oliver Twist*. His mania cuts him off from true relationship. Subtly enough, not only money as a means, but the means to the means, perverts its end. Dickens skilfully exhibits obsession undermining the love it purports to serve, when old Trent, attentive only to his inner voice, crazily igores the girl's living presence:

'She is poor now . . . but the time is coming when she shall be rich . . . it surely must come. It has come to other men who do nothing but waste and riot. When will it come to me!'

'I am very happy as I am, Grandfather,' said the child.

'Tush, tush!' returned the old man, 'thou dost not know—how should'st thou!' Then he muttered again between his teeth . . . (Ch. 1.)

The gambling mania (surely, on a personal level related to John Dickens's fatal combination of carelessness and industry) slips easily into the murder impulse. Nell, overhearing the old man's intention to rob Mrs. Jarley, is

distracted . . . with fearful thoughts of what he might be tempted and led on to do . . . detected in the act . . . with but a woman to struggle with. (Ch. 42.)

Quilp's demon activities do not of course extend to murder, though his outrages with gimlets and red-hot pokers against the figurehead are suggestive. What he does do is murder the proprieties of the novel. Granted Nell's 'saintly precocity' (Chesterton), his sardonic lawlessness is more destructive than murderous impulses in the grandfather because it threatens her not so much with martyrdom as with monstrousness. Monster begets monster, and Nell in her turn, as a monster of goodness, similarly exposes Quilp's gargoyle evil.

Dickens has real insight into the emotional chaos of a child's mind. In his early novels he also shares this chaos. The trouble with his insights is not that they are especially subterranean, as compared, say, with Swiveller's humour taken as a superficial norm, but that they are unevenly developed. He allows ambivalence in what Nell sees in others but none in herself. The grandfather's ambivalence looks like violence splitting because there is no answering ambivalence in Nell. Were she even potentially woman, she would be compromised by contradictory impulses, like Mrs. Quilp's, 'who had allied herself in wedlock to the dwarf in one of those strange infatuations', and who acknowledges to her woman critics that

'Quilp has such a way with him when he likes, that the best-looking woman here couldn't refuse him if I were dead, and she was free, and he chose to make love to her.' (Ch. 4.)

Mrs. Quilp is starkly enough implicated in sexuality. The account of Quilp keeping his wife up all night by him while he indulges his 'smoking humour' ('I shall probably blaze away all night') till the end of his cigar becomes 'a deep fiery red' is the closest we get to downright copulation in early-Victorian fiction. Dickens protects

Nell from sexuality by early sounding the mortuary note that is to keep her for ever a child. Yet neither is she merely a child. At fourteen she is ambiguously poised. The Marchioness, as soon as she appears, disables Nell's childhood by showing what real hardship and terror can do. She too is poised between childhood and womanhood, but her ambiguous state is not protective but fully justified both by her savage ill-usage in Sally Brass's underground torture-chamber (treatment more coldly sadistic than anything Oliver endures and intensified by Dickens's slightly prurient harping on Sally's virginity when she is in fact her mother) and by her subsequent tenderly adolescent ministrations over Dick. Nell never has to earn gratitude and veneration. She simply commands these qualities from the author himself. Whereas Mrs. Quilp and the Marchioness have to act and suffer, thus introducing an element of plot in the novel later developed by Dick. They seem to stand in for the unrealized human potential of the desperately etherialized angel martyr, to represent her in the Quilp world, one as his wife, the other as his child. They suffer real pain or hunger. Mrs. Quilp's 'arms . . . were seldom free from impressions of his fingers in black and blue colours'. (Ch. 13.) Likewise, Dick Swiveller's food is really gobbled by the starved Marchioness. In contrast, at the end of *her* agony, Nell 'felt that the time was close at hand when her enfeebled powers would bear her no more'. Diction abstracts pain. In the end, despite heavy underwriting, some complication of relationship and various substitutes to connect her with London where the life goes on, Nell suffers under the glaring strategy of an action designed to keep her from the intolerable scrutiny of Quilp—a critic whose caustic irreverence makes Oscar Wilde and Aldous Huxley sound tame.

Out of London, Nell can operate, if not as a person, at least as an aroma of consciousness. Contact with Quilp condenses her into the object of his grotesquely insolent and aggressively sexual humour. Dickens has to separate them; and this separation accounts for the sensational reverse in what has been valued in the novel. Certainly, it affects its whole structure. Devil and angel cannot be exposed to each other, let alone fused in one personality, without sending Dickens's whole moral cosmology crashing. Yet, despite this basic flaw, Nell connects with Quilp through old Trent's demoniacal possession and Quilp with her through the wax-works, the dwarfs who bite the giant's legs, the shop-lumber, and the church gargoyles. But Nell cannot withstand for long a direct assault on the values she embodies. Down they go beneath Quilp's withering contumely. Sometimes this assault is directly sexual, as when he invites her ('lures' is the word Dickens uses) to be his second Mrs. Quilp or occupies her 'bower' (again Dickens releases the erotic implications of the word) and defiles her bed with furious smoking. It is not exposure to contemptuous lust that damages Nell, but the way he builds images of her that utterly contradict the suitably slight and pallid martyr. 'Chubby, rosy, cosy, little Nell'—we can hear Quilp's sensual vowel-play positively putting flesh on her.

Quilp undermines Nell-values by his general war against woman-kind ('I'll have man-traps cunningly altered and improved for catching women'); against marriage ('I'll be a bachelor, a devil-may-care-bachelor' certainly puts the pro-Nell party of Master Humphrey, the Single Gentleman and the Bachelor himself in their place); against kinship, one of the most strident Nell-values ('. . . so much for dear relations. Thank God I acknowledge none'); and against namby-pamby goodness in the form of Kit ('I hate your virtuous people!' said the dwarf, throwing off a bumper of brandy, and smacking his lips, 'Oh! I hate 'em every one!'). Kit, like the Mar-chioness and Mrs. Quilp, represents Nell in London; and Quilp's plot against him, though feebly handled, deserves its prominence. He does represent real values like family loyalty and laughter. Yet at times his goodness looks a little oily like Rob the Grinder's in *Dombey and Son*. He is contained by Quilp's boy who somersaults in derision against respectable society, and even against Quilp himself, though 'there existed a strange kind of mutual liking between them' which links him oddly with Mrs. Quilp and Sally. He concludes by countering Kit's connubial felicity and joining a circus. Nothing shows more clearly than this pair how Dickens's sympathies can go two ways at once. The circus remains Dickens's one inadequate representation of artistic life. Quilp's boy, a bit like Dickens himself, 'afterwards tumbled with extraordinary success and to overflowing audiences'.

Quilp's very vitality savages Nell's pallid heroics. She is the puking heroine terrorized by that childhood arch-knock-about comedian, Punch. With his flailing fists and sticks, his coarse railery, his ferocity to dogs and women (his wife, Mrs. Jiniwin, Sally Brass, and Nell all play Judy to him), what else can he be? Though busy subverting Nell from the moment he orchestrates her sobbing lament to Mrs. Quilp with the creaking of the door (so that Nell's blank verse pathetics ought never to strike the inner ear without a derisive commentary of Quilpine creaking), his deadliest thrust against her comes in the shape of Punch himself, who, 'perched cross-legged upon a tomb-stone',

seemed to be pointing with the tip of his cap to a most flourishing epitaph, and to be chuckling over it with all his heart. (Ch. 16.)

A sketchy intrigue and an action designed to separate its two main protagonists seems largely to exhaust the novel. But only if one thinks with Chesterton of Dick Swiveller in terms of 'a lonely literary pleasure in exaggerative language'. Dick, however, assumes a more significant rôle—at first concealed by Dickens's almost reflex type-casting, verbal-labelling, and implication in cockney-pastoral sub-plot—as something like an initiator of plot. True, he is not a moral agent in any developed sense. He inflects and colours rather than transforms and sustains. He remains, however, with the Marchioness, the one person in whom potentialities are released and who changes his situation by changing himself. Initially he is stereotyped as comic relief in the rôle of Fred's fellow-tormentor of old Trent: 'The watchword to the old min is—fork.' Quite late he is still dismissed as a 'careless profligate . . . a brute only in the gratification of his appetites'. (Ch. 23.) Horne in 1844 (*New Spirit of the Age*) noted that in Dickens 'the first words that [a] man utters are the keynote of his character'. Dick in a sense is never more than the expansion of his original formula, a 'running on . . . with scraps of verse as if they were only prose in a hurry'. What happens is that with the disappearance of Fred, whom he was to support, he gradually shifts over to occupy the centre of the field of force created by the opposition between Nell and Quilp. His stream of patter choked with half-digested gobbets of quotation subtly becomes a subversive commentary against them both.

His anti-Quilp status is confirmed by his being the one person to trounce Quilp in open fight. Further he recognizes him as an evil spirit:

'If you're any sort of spirit at all, sir, you're an evil spirit. Choice spirits . . . are quite different sorts of people. . . .' (Ch. 23.)

In the same chapter, he drunkenly mimes Nell's predicament:

'Left an infant by my parents, at an early age . . . cast upon the world in my tenderest period, and thrown upon the mercies of a deluding dwarf, who can wonder at my weakness! Here's a miserable orphan for you.'

'Then,' said somebody hard by, 'let me be a father to you.'

The 'somebody' is Quilp, who attempts to complete the confused pattern of parents and children that dominates the book. Quilp is an evil parent-figure: to Nell, Kit, Fred, the Marchioness, and Quilp's boy. Opposed to him are 'good' parents: Grandfather, Schoolmaster, Single Gentleman, Bachelor, and Garland. This opposition Dick firmly escapes both by virtue of his early lawlessness and his subsequent rejection of Quilp and Sally in favour of the Marchioness. Till nearly the last he remains suspicious of Kit and veers over to his side only when Kit is in prison: but not, like the others, because he believes Kit innocent.

Dick is confirmed as a third force in the novel from the moment he confronts the Brasses. From then on, through his lonely bedtime fluting, through his discovery and succour of the Marchioness and hers of him, we are *with* Dick as we are with no one else. Dick's 'lonely literary pleasure' in parody and theatrical burlesque gives him a kind of double consciousness where Quilp and Nell utter themelves single-mindedly through caustic snarl or pallid diction. Dick, like the young Dickens (the likeness in names is suggestive), is stage-struck to the point where he must perform too. But to have an actor acting an actor on the stage is to risk sending up the total illusion; it undermines the rest of the cast. This is what happens. Ch. 55 ends on strong mortuary chords with Nell gazing 'at the declining sun' in anticipation of early death. Ch. 56 discovers Dick 'in a theatrical mood' wearing black crêpe round his hat as an 'emblem of woman's perfidy'. Succeeding dialogue with Chuckster seems to prolong in burlesque the subject of the previous chapter:

'All alone. Swiveller solus. " 'Tis now the witching——" '
' "Hour of night!" '
' "When churchyards yawn," '
' "And graves give up their dead." '

Dick's own parody poetics and theatricality establish themselves in endemic, neutralizing opposition to Nell's blank-verse elegiacs. The good work is taken up by Mr. Slum's bardic professionalism ('. . . it's the delight of my life to have dabbled in poetry . . .'; 'Five shillings', returned Mr. Slum, using his pencil as a tooth-pick. 'Cheaper than any prose.'), and Mrs. Jarley's high dedication to her wax-works as literature:

'It's calm and—what's the word again—critical?—no—classical, that's it—it's calm and classical. No low beatings and knockings about, no jokings and squeakings like your precious Punches, but always the same, with a constantly unchanging air of coldness and gentility . . .'

The last phrase could describe Nell herself. Dick, by contrast, does change: by his gentleness to the Marchioness, though as something of a gent and without ever being quite genteel, he is on his way to becoming that Dickensian ideal—a true gentleman. And so he disrupts the static and primitive moral duality of Quilp and Nell, and establishes between them a growing point towards the integrated and morally complicated personality.

Dickens effects Dick's transition from comic prototype to genuine personality deftly enough. After being introduced to Sally by Quilp as 'a gentleman of good family and great expectations', Dick is left alone with her and his horrible fascination with her 'intolerable brown head-dress':

Mr. Swiveller by degrees began to feel strange influences creeping over him—horrible desires to annihilate this Sally Brass—mysterious promptings to knock her head-dress off and try how she looked without it. (Ch. 33.)

He then swings at the preoccupied Sally with a ruler until his 'agitation' is 'calmed'. One can never quite unravel these peculiarly Dickensian knots of irrational impulse. Here they serve, by making the reader share Dick's irritability and tedium, to abolish the rather leisurely conventional time of the novel in favour of the subjective time of one of its characters whose identity is thus established to itself as well as by virtue of a function and a style. One suspects that here Dickens exploits the reader's own primitive memories of schoolboy tedium and revolt. Sally, the 'female dragon', acts curiously like a school-marm on Dick's adolescently irritable sense of constricted identity. Dick's clerkship with the Brasses feels like a transposed classroom scene. It rather resembles Paul Dombey's mute dialogues with Mrs. Pipchin.

Thus, however primitively, Dick is shown with an inner world. Early Dickens novels in their entirety often strike one as being all inner world—fantastic hallucinations that correspond only at several removes with the outer world that knocks so lustily against Dickens's senses. But as soon as one voice within the hallucination betrays an inwardness of its own, the distinction between inner and outer begins to reassert itself. It is this that renders Dick's relationship to the Marchioness so firm and moving. Though crudely delineated, they are real people, with independent emotions and a stake in the world. True, Dick burlesques their situation: 'The Baron Sampsono Brasso and his fair sister are (you tell me) at the Play?' But this comes out partly as a defence against difficult feeling (there is enough human data for this sort of speculation) and partly to cut the Brasses and Quilp—'the dismounted nightmare'; 'the evil genius of the cellars'— down to size. Dick's card-game with the Marchioness looks like dismissive commentary on the Grandfather's gambling mania: here the play is *with* the loved one (Swiveller himself provides the stakes), not, under pretext of being for her, against her. Trent had fiercely announced that Nell 'shall have no pittance, but a fortune' and will be 'a fine lady'. Dick—and he does it with delicacy and tact—makes the tortured little servant a lady straightway: 'To make it seem more pleasant, I shall call you the Marchioness.' Thus by simple sympathy he does for her what neither the Grandfather's crazy dreams of wealth nor Dickens's own rhetoric can do for Nell—gives her human status and identity which in turn liberates her into a sympathy and love still, admittedly, adolescent:

'—I'm so glad you're better, Mr. Liverer.'
'Liverer indeed! . . . It's as well I *am* a liverer. I strongly suspect I should have died, Marchioness, but for you.'

Yet it remains a relationship and begins to fill the centre vacated by Nell's and Quilp's incompatibility. These two do unify the novel in a queer negative way by their opposition. But the unity is an impermanent one ready to dissolve into mutual destruction. Out of their death Dick the liverer is born (the connection between Dick's vitality and drinking habits is surely made here) to evolve through Copperfield into Pip and, by circuitous ways, into one term of a mature human relationship. The fact that Dickens never quite got there matters little in comparison with the conflict, adventure, and discovery of the journey itself. Meanwhile Dick, like Dickens, is sustained by a robust facetiousness; though I do not suspect either is punning on Swiveller's gay snatch of quotation that forms my epigraph: 'But let us go ring fancy's knell'. Still, that is just what, with the Marchioness's assistance, I think Dick does.

BARNABY RUDGE

Jack Lindsay

DICKENS IS hardly thought of as an historical novelist; yet he wrote two historical novels which play an important part in his development and contribute something significant to the genre. *Barnaby Rudge* was the work which stabilized his method; *A Tale of Two Cities* enabled him to weather the most difficult moment in his life, expressed personally in the breakdown of his marriage, and to gain a new start which led into *Great Expectations* and *Our Mutual Friend*. Each historical novel deals with a mass-movement, or rather mass-explosion, and reveals the powerful impact of Carlyle. Each owns as its central image the mass-destruction of a prison, Newgate or the Bastille; the idea of liberated prisoners plays a key part in emotional pressures begetting the novel and forming it.

Dickens signed a contract for the work that was to become *Barnaby Rudge* in 1836, before *Pickwick* proved such a tremendous success. The modest terms he was then ready to accept soon appeared hopelessly poor, and next year he had the contract cancelled and a new one made with Bentley. The original title had been *Gabriel Vardon, the Locksmith of London,* suggesting one of the day's conventional romances; now the title became *Barnaby Rudge, a Tale of the Riots of '80.* But Dickens's entanglement with his serials, and perhaps a certain trepidation at embarking on a set full-length novel, kept on holding him up. *Oliver Twist, Nicholas Nickleby,* and *The Old Curiosity Shop* appeared before he got down to *Barnaby,* which was published in weekly instalments from February to November 1841.

The long delay, during which the project incubated in his mind, had a strong effect on the finished product. The previous novels had been picaresque, not attempting the large-scale planning now required. But through them he had learned much about plot-contrivance—though while he had gained in confidence, he must also have felt a deepening of the tensions gathered round a theme on which he had brooded, yet from which he had withheld himself for some five exciting and strenuous years. The fact that he stuck to the project despite so many dispersals of interest shows that it meant a great deal to him, both intrinsically and as a means of proving to himself and the world that he was a mature novelist able to stand up against Scott, not a hectically inspired improviser. His father-in-law Hogarth had been Scott's law-agent; and Scott was the great name against which he felt he must match himself if he were to rise to his full stature. During the feverish years 1836-40 he was comparing himself to Scott with his famous staying powers. 'The conduct of three different stories at the same time, and the production of a large portion of each, every month, would have gone beyond Scott himself,' he wrote to Bentley during their negotiations. In early 1838, in his anguish over Mary Hogarth's death, he consulted Scott's diary, much affected by a passage that seemed to echo his own feelings over Mary's grave. He wanted to find this link, and the finding of it must have strengthened his sense of fellowship with Scott, of continuing his work.

He made a false start in the autumn of 1839, 'going tooth and nail at *Barnaby*' and completing what became the first three chapters. But he was diverted by *Master Humphrey's Clock* and not till January 1841 could he resume the work. At first there were moments of hard going; but on reaching the riots he was swept along, only complaining at the lack of elbow-room in weekly instalments. The manuscript, which survives, shows that he must have carried out much revision on the proofs. He kept on asking Forster to cut. 'If there is anything here you object to, knock it out ruthlessly.' 'Don't fail to erase anything that seems to you too strong.' But nothing of importance seems lost: only occasional points of emphasis and some descriptive passages. At the end, however, he had found intolerable the strain of working out a complicated story so that it was effective and comprehensible in weekly parts.

The Preface shows that it was the riots, with 'their extraordinary and remarkable features', that had attracted him and made him stick to the project. He adds that he did not know of any other fictional treatment. (His diary under 31 January, 1839, at a period when his letters show Barnaby in his mind, refers to 'Gaspey. Chapter on

Executioners'. And though only one executioner, Dennis, appears in Thomas Gaspey's *The Mystery* of 1820, the reference must be to that three-volume novel, where the riots take up four of the early chapters. As however they play no integral part, Dickens doubtless felt that he could ignore the book.) His journalistic experiences had familiarized him with Newgate, which besides he knew from his schooldays. He published an article in the *Morning Chronicle*, 23 Oct., 1834, which was included as 'Criminal Courts' in his second series of *Sketches*; and he visited the jail in 1835 for an article printed in the first series, which shows him moved by the spectacle of three condemned men. Two of these men were later executed, one reprieved. He stressed the massive walls and the hopelessness of escape: here certainly lay the emotional genesis of his novel. In September 1841, in his fervid way of treating his writings as real experiences, he declared in a letter, 'I have burst into Newgate, and am going in the next number to tear the prisoners out by the hair of their heads.' The link with Scott appears in the influence of *The Heart of Midlothian*, with its storming of the Tolbooth and with its Madge Wildfire, who helped in the conception of Barnaby. There was also, noted as early as P. Robertson's speech at the Edinburgh banquet of June 1841, a connection between Barnaby and Davie Gellatley, the daft servant of *Waverley*.

Something of the transition from *Gabriel Vardon* to *Barnaby Rudge* is visible in the way a personal tale of murder, guilt, and discovery is woven into the epical tale of the riots. There are gaps and weaknesses in the interweaving, especially in the use of a five years' interval between the purely personal and the epical sections; yet at the same time a herculean effort is made to overcome the discrepancies. The force and skill of this effort, and its significance in the development of Dickens's artistic method, have not been properly estimated. Rudge, a gardener, has murdered his master at the Warren, Chigwell, and then gone off after making it seem that he too has been killed. His son is born a semi-idiot. Haredale, brother of the murdered man, is a Catholic, living an in-turned life at the Warren and driven by the need to vindicate himself by unmasking the murderer. His niece Emma loves Edward, son of Chester, Haredale's mortal foe. The first section of the book is taken up with accounts of the wandering unknown (Rudge) in his frenzy of blood-guilt, Chester with his machinations aimed at parting Edward and Emma, Joe Willet's love for Dolly Vardon. The scene changes from the Chigwell inn, the Maypole, run by John Willet, to Vardon's house in London, with diversions to Mrs. Rudge's home, Chester's rooms in the Temple, the Warren, and the cellar where Tappertit, Vardon's apprentice, rules his club of rebellious lads. Then comes the five years' gap, the riots seethe up, and all the characters are engulfed.

The two decisive influences are Carlyle and Bulwer. The delays in writing enabled Dickens to read *The French Revolution* (1837) and *Chartism* (1839), and transform his ideas. The hearty romance became an epical novel with a philosophy of history permeating it. From Carlyle Dickens gained the concept of revolt and revolution as an elemental upsurge of the oppressed: a necessary stage, though in itself an explosion of blind retaliatory violence. He could not but respond with every fibre of his being to Carlyle's attacks on the class that monopolized suffrage, land, press, religion, and imposed the Poor Law. He wrote fierce ballads like *The Fine Old English Gentleman,* and in his revulsion from England meditated emigration: 'By Jove, how radical I am getting. I wax stronger in the true principles every day.' Carlyle gave him a perspective which made sense out of his scattered impulses of revolt and criticism, and which remained with him till the end. Without it he could never have grown into the great artist we know; and *Barnaby*, the novel in which he first makes a profound struggle to work out and extend his new understanding, is thus of extreme importance in his development. Carlyle denounced the cash-nexus as the sole link left between man and man in a capitalist world, a link that perverted men and turned them into 'things' in their relations to one another. He declared that every revolution gave the power of 'articulation' to a new class. 'Class after class acquires faculty of utterance . . . so that always, after a space, there is not only a new gift of articulating, but there is something new to articulate.' He was thinking of the contemporary radical and chartist agitations. Dickens, looking back to the last large-scale upheaval before his own period, saw there the embryonic 'articulation' of what was speaking out loud in his own world. To define that articulation he felt the 'natural' Barnaby and the crazed Lord George Gordon as perfect images.

Scott had helped him towards his concept of the Fool; but he wanted to make his fool-figures more integrally connected with the historical theme of convulsion and change than they are in Scott's work. He was trying to return to the Shakespearian Fool, but couldn't assume a folk-tradition. As a result, his Barnaby and Gordon lack the realistic basis of Scott's figures; for he makes them carry a far greater philosophic burden. At the same time, desiring psychological realism, he could not be content with conjuring up a poetic image. It was here that the broken-down remnants of folk-tradition in melodrama and the work of Bulwer came in to help him. The idiot hero was very popular in the melodramas to which he had strongly responded, e.g., in such plays as *The Idiot Witness* and *The Idiot of Heidelberg*. (This was one reason why the issues of *Barnaby* at once provoked dramatizations. The first two were rushed out before the theme of the riots was reached; the third did try to stage the riots. There seems yet another 1841 version of which we know little.)

What Dickens drew from Bulwer was subtler. Bulwer, too, was matching himself against Scott, and many of his positions were very close to Dickens's. His *Paul Clifford* antedated Oliver; his *Last Days of Pompeii* helped Dickens to the idea of private lives caught suddenly up in a universal cataclysm; and he was much concerned with questions of guilt in both a social and a personal aspect. His 'Reign of Terror', published in the *Foreign Quarterly Review* in 1842, had had its main thesis 'put into its final shape at a date much in advance of its publication there'.[1] As well as shrewdly realizing the essential middle-class nature of the French Revolution, this essay set out the position that guilt, whether individual or communal, was the result of previous circumstance. Bulwer responded strongly to *The Old Curiosity Shop*; for his *Night and Morning*, published in 1841, has many similar elements. We meet it in the Old Man and the Young Girl in symbolic union. The Old Man has driven his son into a life of vice by his hard righteousness, but is himself in the grip of greed; he is joined with his grand-daughter, a child-woman Fanny, who, like Nell, is humiliated by her grandfather's actions. Fanny is shown groping pathetically for an understanding of life; her fight through a twilight consciousness is well defined; and as a character she is more convincing than Barnaby, not to mention Nell. As *Night*

---

[1] T. H. S. Escott, *Edward Bulwer* (1910), p. 196; Bulwer was replying to G. Duval's attack on the chief actors of the French Revolution. *Zanoni* appeared in 1842. See my *Charles Dickens*, pp. 196-8, for a fuller treatment of *Night and Morning*. The hypocrite of that novel, Beaufort, looks to Pecksniff, as Bulwer recognized, but also has links with Chester. (The hypocrite, the liar, the self-deceiver become of importance as the plainest expression of the gap between reality and men's ideas of it. Bulwer in the 1845 edition of *Night and Morning* profoundly spoke of 'new regions . . . lying far, and rarely trodden, beyond that range of conventional morality in which Novelist after Novelist has entrenched himself—amongst those subtle recesses in the ethics of human life in which truth and falsehood dwell undisturbed and unseparated'.)

and Morning was published in 1841 during the issues of *Barnaby*, it is hard to decide if it affected Dickens's treatment of his fool; but its position as a halfway-house between *The Old Curiosity Shop* and *Barnaby* is striking, and demonstrates how close in method and outlook were Dickens and Bulwer at this phase. Dickens had now known Bulwer for some years and each man had influenced the other.

The underlying topicality of *Barnaby* needs no stressing. The previous five years had seen a sharp rise in the movements of popular protest, ranging as they did from the Poor Law riots to Chartist upheavals at Devizes, Birmingham, Sheffield, and mass-gatherings on Kersal Moor and Kennington Common. The Newport insurrection, with its aim of freeing prisoners, must particularly have stirred Dickens. The 1840 trial of Edward Oxford for shooting at the Queen had raised questions of legal responsibility and insanity; and Dickens shared the growing abhorrence of public executions. The Protestant Association in 1839 had local branches for 'operatives', anti-Catholic petitions, and large meetings in Exeter Hall. Dickens, who disliked all organized religion, had a special hatred of evangelical puritanism: an emotion not lessened by his sister Fanny's marriage. (He was writing on the eve of the Oxford Movement, which in due time was to stimulate him into an ardent anti-Catholicism of his own.)

The theme of *Barnaby* was thus excellently calculated to encourage him to struggle against the meandering or restricted settings of his previous works and to tackle a theme that brought him squarely up against contemporary reality in its main currents. Where the example of Bulwer was important was in showing how a man could merge deep-going fantasy-motives with a realistic setting in order to define the main social and spiritual trends and conflicts around him. That which in *Oliver* and *The Old Curiosity Shop* was still partly in-tuitional, unconscious of its larger bearings, now became a fully worked-out method. Fantasy was used to stress and give a spontaneous energy to images which were well understood as embodying essential aspects of the life-process: that is, aspects which expressed all that was deepest and most typical in what was happening to men, forming and deforming them. Dickens learned thus to build free fantasy-images, which at the same time included a total judgment of life and touched on the world about him at a myriad points. In perfecting this method Dickens went far beyond Bulwer, but was strongly aided towards the mature comprehension of his aims by Bulwer's example.

He took over from Scott the theme of the private person snatched up, without will or intention, into a great historical movement, so that a profound tension arises between the hopes and ideas of the implicated individual and the historical event realized in its full dynamic pattern. But he had learned from the workings of his own mind, and from Bulwer, how to deepen the whole picture by the infusion of a tense particular atmosphere, by the invention of certain rich poetic images around which the material was organized—or rather organized itself. For those images were not created at random; they arrived as the final point of penetration into the total meaning of the historic event, the pattern of social conflict. Henceforth Dickens's struggle as an artist was to press through the medley of images and ideas generated by the fascinating hurly-burly of life to that point of significant image-concentration. Then at last he knew triumphantly that he had grasped what he was after: a conception which satisfied both his imaginative sense and his social realism, which stirred his wild fantasy-powers and yet was ratified as a valid judgment of his world. Thus he succeeded in expressing, not merely the endless oddments of the world that for one reason or another excited or interested him, but the central formative forces at work in and on people.

The Fool-image was the key to Barnaby. But to use it effectively he had to find ways and means of unifying the aesthetic texture, of bringing dynamically together within a single focus the personal and the social. This was much more than a matter of plot-contrivance, though that came into it. In working out his plot, he was all the while aware of the pulls and tensions set up by the central images; and this involved an aesthetic as well as an intellectual system of co-ordinations. Bulwer in *Night and Morning* used the change from dark to light to symbolize the progress of Fanny into a new life, into a deepened and more stable consciousness. Dickens in *Barnaby* used Light and Darkness as active principles, which expressed and unified the personal and the social aspects of the theme, merging the struggles of men with the life of nature and at the same time insisting that the specific acts, which were represented, were part of a greater and unending process. (What we may call the theory of this use of Light and Darkness as active principles invading the dead mechanistic Newtonian universe, had been worked out by the line of poets between Thomson and Wordsworth.)

Throughout *Barnaby* the Night predominates. Dickens opens in the tempestuous dark, contrasting the snug Maypole parlour with the dangerous forces outside. (From the outset then the parlour of Willet is made the emblem of the unconscious and tyrannical complacence which cannot even guess at the dark energies gathering to wreck the society it accepts.) Then Vardon's house, seen awhile by day, fades out into Tappertit's night-adventures, the actual schemings that threaten the day-world. We return to the inn with the night-meeting of the adversaries, Chester and Haredale. Joe visits London and returns by moonlight, encountering Edward. A glimpse of Chester at home is followed by the night-scenes of Mrs. Rudge's guilt-haunted home and by more of Tappertit's secret adventures. Vardon's visit to Chigwell darkens into Hugh's dusk-threat to Dolly, the night-journey of the lovers, Hugh's night-visit to Chester. Next day Tappertit visits Chester and the Rudges trudge to Chigwell. The widow's empty house then becomes a renewed centre of night-fears; the comedy of Chester's call on Mrs. Vardon leads into another night-visit from Hugh. Chester visits Chigwell and there is another long night-episode of tension at the Maypole. Joe leaves home next day and in the evening Edward breaks from his father.

The effect is of brief day-complots, of superficial movements in the streets of day, which are swallowed up in a surge of darkness. In the darkness the hidden forces are at work, obscurely and violently, biding their time. There is an extreme tension between the events of the day and those of the night, though the Vardons and the John Willets of the world are quite unaware of it. They are blind to the way in which their day-world of normal acceptances is crumbling away. The darkness belongs to Hugh, Rudge, Tappertit, Stagg: to the oppressed labourer, dehumanized and unable to use his strength rationally on his own behalf; to the frantically driven murderer; to the discontented apprentice or journeyman who indulges in dreams of revenge and social reversal and who comes together with his underprivileged fellows; to the outcast whose blindness has made him materially one with the dark spaces. Rudge, through his alliance with Stagg, merges with the night-world of the Tappertits.

The second and larger portion of the novel again opens with a wild night raving round the smug and snug Maypole. Into that night both Rudge and Gordon irrupt: the hidden guilt and the stirring threat. After a brief passage of light we are back in the darkness of Gashford and Dennis, of Hugh visiting Chester, of the Rudge house. The clash of Haredale and Gashford is necessarily a momentary day-revelation, caught up swiftly in the savage dark. Barnaby appears in a sunset-moment, on to which the menace of Stagg and Rudge intrudes. A flight follows. The fugitives at last emerge out of the night into a London of portentous movement; and we swing into the violent night-patterns of the riots, when the day is only a vain respite from the swarming and accumulative retaliations of the darkness and its denizens.

Dickens is always at home in a night-setting, where sharp and strange lights may pick out with special force the grotesque masks in which he delights, the masks that reveal the truth behind the faces. But here he uses the darkness consistently, with a piling-up rhythm, giving depth and force to the world of Rudge and Tappertit, and making the riots appear as the necessary consequence of the world he depicts. By his heavy chiaroscuro he builds up a great emotional power, which is only partly derived from the explicit activities of his characters in their limited range and scope of reference.

The result is in part a discrepancy between the tremendous force of the poetic motives that surround the characters, and the characters themselves. Tappertit is the figure who ostensibly represents the wrongs and grievances of the workers; but he is a figure of fun and we do not feel any real relation between his fulminations and the shattering upheaval—except in the sense of a parody. Dickens is chary about showing what is driving the people into revolt—though at a few points he is so overcome by his emotion that he breaks through his petty-bourgeois cautions and reticences, and makes the underdog speak in accents that are in accord with the fundamental Carlylean theme: when Stagg utters his bitter comments to Mrs. Rudge and when Hugh bursts out before his hanging.

His chiaroscuro—a briefly flaring light in the midst of a great darkness—provides, then, the dynamic method by which he brings out the unrealized tensions of the world and defines his people in their sharp stripped essences. Pictorial precision is not just something added to the narrative; it lies at the heart of the method and is a form of spiritual vision. The houses have as much character as the people they enclose; they own something of the darkness that has settled into their ancient nooks and crannies. The Maypole and Willet, the Warren and Haredale, the house-workshop and Vardon, the Temple chambers and Chester, the Rudge house and Barnaby, the cellar and Stagg—all these are integrally related. In the end we feel Willet and the Maypole as in effect the same flesh; the wrecking of the inn is one with its master's collapse from a self-righteous petty tyrant into a stupefied acquiescent hulk; we are convinced of the breakdown of a world. The picture of the inn-talkers at the outset, caught in a mass of darkness and flickering light, exemplifies in a small space the method of the whole novel and sets the key in tone and texture. While Joe's last night in the inn, with the furniture creaking into a life of its own, stresses the union of men and the things they make, as well as the alien life in the things, which can subdue men and pervert their humanity. Chester's complaints about the dead winds lurking in the creviced house jestingly underline the same point. Throughout we feel evoked the complex relations of men and their homes, men and things, men and nature.[1]

The saturation of this world by darkness, with fitful moments of deceptive or revelatory light, harmonizes with the central conception, which reposes on Barnaby and Gordon. It expresses in the last resort the mental processes of those two Fools, with their painful struggle against dark pressures into a new understanding of the world—a struggle which, in Carlyle's words, begets not only a new gift of articulation, but also something new to articulate. In making his traditional use of the folk-fool as the mouthpiece of wisdoms rejected by the world of privilege and money, Dickens indeed seems haunted by some further words of Carlyle:

. . . it is a question which cannot be left to the Collective Folly of the Nation! In or out of Parliament, darkness, neglect, hallucination must contrive to cease in regard to it; true insight into it must be had. How inexpressibly useful were true insight into it; a genuine understanding by the upper classes of society what it is that the under classes intrinsically

---

[1] The Bastille and Newgate are merely large-scale 'historical' versions of the house-image that runs through Dickens's work. The House (representing the Family and above all the maternal body) is for him a refraction of the whole of society. The 'imprisonment' in the House is directly expressed in Mrs. Clennam and Miss Havisham—cf. Bleak House, the House of Dombey, the Marshalsea, etc. Here the House comes to stand for all that is most enclosing—restrictive, repressive, alienating —in Victorian society. (At a lighter level is the series of nagging wives, to whom Mrs. Vardon belongs, who compose Dickens's picture of actual Victorian family-life as compared with the dream-picture that never comes down to earth. We may note in Mrs. Vardon's accomplice Miggs how easily Dickens could have slid into sexual frankness; he depicts her as continually itching to be ravished.)

mean; a clear interpretation of the thought which at heart torments these wild, inarticulate souls, struggling there, with inarticulate uproar, like dumb animals, in pain, unable to speak what is in them.

Barnaby and Gordon thus represent the future striving to be born, the wild confusion of hopes and desires which can as yet be articulated only in the tones of 'wild animals, in pain'. Their dark world can only be oppressed and distracted by the cold daylight which is identified with Chester's wily rationalizations and deliberate distortions. As fool-figures they are meant to supply the positive aspect which Dickens feels unable to impart to the direct revolt-formulations of Tappertit and his comrades. (The trade-unions of the 1830's still used initiation-ceremonies not unlike those of Tappertit's society.) Dickens worked hard at a thorough documentation of his account of the riots; but he refused an offer of the *Trials* after he had made up his mind about Gordon. He didn't want anything to disturb his conviction of the dual fool-figures as the inarticulate future speaking at both the upper and the lower levels of society. The importance of those figures for him was further brought out by his passing plan, luckily obstructed by Forster, of setting three loons, liberated from Bedlam, at the head of the rioters. (He had visited Bedlam for the *Sketches*; and the image of destroyed Bedlam merges with that of destroyed Newgate.) Gordon's ultimate death in the prison which the people had broken is the final touch of irony, of faith in the fool-wisdom uttered through the torments of 'these wild, inarticulate souls':

There are wise men in the highways of the world who may learn something, even from this poor crazy lord who died in Newgate. (Ch. the Last.)

Dickens stresses the relationship of Barnaby and Gordon by the two scenes of confrontation, at the start and at the end of the insurrection. Barnaby's selfless loyalty, leading to a useless martyrdom, is paired off with Gordon's selfless devotion to a deceptive idea; but beyond the irony Dickens seeks to evoke that in the loyalty and the devotion which transcends the historical situation and looks to a real goal of brotherhood, where the bitter cheat is ended. His method for expressing Barnaby's consciousness has affinities with that of Bulwer for expressing Fanny's, and both methods derive from the reverie-idiom of the Romantic poets. Barnaby sees strange forms of life in the washing that tosses on the clothes-line, in the convolutions of fire, in the shadows that are the doubles of people, in Grip's struggle with the wind:

The strange imaginings he had; his terror of certain senseless things— familiar objects he endowed with life; the slow and gradual breaking out of that one horror in which, before his birth, his darkened intellect began. . . . (Ch. 25.)

His obsession is thus directly linked with the motive of the curse, the blood-guilt; it reveals in nightmare-form that ambivalence we noted in connection with the Maypole on Joe's last night. Barnaby is over-powered by things, by the existentialist *nausée*, in which the depths of alienation are sounded; his struggle into articulation is the effort to defeat the nausea by gaining a wholly new start. Such a start implies a total rejection of existing relationships, so that a new humanity may be achieved, overcoming the horror of the deadly isolation and yet no longer caught in the old network of corruptions and divisions. The problem for the neurotic (or the poet) is not to eliminate inner conflict by an adaptation to things as they are, but to realize that in existing things which precipitates the conflict and inhibits a fuller humanity, he has to adapt himself to that which as yet doesn't exist—which he must struggle to bring into existence as the sole guarantee of his own security and happiness. Barnaby's domination by the guilt-anguish thus holds the clue of innocence renewed on the level of a new liberated or integrated consciousness. There is tragic irony in his confrontation with his father, which solves nothing, though it deepens his problems; there is irony again in his anxieties over blood and money, in his conviction that by join-ing the rioters he will gain gold and redeem his mother.[1] His inno-cent hope, which seems a sort of pious parody of the actual looting, yet expresses that in the rioting which despite everything breaks the vicious circle of violence against violence, greed against greed, and looks to a true brotherhood. His belief that the redemption, some-how purifying gold of its bloodiness, lies in the gathering of people, is the high point of affirmation in the book, ' "A crowd indeed!" said Barnaby. "Do you hear that, mother?" ' (Ch. 48.)

---

[1] Barnaby, hoping for the gold in the sunset-sky, says, 'I wish I knew where gold was buried. How hard I'd work to dig it up!' and looks 'from the redness of the sky to the mark upon his wrist as if he would compare the two'. (Ch. 45.) This leads into the remarks of Stagg that turn his thoughts to London. In *Night and Morning* Fanny asks, 'There is one thing that always puzzles me—I want you to explain it. Why does everything in life depend upon money?'

Inextricably linked with the distracted movements of Barnaby's mind is the guilt-flight of Rudge. The flight-motive, supplanting the scheme of an amiable Pickwickian wandering, had been strong in Dickens ever since Mary's death. Bill Sikes, after murdering Nancy, rushes off in the same direction as the stricken Dickens, and sinks at the same spot as he did; Oliver runs blindly from a cruel world; Nell and the Old Man hurry from a private persecution into the actual hell of the industrial system. In *Barnaby* Rudge is at last trapped by the light of the fired Warren; the secret of personal blood-guilt is brought into the open simultaneously with the climax of mob-violence. The private and the social patterns coincide in the last resort.

Barnaby and Tappertit, we saw, make up together what Dickens feels the motive force of the revolt: that which is limited to particular circumstance and the sense of personal wrong, and is treated humorously, satirically, and that which holds the pure human aspiration and is treated poetically, sympathetically. But other figures are needed to fill the wide gap between these two levels of life, and so Hugh and Dennis are brought in with Stagg providing the link with Rudge. Hugh is depicted as a great hulking semi-brute, a 'natural' man distorted by a callous world, Caliban in an eighteenth-century setting. His significance is underlined by his position as Chester's bastard: a relationship given depth, through his reluctant fascination by his unknown father. He is swung between good and evil in an uncomprehended world; but his humanity survives in his feeling for Barnaby, whom alone he can respect, and is strengthened, then finally released, by his experience of revolutionary comradeship. His last-minute awareness of the forces that have shaped him does not show Dickens stepping outside the confines of his character to point a moral; the changes are validly determined by Hugh's experiences and form a necessary part of the novel's pattern, merging with the pangs of the new life in Barnaby and Gordon. Hugh becomes the pledge of a mass-force which in due time of articulation will no longer be merely destructive, retaliatory, and misdirected.

Dennis on the other hand represents that in the people which has become hopelessly corrupted. As public hangman, he is the emblem of the State and its force, of the evil thing which has begotten the maddened retort or the rioters. His sliding over to the side of the latter then expresses that in them which is condemned to the vicious circle. When however they liberate the prisoners. he slides back in outrage to his original allegiance. That is, he realizes that in the outbreak which implies in its ultimate objective the end of the use of force altogether, and so he turns against the whole thing. Dickens thus uses Dennis with brilliant irony, not only to bring out the way in which both State-power and mob-violence have a common element, but also to bring out the point of divergence, the Barnaby-element which despite everything moves the people in their depths.

In discussing the symbolic significance of these characters we must not however forget the great power of their draughtsmanship. Here is splendidly achieved the clarity of contours that makes Dickens's people more sharply memorable than the creations of any other writer—in the simple and profound sense of a definite palpable identity. But the precision and the force of outline are never isolated from the total plastic and dynamic effect. Failure to grasp the vital interaction of parts, the textural richness of the whole indivisible picture, is what has led critics to describe Dickens's characters as two-dimensional, as cut-out figures lacking an inner life.

The persons in the novel who define the acceptance of the *status quo* are all, apart from the plain honest Vardon, despicable: Chester, Willet, the Lord Mayor, the country-gentleman who persecutes Barnaby.

We may sum up then by calling *Barnaby Rudge* a work on a grand scale, even if it is not a complete success. An historical novel requires somewhere in it a more objective assessment of the social forces involved; and Dickens attempts to define the essence of the situation almost entirely through symbolic devices, dynamic chiaroscuro effects, clusters of poetic imagery. The folk-fool, who is prophet and liberator, Merlin and Parsifal, is a potent symbol in the medieval world, and so is still available for the tragic universe of Shakespeare; but in the world of developing industrialism his magic dwindles. (Perhaps the last adequate use of him on a grand scale is in the Coster's *Tyl Eulenspiegel*; after that he becomes Chaplin's little man or the Good Soldier Schweik.) Dickens conjures him up valiantly in Barnaby, but is unable to make him carry all the weight of meaning that the fable demands. Part of the reason for the novel's weaknesses lies in Dickens's ambivalence towards the theme. At his deepest creative levels he is drawn with intense sympathy and understanding towards the depiction of a popular uprising, yet at the same time he fears such events as merely destructive and revengeful. In choosing the Gordon Riots he took in fact the best possible instance to justify his ambivalence; for these riots were carried out by people who had lost the clear and naïve radical aims of the Wilkite 1760's, but could not formulate yet the demands and projects of the 1830's, when the industrial system had arrived and working-class organization was becoming a reality. In a way the dissociated and divergent forces represented by Barnaby, Tappertit, Gordon, Hugh, Dennis, and Stagg do add up to something like the actual situation; and we might claim that Barnaby and Gordon do stand truly for the confused last-remnants of medievalism in the perplexed scene. But when all is said, there is an element of disorder as well as of deep intuitional integration in Dickens's massing of his symbols and images. This disorder is what prevents *Barnaby* from being a very great work. It cannot however prevent it from being an impressive achievement. Here Dickens arrives at the maturity of method which makes possible the great series of symbolic characters and settings in which he defines with masterly insight and compression the essential conflicts and transformative forces at work in his world.

We can see then why his two historical novels, though not among his best works, have an importance all their own in his development. They express moments of great inner strain and advance, when he made decisive efforts to grapple with a total historical pattern. Transitional works, they show him in the process of achieving a new stable level from which he can confidently return to the contemporary scene. They ensure his grasp of symbolic character, of imagery that goes to the heart of the human condition. At the same time they are contributions to the historical genre itself, adding a symbolic interplay and an enrichment of aesthetic elements to the methods developed by Scott. In the last resort we find that Dickens, as much as Balzac, was building on the ground that Scott had cleared with his strong sense of the dialectical interrelation of individual and society at a specific crisis-moment of national growth. Balzac, though not lacking his own important fantasy-element, added just that clear-sighted analytic quality which *Barnaby* lacks. Dickens, with greater reliance on poetic symbol, added the subtle and unifying plastic element which we discussed in his use of chiaroscuro, of dynamic light-effects. Here he was building directly on the method of the Gothic Novel at its highest level of development in the hands of writers like Anne Radcliffe, where emotional conflict or crisis was always linked with transformative light-effects (sunrise, sunset, moonrise, storm-light). Dickens used the Gothic aesthetic with an enormously enhanced power and consistency; and in so doing he brought something new into the historical novel and the novel in general—an intensity and a unity of movement and pattern which are carried on in turn by Zola and Dostoevsky in their best work. The more one considers his work in detail and in breadth, the more consummate an artist he appears.

Note on Thomas Gaspey. Dickens could hardly not have known *The Mystery, or Forty Years Ago*, by Gaspey, who was a member of the *Evening Chronicle* staff. Its hero, Charles Harley, gets into a brawl with the rioters, is arrested and jailed, and finally released after his friend, Sir George Henderson, turns up to vouch for him. Dennis (a real character, who was in fact tried but reprieved) is taunted by the rioters about the freeing of the prisoners. 'No, but I say, Ned—this is a serious thing for you. There'll be no hangings on Thursday; I suppose you know that? That's bad news for you. The fellows that was to be tucked up is let loose.' Ned demurs: 'I shall have my quarter all the same.' But a Negro points out that he won't get the men's clothes, 'and you won't bleed 'em before they go off'. Ned replies, 'You'll be black in the face before you're turned off.' There is a fight and Dennis makes off. Out of this piece of rough byplay Dickens constructs his Dennis, turning the jokes into the basis for his subtle characterization.

Harley may have contributed to the picture of young Chester; he denounces at length the 'wife-trade' whereby a man sells himself in marriage. A naval officer, he goes off to Africa: the second volume is almost wholly made up of his wanderings there. In Vol. III, Ch. vi, a countrywoman goes mad and threatens to kill a child when the straight-jacket is fetched. *The Mystery* is a typical piece of romantic contrivance in which the excitements of an incestuous situation are conjured up, but high morals are preserved. The girl in Harley's passion is revealed as his half-sister, then turns out not to be related at all. (In Vol. I, p. 41 there is a discussion about the equal sharing out of wealth, in which it is decided that very soon inequality would reassert itself. Britain's position in India is defended, though there are some strong comments on cruelties there, as in the Africa of the slave-trade.) In Gaspey's *George Godfrey*, 1828, there is an execution-scene, with last-minute reprieves.

MARTIN CHUZZLEWIT

Barbara Hardy

AT THIS time in critical history it seems impossible to begin, as I should like to, with the assumption that most readers of Dickens will agree with John Forster, Gissing, and various other critics, that *Martin Chuzzlewit* is a badly organized novel. This formal judgment is one I endorse, though I believe that it can do with careful scrutiny. What does this failure in composition amount to, and does it matter? If this really is the fabulous beast, James's large loose baggy monster, ought we not to ask whether the novel cannot afford more bagginess than most other forms, and especially the comic novel, with its special functional mannerism which gives full effect to local assertions of wit and farce. Dickens's comic purposes make for a certain formal relaxation which flourishes many bright particulars, not all of which are subsumed by the central themes, and it is therefore no mere piety which makes me say that this novel, unusually disintegrated though it is, gets by on its patches of compelling gusto, comic and also grim. Nevertheless, its defects of form are important, largely because they expose, in several ways, some of Dickens's weaknesses of feeling and dramatic power.

But not all readers would agree that there is a formal failure. Many of the recent interpretations by close and serious critics have claimed for *Martin Chuzzlewit* a depth and coherence of thought and feeling which makes me wonder whether I have read the same book, and before I say anything about my own views, I must look briefly at some of those strange images of Dickens—as they appear to me—so freely bred by post-Jamesian criticism. For though James rejected many nineteenth-century novels as shapeless and uneconomical, it is probably his insistence on the totally relevant narrative structure which is now partly responsible for our attempts to deny the looseness and bagginess of so many of the Victorians.

It is not a mere formal exaggeration which is at work in criticism of the novel. Several recent critics have established Dickens's formal power by trying to prove that his novels have a consistent and unified ideological structure. I can truthfully say that the *Martin Chuzzlewit* of Jack Lindsay (*Charles Dickens*), Dorothy Van Ghent ('The Dickens World: A View from Todgers's,' *Sewanee Review*, LVIII (1950)), and J. Hillis Miller (*Charles Dickens*), is a novel—or rather, three different novels—which I should like to read. Lindsay's novel, in which the young Martin represents the adventurous enterprise of capitalism, Jonas the dark usorious exploitation, and Mark Tapley the unbreakable common man, has coherence of symbolic characterization and social analysis, though in his fine observations on Dickens's transmutation of tension and fantasy he recognizes Dickens's instability. The visions of disintegration explored by Dorothy Van Ghent and Hillis Miller, while illuminating many aspects of the work, suggest a psychological subtlety and grasp. And there is Sylvère Monod's poetic novel (*Dickens romancier*) with its beauty and gaiety—Dickens's worst flights of gassy rhetoric sound controlled and elegant in French—and Edgar Johnson's morally unified novel making the transition from gloom to warmth.

Critics like these, standing well away from the lunatic fringe, suggest the appearance of a vast parasitic growth, a super-criticism which blurs analysis in re-creation, and scarcely needs to consider judgment. I know of no Victorian novelist who has been recreated in the image of his critics so frequently and so strongly as Dickens. It is not just a matter of our current obsession with total relevance which makes us consider all the Victorians as if they were formal artists after the manner of Turgenev, Stevenson, and James himself. The interpretations I have just mentioned are ideological rather than formalist exaggerations. Dickens's combination of striking satire and animistic description tempts us to think that he must have a more coherent moral scheme than he really has. His attempts to combine a moral action with his strong static social portraiture, his vague gestures towards *Bildungsroman*—all coming in part from his lack of intellectual quality, and all particularly conspicuous in *Martin Chuzzlewit*—attracts the force of more methodical and original minds.

But the critic who is wary of imposing an intellectual scheme—or who may not have one to impose—may be as guilty of free distortion as the Marxist or existentialist arguing his thematic unity. We now have ready to hand the apparently objective techniques of formal analysis, and the thematic defence of Dickens's form in *Martin Chuzzlewit* ranges from the subtle to the simple. Edgar Johnson, for instance, has this to say:

> With the exception of the rather disgressive American episodes (and a little special pleading might bring even them into the pattern), all the characters are linked by their relationship to the theme of selfishness. In a curious way this rendition of a generalized vice gives *Martin Chuzzlewit* affinities with novels otherwise so different as George Meredith's *The Egoist* and Jane Austen's *Pride and Prejudice*. . . . His exposure of selfishness is as sharp, if not as subtle, as Meredith's dissection of egoism, and his method is identical with Jane Austen's, whose characters are all mutations on pride and prejudice. (*Charles Dickens*.)

The resemblance between these three novels is indeed peculiar, unless it is merely obvious. Dickens does state formally that he is setting out to explore the theme of selfishness, but there are a very large number of novels, and many other forms of literary and non-literary discourse, doing the same thing. I am sure it is harder to find novels which lack the unity of theme than novels which possess it. It does not distinguish the novel from other forms, nor does it distinguish the good novel from the bad. Moral unity is the unity of the writer's categories, and it is only one aspect of narrative form. It need not affect the action of the novel, which has to display these categories in a tense progression, and once we leave problems of form, of which it is only a part, it has no relevance either to the moral and psychological insight of the artist, or to his dramatic, poetic, or critical handling. To say that a novel has the unity of its moral categories is to say only one minimal thing about its structure, and is certainly to decide nothing about its merit.

The formal critic may of course use this reductive concept more critically, and relate it to the Aristotelian relations of beginning, middle, and end. This is what Edgar B. Benjamin does in his article, 'The Structure of *Martin Chuzzlewit*', *Philological Quarterly*, XXXIV, 1955. He looks at moral unity in terms of formal progression, interpreting the main humour as Hypocrisy, and describing the structure in terms of Hypocrisy's rise and fall: Hypocrisy Ascendant, Triumphant, and Unmasked. But his attention to action, I think, is only specious: he picks out the changes in the situation of hypocritical characters but seems to assume that these changes, and their exemplary significance, determines the movement of tension in the novel. This is something which I doubt.

We cannot—especially in Dickens—make an automatic correlation between moral change and narrative action. I would of course agree that the characters have this extensive moral commitment to the general theme of selfishness and often to the more specialized variant of hypocrisy. The comic characters (the Pecksniff family, Mrs. Gamp, the Moulds) express the theme in their personal, professional, and social rôles; the grimmer characters (Jonas and Tigg Montague) do the same. And there are a few characters (old Martin, young Martin, and Mercy Chuzzlewit, with the possible additions of Tom Pinch and Mark Tapley) who may be said to undergo some change in their attitude to their own or other people's preoccupation with Self. Some of the changes in the novel involve the delineation of a change of heart, others seem to involve the change from a comic to a serious mode. Action which depends on a change of heart is plainly an example of tension provided by moral interest, and if we pick some obvious examples of novels having this kind of moral action we might add *Great Expectations* and *Hard Times* to a list including *Emma, Middlemarch*, and *The Ambassadors*. The problem of moral action in Dickens as a whole is too intricate for me to discuss here, but I want to make it clear that what I see as the gap between moral theme and action in *Martin Chuzzlewit* is not a dislocation invariably characteristic of Dickens. Dickens is concerned with showing moral change: how does he do it? We need to ask further questions too. How far are the tensions, expectations, and surprises which make the curve of our attention—the line of action—concerned with the moral subject?

The action is concerned with moral causality: it is in part at least precipitated by the theme of Self. The impersonations of the elder Chuzzlewit, the exiles of Martin, Mark Tapley, Tom Pinch, the attempted murder of Anthony Chuzzlewit, and the actual murder of Tigg Montague, the speculator and blackmailer, are all caused by selfishness, unselfishness, or by the desire to test, expose, and reform selfishness and unselfishness. Selfishness is also given its forms of Nemesis, including the public Jonsonian exposure of Pecksniff's deceit and hubris, the punishment of Mercy in her marriage to Jonas, the ordeal of Martin in Eden, and the stern advice given to Mrs. Gamp. On the credit side there are the rewards of Tom, Ruth, John Westlock, Mark Tapley, and the young Martin. The theme expresses itself actively—apart from the content of character—in the demonstration of a change of heart and in this use of moral cause and effect. But how much of our reading interest depends on this moral significance? And how is the moral action handled, and with what conviction and plausibility? I should like to try to answer both questions together.

The only important part of the action which runs right through the novel is the impersonation of Old Chuzzlewit, and its consequences in the duping of Pecksniff and the exile of Martin. It provides some mystery, some irony, and some scenes which enact the humours. There is the hypocritical domestic show put on for Martin's benefit, several scenes of moral antithesis between young Martin and Tom Pinch, the splendid quarrel scene in which the predatory Chuzzlewit hypocrites fall out, the scene where Old Chuzzlewit lies to Pecksniff while Pecksniff is lying to him. Such scenes are frequent at the beginning, then thin out, and reappear in a conspicuous huddle towards the end when we have the revelation of Martin's trick, the exposure of Pecksniff, and the general apportionment of rewards and punishments. This one over-arching piece of action does indeed over-arch. It is important at the beginning and end but stays more or less out of sight for a large part of the novel; and when it does appear it is markedly unproductive of tension. There are indeed so few rising intonations of curiosity, doubt, and expectation at the beginning of the novel that it is not surprising that the novel was not a success as a serial, though no doubt all the other reasons which have been suggested for this relative failure—disappointment with *Barnaby Rudge*, reviewers' hostility to *American Notes*, the change to monthly publication, harshness of satire, lack of pathetic children and deaths—may also be important. But the striking difference between this novel and almost all Dickens's others is this absence of initial tension. Most of the others present a rising curve of attention, and do this, I think, by presenting at the beginning both strong incident and some point of emotional identification. Incident and human emotional centre are both present, for instance, in the death of Mrs. Dombey, the mystery of Esther's birth, Pip's encounter with Magwitch, the first river scene in *Our Mutual Friend*. Sometimes the incident alone is arresting, as in the workhouse scene in the first chapter of *Oliver Twist*, sometimes the introductory scene is symbolic, as in *Bleak House* and *Little Dorrit*, but in all these novels we also move swiftly forward to a strong human identification. Leaving aside the tiresome exercise in sarcasm which is the prelude to Martin Chuzzlewit—its focus now seems blurred—there is no exciting incident in the early chapters. There are indeed very few strongly exciting situations anywhere in the novel, apart from Martin's trip to Eden and the criminal career of Jonas Chuzzlewit—and neither of these sources of tension is anticipated by any early trailers. The human centre is missing too: the most interesting and conspicuous character is Pecksniff and he is as useless for purposes of identification as Micawber, presented as he is from the outside, and in a strong harsh stereotype. Martin is too neutral and uninteresting, and is also scarcely ever seen from the inside, at least until his traumatic experiences. The one character whose emotions are dramatized with any strength is Tom Pinch, and he is not only a grossly sentimental figure but is also given practically nothing to do. In these three characters, as they appear, there seems to be no potentiality for either tense action or emotional identification, but the wasted opportunity lies in the conflict and impersonation of old Martin. This impersonation is neither prominent nor made productive of much mystery, influence, or dramatic irony—the comparison with the brilliant impersonation of Boffin's miserly humour in *Our Mutual Friend*, which is mysterious, affects other characters, and is rich in irony and innuendo, should make this clear. Boffin's assumed humour is motivated—engineered by Harmon for the cure of Bella. It is influential—it does cure her. And as an impersonation it is like Malcolm's in *Macbeth* and provides a special exaggerated moral symbol of the prevailing evil in the novel. Martin's impersonation is much more weakly motivated, and has barely more than a concluding pantomimic resolution in action.

If the moral content does not terminate in action, as I am arguing, what then constitutes the incident of the early parts of the novel? There are brilliant comic scenes, with a great deal of satire, linguistic humour, and farce. But although these scenes usually have thematic relevance they seldom move—and why should they?—beyond a self-contained action which raises no questions and leaves no disturbing loose ends. There is certainly some attempt at the moral conflict which in other novels produces its tension, in personal relationships which have a moral antithesis: Nicholas and Smike, Dombey and Florence, Hexam and Lizzie, and so on. But the moral antithesis in *Martin Chuzzlewit* strikes me as purely formal. There is the moral opposition of old Martin and Pecksniff, of young Martin first with

Tom Pinch, then with Mark Tapley. None of these morally significant pairs is shown in the tension of personal relation—there is no human antagonism, or love, or fear, or any of the conflicting emotions which mark the relations of Oliver and Fagin, or Pip and Magwitch, or Florence and Dombey, where the moral antithesis is expressed in human relations, and changes accordingly. The only parts of *Martin Chuzzlewit* which show a personal as well as a moral conflict are either presented offstage in exposition, like the relationship between Martin and his grandfather, which is potentially of the same mixed human and moral tension as these examples from the better novels, or are not primarily explored for moral antithesis. Mercy's relation to the sadistic Jonas with its pleas and cries on behalf of outraged sacred womanhood, or the relation of Mary Graham to Pecksniff in his rôle of repulsive furtive lecher, are not moving as *moral* dramatizations.

It might be argued that although Martin started off as a neutral character, he does come to provide a point of identification: he is the only character shown in the process of change. Dickens nearly always makes his gestures to *Bildungsroman*, and *Hard Times* and *Great Expectations*—I am not so sure about *Our Mutual Friend*—make much more than gestures, in Dickens's Jacobean mode of conventionalized psychology. Martin's need for change is shown right at the beginning, but when the change comes it is segregated from the rest of the action, both in place and in effect. Martin's conversion is made visible only to Mark Tapley, in Eden. It does up to a point constitute a self-contained action with a beginning, middle, and end: Martin's is the responsibility for going to America and then to Eden, though the moral weakness which emerges here is impetuous innocence rather than selfishness. It is followed by his climactic vision of Self, after sickness, disillusion, and admiration for Mark, his moral opposite, and culminates in the triumphant affirmation of some belief in America's possible Phoenix-like rebirth. But this account of the action, like Benjamin's account of the rise and fall of hypocrisy, is misleading because it ignores the method of presentation. Action is implied rather than dramatized in this moral change, and although the abruptness, the crisis, and the use of external example in Mark, are characteristic of many of Dickens's sudden conversions, the absence of any sense of time is particularly noticeable in this novel because of the general superficial treatment of Martin's moral conduct. Dickens tells us that the change of heart did not come about in a moment, but this is telling, not showing, and the process of months is jammed into a few paragraphs with no correlative for the passage of time:

> It was natural for him to reflect—he had months to do it in—upon his own escape, and Mark's extremity. This led him to consider which of them could be the better spared, and why? Then the curtain slowly rose a very little way; and Self, Self, Self, was shown below . . . It was long before he fixed the knowledge of himself so firmly in his mind that he could thoroughly discern the truth; but in the hideous solitude of that most hideous place, with Hope so far removed, Ambition quenched, and Death beside him rattling at the very door, reflection came, as in a plague-beleaguered town; and so he felt and knew the failing of his life, and saw distinctly what an ugly spot it was. (Ch. 33.)

The suddenness is common, as I say, and there is no point in comparing Dickens's conversions here with the slow and often eddying movement traced in George Eliot or Henry James. But I think this change is even more abrupt in exposition, relying heavily on compressed rhetoric, than the fairly abrupt conversions of David Copperfield or Bella Wilfer, though the important difference lies in the context of dramatized moral action. Dombey, Steerforth, Gradgrind, Pip, and other major and minor examples of flawed character—not necessarily changing—are demonstrated in appropriate action, large and small. Steerforth, for instance, is not given only the decisive action of seducing Emily, but various other significant acts of selfishness—baiting the poor usher, making David read to him at night, and so on. Martin's violent change appears in a very different context of action, for Martin is given very little to do. His selfishness, like his grandfather's, is shown in exposition in the moral contrasts I have mentioned and in a series of trivial physical gestures which are closer to theatrical business than to dramatic action: twice he keeps the fire from Tom, once he lets Tom carry his greatcoat. Small details like this have a place in moral delineation, but here they carry too large a load.

Martin's selfishness is also motivated, showing Dickens's interest in environment and heredity, but the origins like the effects are also presented in exposition, in contrast with, say, David Copperfield or Great Expectations. And his actions as a changed man are again expressed mainly at the level of business—he surprises Mark by expressing sympathy for Tom, he rebukes Mark for staying on the windy side instead of taking turn and turn about. There is no active effect. When Pip and David change there are repercussions throughout all their relationships. But the inconspicuous relation between Mary and Martin is totally unaffected by his change, and so indeed is his relation to his grandfather. Although his admission of wrong and change are made at the end, he is a passive figure. It would not be true to say that he is always passive: in his rôle as lover and as a selfish man undergoing change he is given inadequate expression in action, but he has a very important rôle in the American episodes. But there is something a little odd here: although America provides the test and ordeal, the sense of responsibility, and the endurance, there is no visible relation between Martin's selfishness and the dramatization on a national scale of the hypocritical and aggressive selfishness of America. His main rôle here, as he is lionized like his creator, is to act as spirited and zealous critic of America, given the *ex -officio* wisdom and objectivity of his Englishness. There is indeed, as we all know, this thematic connection between the social satire and the individual types of selfishness, but it is worth observing that Dickens makes no dramatic acknowledgment of the resemblance in the presentation of Martin. He temporarily drops his humour and is humane and zealous as Mark. It shows the superficial and imposed nature of his selfish humour, and shows too a dislocation characteristic of this novel.

The third important part of the action is of course the blackmail and murder. Percy Lubbock, who writes all too briefly about Dickens, observes that in all the novels except *David Copperfield* it is 'his chosen intrigue, his "plot" that makes the shape of his book', and although I think this is a simplification which ignores Dickens's use of contrast and cross-cutting, the formal 'streaky bacon' as he calls it in *Oliver Twist*, it is a sound comment which once more emphasizes the importance of action. It is true that the intrigue, the sensational and intricate web of plotting and mystery, usually occupies only one part of the usual formula in a Dickens novel. The formula is made up of this kind of plot, and some moral process, a love-story or two, and a specialized social satire, not to mention the more or less connected comic scenes. In the late novels, from *Bleak House* onwards, the plot is inextricably related, in symbolism and causality, to all the other narrative elements, and it seems to be true—in one sense at least—that the tensions and expectations of the intrigue 'give shape'. They compensate for the lack of continuous moral or psychological action and for the essentially static and self-contained nature of most of the satiric and comic action—some parts of *David Copperfield* and *Great Expectations* strongly excepted. In *Martin Chuzzlewit* the only tense and dynamic action starts too late to have this kind of total structural compensation. It is presented in a chunk, rather like the American episode, though interwoven of course with all the other pieces of what I hesitate to call action. Jonas's story is a well-handled exercise in the manner of Poe: a study in the psychology of guilt, fear, and the perverse imp that tempts to self-exposure. It has small beginnings in Jonas's aggressiveness to his father, and in his threat after the proposal, then moves mysteriously through the death of Anthony, the blackmail of Tigg Montague, his murder, and culminates in one of the best unmasking scenes in Dickens, with the brilliant use of Mrs. Gamp, for once trembling with more than gin, and the comic-sinister announcement of the actual appearance of Mrs. Harris. It is not as various and subtle as the analysis of the passions of Bill Sikes or Bradley Headstone, but it exposes its limited passions with hallucinatory power: Montague's fear of the door, Jonas's fear of the locked room, his beating heart, and his telltale face (*The Telltale Heart* was published in January 1841, the month when the publication of *Martin Chuzzlewit* began, and though I know of no evidence that Dickens read it, there seems to me to be as striking a resemblance between the Jonas parts and Poe's story as between that story and its supposed Dickens source in *The Clockcase*—a nice case, if true, of a source with its tail in its mouth). The criminal psychology is finely done, and so too is the revelation of the card up the author's sleeve. Jonas discovers that he has not really killed his father and so need not have killed Montague, and the combination of expectation and surprise here is worthy of the more dexterous double trick pulled off in *Our Mutual Friend* (the novel for which *Martin Chuzzlewit* acts as a source in several ways). This part of the action has also been described as thematically insistent: this is selfishness carried to the extreme of murder, and though I do not think that this depends for its excitement and tension on this moral significance, it is true that selfishness precipitates the action. This is not remarkable—murder is rarely selfless. The theme fits where it touches, and I would have thought that what engages our interest—what is central—is the psychology of crime and punishment rather than the anatomy of selfishness.

There is another way, apart from the mechanical unifying source of family relations, in which this action is related to the rest of the novel. Jonas is shown as the sadistic husband of poor transformed Mercy/Merry Chuzzlewit. If one of the formal characteristics of this novel is the lack of integrating action, another is surely a very characteristic lack of continuity in character. Is there any other novel where the characters are so made over for new rôles? Mercy and—to some extent—Jonas, seem to begin as comic characters, and become players in the grim melodrama. Montague Tigg becomes Tigg Montague. Chevy Slyme becomes a policeman. Bailey of Todgers's becomes the boy who travels with Jonas and Montague, who is believed dead, and who is joyfully resurrected at the end. Jonas is perhaps the only successful example—he moves quite convincingly from mean and furtive aggressiveness to a large predatoriness and brutality, and there is no difficulty about moving from his outside to the inner point-of-view: it is the same technique Dickens used earlier with Bill Sikes. Apart from *David Copperfield* and *Great Expectations*, Dickens's psychology is most convincing when he is dramatizing sensations of guilt, fear, and panic. Mercy, Tigg, Bailey, and Chevy are each merely two characters joined by being given the same name: there are the bridging explanations that Mercy is getting her punishment for her frivolity, that Tigg was given the money by old Martin to start him off in large speculation, that Chevy is still resentful at having to take on a job unworthy of his powers, but these are imposed. Bailey as the comic boy of Todgers—'There's a fish tomorrow. Just come. Don't eat none of him!'—bears no resemblance to the pathetic boy who is merely a silent dummy used to arouse pity and fear. The use of Mrs. Gamp in the dénouement is the most successful example of Dickens's habit of making a character do overtime, and here there is not only the careful preparation in Betsy Prig's terrible attack on the substantiality of Mrs. Harris—'I don't believe there's no sich a person'—but also a certain turn of the screw in the melodramatic use of the invisible comic alter ego. These are instances of loose ends being so carefully tucked into the wrong place that their looseness, and their mechanical structure, is revealed. Dickens is both careful and slap-happy about some aspects of composition: there is indeed a good passage where he seems to be parodying and anticipating certain excesses of thematic analysis:

From Mr. Moddle to Eden is an easy and natural transition. Mr. Moddle, living the atmosphere of Miss Pecksniff's love, dwelt (if he had but known it) in a terrestrial Paradise. The thriving city of Paradise was also a terrestrial Paradise, upon the showing of its proprietors. The beautiful Miss Pecksniff might have been poetically described as a something too good for man in his fallen and degraded state. That was exactly the character of the thriving city of Eden. . . . (Ch. 33.)

Dickens's transitions, in this novel and in others, are handled in a variety of ways. This example is characteristic of a certain mechanical composition which often derives from a relationship of theme but very seldom from a continuity of feeling. The transitions in character are managed with a similar superimposition of theoretical relation: Mercy is both changed and punished by her marriage, Tigg becomes Montague—with a drastic linguistic change and a similarly imposed explanation after the fact. What really seems to happen is that Dickens switches from the comic to the melodramatic mode: there is a purely intellectual movement made possible—though we cannot do more than guess about the causality—by the absence of what Coleridge called the unity of feeling. Form and psychology cannot be divorced: the difference between George Eliot's transitions from Dorothea to Casaubon, and Dickens's from Eden to Moddle, or between the thematic unity of characters like Lydgate and Raffles, and characters like Martin and Pecksniff and Mrs. Honimy, is that George Eliot's unity is one of feeling: her characters are conceived imaginatively as made out of the same relation to environment, the same aspirations, fantasies, and selfish and selfless urges. Dickens moves from one mode to another, and sometimes makes his connections work in theme rather than action.

At times they do not work. His tidiness may be plausible, as in his final use of Mrs. Gamp, or may be tolerated though implausible, as in the exploitation of Bailey as the pathetic child-figure for which he is scarcely qualified by his earlier appearances. But at times there are glaring examples of contradictions left unreconciled, or of resemblances of which Dickens seems unaware. One of these is Martin's dual rôle as selfish man and critic of selfishness. Another is the conspicuous transition from the satirical use of hyperbole and rhetorical question and metaphor in Pecksniff and the totally identified linguistic extravagance of Tom Pinch. Or there is the very last juxtaposition in the novel. In the last chapter we have Moddle's very funny flight from the altar—'Unalterably, never yours, Augustus'—and then immediately afterwards comes the last bid for pathos in

Tom Pinch's equally romantic unrequited longings for Another who is Another's. Pecksniff's exaggerations are a correlative for insincerity, Dickens's exaggerations on behalf of Tom are in deadly earnest, and here coincidence shows the lack of imaginative comparison and judgment of emotion and style. The great satirist can turn to gross sentimentality without his left hand knowing what his right hand is doing. The content of Moddle's yearnings and isolation come unhappily before the final full-blast appeal from Tom's plight: Moddle's 'e'en now' and the author's 'Thou wert by her side' to Tom, are dangerously close, and Moddle's comic 'Unalterably' changes to the ecstatic vision of final reunion in Heaven. The differences are as revealing as the resemblances: Moddle's farewell is studded with bathos: '300 tons per register—forgive me if in my distraction I allude to the ship', whereas our farewell to Tom plays on the associations of religion, gardens, music, and—of course—children. There are no major death-beds and pathetic children in the novel, but Dickens deliberately used—or felt intensely—their powerful appeal when he introduced Mary's child, who is significantly 'slight' and (on one occasion, calling for Tom to be her patient nurse) on a sick-bed. The *vox humana* of the pathetic mode and the comic exaggeration of its opposite are good examples of Dickens's formal completion and fundamental failure to connect. The result is unintentional self-parody.

The acceptability of the Dickensian sensibility, and its relation both to his sense of audience and his private fantasy, is still a problem: we mostly agree with Oscar Wilde that one must have a heart of stone not to laugh at Little Nell, but we still disagree about Paul Dombey. But admitting the variability of individual thresholds of sensibility and taste, I should like to suggest the relevance of formal analysis to this question of Dickens's emotional taste. In the first chapter of *Oliver Twist* there is the death-bed and the birth, with the theatrical rhetoric of 'Let me see the child and die'. Out of context this may seem regrettable, but in the context the pathos is not only contrasted with the institutional satire of workhouse officialdom, but rooted in it: the mother is unparticularized but the matter-of-factness of the doctor and the beery old women gives the situation a particular reason for its pathos. Another example comes from *Dombey and Son*. When Paul tells Toots about the wild waves there is the particularity and contrast of the two odd, not to say touched, children, one babbling his sick vision, the other with his practical obtuse inability to share it. This may be in part a matter of aesthetic distance, but I believe it is mainly a matter of particularity. Intense emotional appeal, in realistic arts like fiction and drama, may well need the particularity of social situation and human contrast. The workhouse doctor and Toots act rather like the Nurse in *Romeo and Juliet*, and reveal both the rareness of the intensity and the solid human habitation from which it springs. The separation of the comic, pathetic, and melodramatic modes in *Martin Chuzzlewit* means that this constant checking and solidifying of pathos very seldom takes place. And the novel acts as a self-made analysis of Dickens's defects of archness and pathos, exposing them in their nakedness, and showing by contrast how he so often manages the same emotional appeal in a way which comes off in other novels.

On the whole, the comedy has nothing to say to the arch love-story of Ruth and John or to the pathos of Tom Pinch, who stands in for the innocent and pathetic child. Together with the melodrama, and surpassing it in its variety and concreteness, it is the main source of vitality in *Martin Chuzzlewit*. Its resilient and compulsive caricatures are not altered by their contact with the serious characters: Mrs. Gamp is warned and Pecksniff exposed and degraded, but the two main comic characters are spared the shift of mode which disintegrates Montague Tigg, Chevy Slyme, and Bailey. The comedy provides its own special source of tension—we await the return to its self-contained comic farce and continued mannerism as the one firm line of interest in the novel. There is more and less than thematic continuity here: even Mr. Pecksniff's drunken longings to see Mrs. Todgers's idea of a wooden leg depends in part on our recollection of his instructions to Martin to produce his idea of a monument to the Lord Mayor, or a tomb for a sheriff, or a nobleman's cowhouse, but Mrs. Gamp's husband's wooden leg is, I hope, as essentially unrelated to Mrs. Todgers's 'idea' as Mrs. Gamp is to a White Goddess. Satire and sick humour flourish in the most influential of Dickens's comic prototypes—she is the Dogberry of syntax, the drunken nurse full of gorgeous child-bed morbidity—and there is, I hope, social realism granted, no symbolic resonance in the umbrella (*pace* Mr. Miller), the cowcumber, or Mrs. Harris's portrait. The farce, the brilliant linguistic incongruity, parody, and zany oddity, on the one hand, and the harsh unfair splendid American satire, on the other, show a sure handling and an expansiveness which other parts of an ineffectual action sorely need.

DEALINGS WITH THE
FIRM OF DOMBEY AND SON:
FIRMNESS *versus* WETNESS

Julian Moynahan

LET HIM be as absorbed as he would in the Son on whom he built such high hopes, he could not forget that closing scene. He could not forget that he had had no part in it. That at the bottom of its clear depths of tenderness and truth, lay those two figures clasped in each other's arms, while he stood on the bank above them, looking down a mere spectator— not a sharer with them—quite shut out. (Ch. 3.)

'Aye,' said the Captain, reverentially; 'it's a almighty element. There's wonders in the deep, my pretty. Think on it when the winds is roaring and the waves is rowling. . . . Lord help 'em, how I pitys all unhappy folks ashore now!' (Ch. 49.)

I

Dombey and Son was the first of Dickens's novels to follow a deeply considered plan. He was becoming conscious of what we call nowadays the problem of focus, and his letter to Forster of July 12, 1842, explains what that focus is to be. He will show Mr. Dombey's obsession with 'that one idea of a son'; will show him first frustrated over Paul's clinging attachment to Florence; and then show his dislike of Florence changing to positive hatred following Paul's death. The story will move on 'through all the branches and offshoots and meanderings that come up' until it culminates in the proud broker's agonized discovery that the despised daughter has all along been 'his only staff and treasure, and his unknown Good Genius'.

Such was the plan and it tells a good deal, but it does not explain the two central mysteries of the book: the mystery of iniquity contained in Dombey's fantastic treatment of his daughter, and the mystery of Florence's enormous power over nearly every important character in the book except Dombey and Carker, and in the end over Dombey. I shall take that back. Florence seems to hold her power over Dombey from the beginning:

He almost felt as if she watched and distrusted him. As if she held the clue to something secret in his breast, of the nature of which he was hardly informed himself. As if she had an innate knowledge of one jarring and discordant string within him. . . . Perhaps—who shall decide on such mysteries!—he was afraid that he might come to hate her. (Ch. 3.)

Extraordinary as this fatherly reaction to a meek daughter of six may be, the deliberately obscured point of vantage from which the characters are viewed is equally so. Here and elsewhere the tone recalls Hawthorne at his most hedging, and the *trompe d'oeil* technique of Melville in *Benito Sereno* and *The Encantadas*. What *does* Dombey feel? Can we be sure that Florence holds a clue? All is hidden under a veil, like the handkerchief with which Dombey conceals his face in the scene whose running title is 'The Statue Melts'. Who *shall* decide on such mysteries? Certainly not Dickens in his sybilline preface—'The two commonest mistakes in judgment that I suppose to arise from the former default, are, the confounding of shyness and arrogance . . .' If this glances at Dombey it either says that Dombey is shy rather than arrogant, or arrogant rather than shy. Is it shyness that makes him strike his daughter a bruising blow on the breast? Is it arrogance that causes him to conceal the outward signs of awakening feeling beneath a handkerchief? Obviously, Dombey is both shy and arrogant to an unnatural degree, and besides, Dickens may not be including him at all in the opening paragraph of his preface where the remark appears..

Dombey and Son is a very disturbing book, and its mysteries of characterization and narrative treatment are a part of what makes it disturbing. These mysteries must be faced, if not finally reduced to plain sense through analysis. Before attempting that, however, I should like to proceed first in the opposite direction, pretending that the problem of Dombey's ill-nature and the problem of Florence's power contain no residual mystery.

Why does Dombey behave so vilely to his daughter? He is proud, and the novel is in some sense a splendidly organized study of this 'master-vice'. Dombey's pride in self-love is played off against the self-lacerating pride of Edith Granger, the covert paranoiac pride of Carker, the appalling physical vanity of Mrs. Skewton, the comic self-complacency of Joey B., and so forth. Dombey's schemes for Paul are a monstrous self-assertion, and Paul's death is as much a blow to his ego as to his affections for his son. He has been jealous of Paul's preference for Florence even as he was jealous of the wet-nurse's closeness to his son. This jealousy becomes hate when, from his point of view, the wrong child dies, and the hate overpowers his cold reserve when his second wife flaunts her passionate regard for Florence and her contempt for him on every possible occasion.

All this is obvious. But Dombey's pride does not explain why he should have been afraid early on that he might come to hate Florence. Whatever Florence challenges in him, it is not mere pride. A man consumed with lofty self-regard should at least be able to tolerate the deep, uncritical love of someone asking so little in return as Florence. Jane Austen's odious Sir Walter Elliot would have romped in it like a sportive walrus in the sea.

Mr. Dombey's second sin is his habit of governing his domestic establishment and private affairs according to firm business prin-ciples. He had acquired his first wife to breed an heir for the Firm and took a second to display the power of his wealth before his associates in The City and his new circle of seedy-aristocratic acquaint-ances in the West End. But the wives do not live up to a viable business ethics. They default on their contracts. The first wife dies after delivering a faulty piece of goods called Paul; Edith sells her resplendent self but then quite literally refuses to deliver the mer-chandise Dombey has paid for.

Nevertheless, there is nothing here to explain why he avoids, fears, and hates Florence. Early in the story his one wish is to keep Paul alive, and Florence performs prodigies of surrogate mothering in the furtherance of that aim. Later on she grows into a beautiful young woman who could have been an ornament to the establishment of conspicuous consumption he created in his house near Portland Place if he had required it of her. From the standpoint of business she is an unexpectedly sound investment.

A third and more 'up-to-date' line of explanation is possible. Florence has an enormous capacity for tender feeling, while Dombey, for reasons never explained, is afraid of feeling. He has built a stone

façade—of rigid views, rigid habits, rigid stance, and a rigid countenance—between his inner self and the people around him. The
eccentric psychoanalyst Wilhelm Reich named this curious and
perhaps characteristically English defence against feeling through the
erection of a frozen façade 'character armour', and developed a kind
of therapy for it which combined direct physical massage of the unnaturally stiff face and body of the patient with more usual kinds of
treatment. He found that his patients feared love more than loneliness. It was easier for them to feel nothing or to hate than to shed
their armour and enter naked into what Dickens calls 'the community
of feeling'.

In *Dombey and Son* Florence assumes the rôle of the therapist and
suffers the hostility that neurotics of this sort are ready to vent on
anyone willing to challenge their essential isolation. The usual expression of her love is tears, and she would dearly love to weep with
or over Dombey at several important turning points of the story. But
he cannot abide her tears or even her tender look. Until the end she
has only seen his face relaxed from its expression of defence one time
—when he lay helpless and unconscious after being thrown from his
horse. He has been able to study hers only from behind a concealing
handkerchief. His brief change in that scene is described as a melting.
Clearly, he is afraid that if he once lets go he will be dissolved or
drowned in a sea of feeling. The first quotation at the beginning of
my essay shows this with great precision. Dombey is recalling how
his wife had died while clasped in his weeping daughter's arms. He
feels shut out from that close embrace. But he also sees the two figures
as if they lay drowned at the bottom of a body of water. Standing
above on the high bank he is lonely yet safe. For Dombey at this
point the sharing of love seems a death by water. To be saved from
his own stoniness he must leap from the bank and dissolve his proud
self in his daughter's tears.

This, of course, is what he comes to in the end. The 'imperfect
shapes' of his fantasy in Chapter 3 adumbrate the true form of his
deliverance at the end. After attempted suicide he passes into the
arms of Florence. She teaches him to weep. On the last page of the
book he is alone with the new Florence. She asks him, 'Dear grandpapa, why do you cry when you kiss me?' He evades this sensible
question but we can answer for him. He has been reborn from the
damp pillow of his invalidism into a new career of sentiment. Father
and daughter are finally alike, with a genius for weeping. Dombey

has at last come to terms with the watery element—sea, river, and tears—on which Dickens's curious message is floated, and the terms are unconditional surrender.

It seems a dismal conclusion to a career which had matched Stavrogin's and Coriolanus's in its superb desolation of pride and obstinacy; not merely inadequate to the man who elicited Edith Granger's purest response of utter hate, but unwholesome as well. I shall have more to say about that later. Here I want to point out before turning to the linked question of Florence's power that 'coming to terms with the watery element' is not only Dombey's trope of salvation. It is fully autonomous in the novel as a whole. Nearly every character who is to be saved or is assured of salvation from the first must establish or has already established close relations with the element of water. As the saintly Captain Cuttle says reverentially, 'Lord help 'em, how I pitys all unhappy folks ashore now.'

II

A nineteenth-century reviewer found Florence's willingness to go on loving a father who hated her morbid. D. H. Lawrence might have found it obscene, and a doing of dirt on life. It is morbid at one point—when Florence while staying at the Thameside villa of Sir Barnet Skettles sees the workman's tenderness towards his wretched, sickly daughter and imagines she might gain her father's love by dying. But at the same time her daughterly affection, up to the time of the final break, remains remarkably constant. It becomes tinged with despair but never becomes adulterated with feelings of annoyance or impatience. Well, Dickens's sentimental heroines are like that, all soul and giving. This comment is all right as far as it goes, but it ignores Florence's power and its mystery. The point is, she keeps at Dombey until she gets him; just as Milly Theale in *The Wings of the Dove* gets Densher and Kate Croy in the end. She is on the scene at every crisis of his life. On the night of Edith's elopement he shatters her gift of tears with a blow, but not even Dombey can summon the strength to repeat so diabolical a gesture. Florence's magical reappearance at the very moment he turns his hatred against himself is a necessary coincidence. It expresses the fact that her magic is stronger than his. The whole scheme of the book requires that she be in at the kill. One needs to put it this way even at the cost of being barred from the pages of *The Dickensian* for life.

What does Florence want of her father? The question has the stupidly perverse ring of an unrepentant Dombey. But it can be enlightening with Dickens to answer even stupid questions in the context of physical action rather than 'inner motivation'. He often arranges his most important meanings on the outside, where they become palpable in gesture and movement. Florence wants to get Dombey's head down on the pillow where she can drown him in a dissolving love. She has done this with her mother at the point of death and with Paul at a similar juncture. And she has done this with Edith, from whom, we are told, she strikes tears as Moses caused water to gush from a rock, yet whom she cannot save. The dream vision assigned to Florence on the appropriate occasion of the night on which Dombey and Edith return from their wedding trip predicts Dombey's salvation within the context of wetness and the sick-bed, just as it predicts that Edith will throw herself away in despair:

She dreamed of seeking her father in wildernesses, of following his track up fearful heights, and down into deep mines and caverns; of being charged with something that would release him from extraordinary suffering—she knew not what, or why—yet never being able to attain the goal and set him free Then she saw him dead, upon that very bed, and in that very room, and knew that he had never loved her to the last, and fell upon his cold breast, passionately weeping. Then a prospect opened, and a river flowed, and a plaintive voice she knew, cried, 'It is running on, Floy! It has never stopped! You are moving with it!' And she saw him at a distance stretching out his arms towards her, while a figure such as Walter's used to be, stood near him, awfully serene and still. In every vision, Edith came and went, sometimes to her joy, sometimes to her sorrow, until they were alone upon the brink of a dark grave, and Edith pointing down, she looked and saw—what!—another Edith lying at the bottom. (Ch. 35.)

We need not boggle over the detail that Dombey is dead in the dream. The chief thing is that he is on the bed and powerless to move until he agrees to move with and in the running water. If Dombey fears love as a death by drowning the remarkable fact is that he is right. Another remarkable fact is that within the circle of Florence's influence even the sea of death is transformed into a vast welter of eternal love which reaches from the barren shores of this life to the shores of heaven. To claim this is to claim that Florence is more angel than woman, and that is exactly what she is called with damnable iteration; she is a sentimental heroine upon whom angelic powers and attributes have been arbitrarily grafted.

III

If Florence is an angel—the Victorian Angel in the House, Angel of Love, Angel of Death empowered to remove Death's sting, angel of the waves, tutelary divinity of the damp little company who crowd into the *cenaculum* of Sol Gills's back parlour—then Dombey must in some sense stand as a human soul threatened with damnation and struggling to resist an overpowering call to be saved. Unfortunately, Dombey does not interest us as a human soul, just as Florence does not interest us as a human character. We are interested in Dombey as a London business man in an age of railroad building and electric telegraphy, an age of risk-taking capital enterprise on a global scale. These social conditions are some of the determinants of his hardness and matter to us more than any mystery of iniquity he may carry in his breast. We are interested in his appalling adventures as the head of a household, as a widower who makes a bad marriage, as the injured party (technically) in a social scandal which must have rocked The City and been a staple item of gossip in the London clubs for months. We are interested in his possessive jealousy of his son, his nastiness towards his daughter, his capacity to act fairly and unfairly by turns in dealing with matters like Sol Gills's debt and the question of Walter's transfer to the West Indies, in his honesty if not his acumen in all business dealings, in the sheer oddness of his intimacy with Carker. Dombey is complicated and real, and inhabits a real, complicated world. His fate should take the variety of his rôles, the contradictoriness of his nature, and above all his integrity, repulsive as it may be, into account. He deserves a complex fate but does not get one. And if we admit that we shall have to admit further that he had everything to fear and nothing to gain from Florence's love. He was right after all.

The essential movement of the book is from complexity towards a weltering simplicity. This is evident in Dombey's power struggle with Florence and in other situations of the novel as well. Originally, Dickens had planned to send Walter Gay on a downward trek into dissipation and death, and to kill off the vapid Sol Gills half-way through the story. Instead, he sends them out on the sea, whence they return like characters out of late Shakespearian comedy from shipwreck and wandering, the one transformed into a successful business man, the other into a successful investor of capital. We do not believe it. Walter is simply not of executive calibre, as they say nowadays, while Gills is surely one of the suckers born every minute.

Dickens's urge to simplify or to destroy outright the complex is evident in his handling of Carker. On the one hand, Carker is a dark analogy of Dombey himself. If Dombey embodies the rigid respectability of commercial enterprise in The City, England's credit as it were, Carker is a predatory version of the same career, which can lead on through excessive profit-taking, bold speculation, and doctored books to either the Honours List or exposure followed by bankruptcy. On the other hand, Carker, with his knowledge of art, of all games, his mastery of languages, his superb horsemanship, his sure taste in interior decoration, is deliberately built up as a uniquely intelligent and talented character. When he is torn to pieces by a railway engine typifying Death but making better sense as a symbol of the hardness and dynamism of the socio-economic climate which produced both Carker and his Principal, intelligence and a knowledge of refined techniques die from the book along with wickedness.

The 'little society of the back parlour' which Dickens sets up as an alternate form of organization to the hard actuality of mid-nineteenth-century England and its Industrial Revolution consists of two retired female servants, a near-imbecile, a virtuous and very funny retired ship pilot, a vendor of obsolete nautical instruments, and a boring young man named Walter. Florence is less *of* the company than its object of worship. As a quasi-religious society it adheres to strict rules. For one thing all or nearly all the regular communicants must be on good terms with the quasi-sacramental element of wet. Captain Cuttle, who moved from his lodgings near a canal of the India Docks to the ship-like property of Sol Gills presents no problem; nor does Walter, that lad 'flowing with milk and honey', or his uncle. Mrs. Toodle has been the wet-nurse and 'common fountain' of the infant Paul, and Toots qualifies by virtue of his intimate association with the sea-struck Dombey heir. Besides, the vagaries of his mental processes resemble the shapeless surgings of the sea. And even Florence, who is the genius of the society rather than a dues-paying member, has stepped down from her niche to undertake a year's voyage on the sea, returning with a new and very vigorous boy child named Paul.

This quasi-religious community subscribes to a narrow and exclusive standard of values. Its values are simple good nature and simple-mindedness. It leaves out of account intelligence, forceful masculine energy—its males are old men, a simpleton, and Walter— as well as sensuality. Edith is barred not only because her career skirts adultery but also because there is an aura of sensuality about her. Her habit of beating herself about the breast and bruising her hand on marble mantelpieces suggests that she has a body and feels things there. She may be sexually frigid but the possibility of a thaw remains.

To enter this community and drink of the wine rescued from the hold of a sinking ship, Dombey must experience a change of heart that reads like a second childhood. He must surrender all those qualities of hardness, self-control, and pride that have made him both human and actual, and inhuman as well. Not merely the excess of those qualities but the qualities themselves. The spectacle is depressing. The only consolation for the reader is our awareness that in his contest with Florence he has been overmatched from the first. At his prime he could freeze the water in the baptismal font and set Miss Tox's teeth chattering during the cold luncheon over which he presided after Paul's christening. The icy current of his selfish nature could freeze for a time around his son 'into one unyielding block'. But Florence has the ocean at her beck and call and he cannot freeze that. Like tears it is too salty. The breaking of the Firm is described as the foundering of a ship. One might similarly describe Sol Gills's establishment towards the end of the novel as an ark commanded by a plurality of sweet old Noahs and floating on a fathomless sea of sentiment.

IV

In Dombey, Dickens created a permanently valid image of nineteenth-century Economic Man in all the unyielding pride of his power and the pathos and repulsiveness of his blighted heart. But *Dombey and Son* is also a vision of the transformation of society by love, and as such is something less than adequate. One difficulty is that the vision is neither genuinely religious, with a full commitment to the idea that the ultimate source of human love is divine love, nor genuinely secular, with a firm commitment to the idea that human destinies must work themselves out within the world of actuality and without the help of heavenly grace or miraculous interventions. The book seems to me to exhibit Protestant piety divorced from its doctrinal foundations, Christian sentiment divorced from the rigours of a creed and from Christian practice. Religion has become a set of loose analogies and tropes employed to conceal faulty argument by analogy: people who act like saints will be rewarded like saints in the end. The meek shall inherit the Industrial Revolution. One tires of hearing Florence or her 'umble compeeress Harriet Carker called an angel. On a harder view, Florence is not a conduit of Grace. The miracles she performs are all arranged for her by the intrusive author. Remove her pall of quasi-religious mystery and Dombey's daughter is at best a sentimentalist lacking decent self-respect, at worst a masochist. She is an image of human feeling devoid of energy, segregated from intelligence and the life of the senses, isolated from the sphere of actual social existence which must be transformed if Dickens's project for the transformation of society by love is to work.

Before his collapse Dombey inhabits a world of power, a world where hard practical intelligence and will have run wild, issuing in spectacular inventions like the railroad, in spectacularly predatory careers like Carker's. This is a tensely masculine world, a society of heads without hearts. Florence's sphere of influence is a slackly feminine one, consisting in a society of hearts without heads. Dickens's attempted solution of this cultural impasse merely perpetuates it. Dombey moves from hardness through debility to a maundering, guilt-ridden submission to feminine softness. A Victorian patriarchy of stiff and tyrannical men of affairs surrenders to a matriarchy of weeping mothers and daughters. Translated into socio-economic terms this would mean that the control of railroads, shipping lines and investment houses would pass under the control of softies like Morfin, adepts in guilt like Carker the Junior, milky young men like Walter Gay. The prospect is amusing but dangerous as well. Even with Mr. Toodle at the controls railway engines would destroy far more people in an era of unlimited sentiment than one of economic imperialism—provided they ran at all. In the long run an ocean of tears is positively frightening as an image of the good society.

Like Lawrence several generations later, Dickens confronts the divisive and anarchic phenomena of industrial society with an over-simplified idea of human community. At the end of *Lady Chatterley's Lover* Mellors writes Connie that things would be all right if men wore tight scarlet trousers and learned to dance and hop and skip, 'and amuse the women themselves, and be amused by the women'. At the end of *Dombey and Son* Dickens is saying that things would be all right if men of Dombey's class and function made their daughters their mothers and lay down. In both cases man turns back boyishly to woman and is saved. The vast resources of human energy and wit that have been trapped within an unjust and destructively oriented socio-economic system are not released or transformed but merely abandoned. So that the problem each writer set out to solve is merely perpetuated in a new, grossly sentimental form.

DAVID COPPERFIELD

John Jones

DICKENS SAID in the preface to the second edition of *David Copperfield* that he liked this the best of all his books. He must have felt, and he may have intended to acknowledge, with due discretion, his autobiographical intimacy with its story; at any rate here, and nowhere else, he made covert exposure of the childhood shame of the blacking factory, and perhaps comforted himself thereby; and here he used his infatuation with Maria Beadnell, and his unhappy marriage, and his father's buoyant fecklessness and sublimely pompous idiom; and here he argued out—with more thoroughness than has been recognized—his career and vocation as a writer. But more of that later. My immediate purpose is to suggest that in liking *Copperfield* the best, Dickens believed it *was* the best (his unsolemn seriousness about his work points to this conclusion); and to refer so high an estimate, which very many of his readers have shared, to a yardstick respected by him and by them—the one that informs the old serial-writer's admonition: 'Make 'em laugh. Make 'em cry. Make 'em wait.'

Make 'em wait, rather than make 'em cry, lies at the root of our confused urge to hem and haw, to reach for qualification, when we contemplate Dickens in his rightful place among the great novelists of the world. Being easily isolated and made a talking point, his bad pathos (make 'em cry) gets overstressed in critical discussion; whereas the truth is that, being easily isolated, his bad pathos seldom matters. The other question is more complicated, especially in *David Copperfield*. Not that this novel has more than its share of gross and protracted solicitings like: who is Betsey Trotwood's shadowy persecutor? what is the truth about the Strong marriage? when will Mr. Peggotty find his Emily? The rouble, primarily, is the longed-for discomfiture of the Murdstones, which is the most artful make-'em-wait in all Dickens and brings home a brilliantly spare narrative of sixty thousand words.

At this firm close *Copperfield* shudders helplessly, motionless like a sailing ship in irons. Miss Trotwood's abhorrence of donkeys is the first bit of tired fantasy in the book. The attempt to construct a benign anti-self to Salem House dies at once on the ear:

> Doctor Strong's was an excellent school; as different from Mr. Creakle's as good is from evil. It was very gravely and decorously ordered, and on a sound system; with an appeal, in everything, to the honour and good faith of the boys, and an avowed intention to rely on their possession of those qualities unless they proved themselves unworthy of it, which worked wonders. (Ch. 16.)

And we find Dickens's Prospectus-prose (which is slovenly prose too: consider that second 'it') matched by his description of the Wickfields' house in the Beautiful Homes manner of the women's magazines:

> We accordingly went up a wonderful old staircase; with a balustrade so broad that we might have gone up that, almost as easily; and into a shady old drawing-room, lighted by three or four of the quaint windows I had looked up at from the street: which had old oak seats in them, that seemed to have come of the same trees as the shining oak floor, and the great beams in the ceiling. It was a prettily furnished room, with a piano and some lively furniture in red and green, and some flowers. (Ch. 15.)

That string of inert adjectives qualifying the unfelt scene is one among many signs of the book's weakened narrative thrust. And here we may observe, alongside its coming to rest in the Murdstones' decisive repulse at Dover where David has found sanctuary (all roads lead to Dover), a general unpreparedness for the hero's shift from a life of suffering to one of action. The following exchange, the first of its kind:

> 'Should you like to go to school at Canterbury?' said my aunt.
> I replied that I should like it very much, as it was so near her.
> 'Good,' said my aunt. 'Should you like to go tomorrow?' (Ch. 15.)

affronts the imagination by its discontinuity with a world in which David never made choices like these; and I am not thinking so much of the compulsions and cruelties themselves as of Dickens's success in the realization of the tough little life always pressing up from beneath the buffeting, with its unquenchable curiosity and self-concern, with its ultimate pertness which is almost blitheness. When David heard his mother was dead he wept long and bitterly—of course, for he was broken-hearted. And next: 'I stood upon a chair when I was left alone, and looked into the glass to see how red my eyes were, and how sorrowful my face.' What piercing genius! How firm the pulse beating through this scene, from Mrs. Creakle's breaking of the news:

'You are too young to know how the world changes every day,' said Mrs. Creakle, 'and how the people in it pass away. But we all have to learn it, David; some of us when we are young, some of us when we are old, some of us at all times of our lives.'

I looked at her earnestly.

'When you came away from home at the end of the vacation,' said Mrs. Creakle, after a pause, 'were they all well?' After another pause, 'Was your mama well?'

I trembled without distinctly knowing why, and still looked at her earnestly, making no attempt to answer.

'Because,' said she, 'I grieve to tell you that I hear this morning your mama is very ill.'

A mist rose between Mrs. Creakle and me, and her figure seemed to move in it for an instant. Then I felt the burning tears run down my face, and it was steady again.

'She is very dangerously ill,' she added.

'She is dead.' (Ch. 9.)

to the swift rallying of the child's bruised consciousness! Dickens never wrote better than he writes here, or than he writes in the sequence that leads from the torment of lessons at home, to the first cut of Mr. Murdstone's cane, to the biting of his hand, to the strange half-peace of banishment upstairs. And nowhere is Dickens's humour more familiar with the painful action than in the oral formulation of Mr. Murdstone's sum: ' "If I go into a cheesemonger's shop, and buy five thousand double-Gloucester cheeses at fourpence-halfpenny each, present payment"—at which I see Miss Murdstone secretly overjoyed.' (Ch. 4.) Indeed, so ample is his conceiving of Nature in these early chapters, that Dickens's treble lack of spirituality and intellect and education grows uniquely unimportant. It is only later in the book that one begins to brood upon what Dostoevsky would have made of Agnes, and what Tolstoi—or even George Eliot —would have done with David's marriage to Dora Spenlow.

But Dickens was able, as were the two Russians (and they saluted the talent in him), to effect a royal directness of statement. It seems an easy thing to say 'a mist rose between Mrs. Creakle and me'. But no English novelists except Scott and Dickens do say it easily. It is Shakespearian. It has something to do with a writer's confidence in his power to present immediately the relationship between physical and emotional events; and this leads to great simplicity and size, and authority, and to what is called Dickens's exaggeration.

Nor am I pretending that all, or nearly all, merit leaves *David Copperfield* at Dover. The book, I suggested just now, stands in irons. Then it pays away, gradually, from the eye of the wind, and its sails fill upon a new tack which it holds to the end; and the end is a completed portrait of the artist as a young man. This early-Victorian novelist, very much a man of his age, is without the concept of the great writer; he holds to that of the great man whose greatness lies in his writing. And therefore the whole fable strikes us a hundred years later as unaesthetic and worldly, and lacking in definition. Certainly we hear that David is unable to discuss his ideas with Dora, she doesn't inspire him; but what looms much larger is her general domestic incompetence; so that we are left contemplating an able and ambitious young man with a half-wit wife round his neck.

Of course the portrait is not entirely devoid of justice to the child-wife, or of modest reserve. While David's single-minded application —the sheer work—is stressed and stressed again, the question of genius is left to his readers. And at the same time Betsey Trotwood is reminding him that he chose Dora for his wife, and Agnes is telling him how sweet and loving she is; he mustn't expect to have everything.

The portrait also has many faults. Probably the emptiest part of this novel, which was published in the same year as *The Prelude*, is David's long retreat to Switzerland, alone with his talent, in search of Nature's healing power. Dickens needed a respectable gap between the two marriages. And to the second and inspiring wife he gave a tiresome religiosity. The portrait would have been clearer, the book would make better sense, if he had not pretended that Agnes, 'near me, pointing upward', was doing other than encourage

David to still greater heights of literary achievement and reputation. Something like his frankness over Traddles's rôle of business manager is called for.

There are two links binding the Trials of David to the Portrait of the Artist: the Peggottys (including Steerforth) and Mr. Micawber. The success of the first is usually, I think, overrated—particularly as regards Mr. Peggotty himself, who remains a mean conception. His 'Thank 'ee, sir' vein points the truth that liberal paternalism *feels* vulnerable where the blackest stand on class and privilege *feels* alien. (In the episode of Murdstone and Grinby's warehouse, which is substantially autobiographical, we experience a malicious urge to stress the pronoun in 'put to work not fit for me', and the adjective in 'with common men and boys'.) Peggotty's enormous superiority to Mr. Peggotty grows out of her office as David's nurse; their relationship transcends class, as happens in life sometimes, and Dickens has no need to spend his vocabulary of rough simple goodness on her. Elsewhere—with Mr. Peggotty and Ham and Emily— factitious rhetoric abounds; Ham is worse than Mr. P., though less important, and even the imaginative stroke of Mrs. Gummidge's sudden recovery from being lone and lorn at the moment of real disaster is dulled by a vamping accompaniment of exclamation. This last, even if exceptionally feeble ('What a change in Mrs. Gummidge in a little time!'), does no more than illustrate Dickens's notorious over-pointing of the logic of his novels; it catches the eye in the last three-quarters of *David Copperfield* because there is so little of it in the first quarter, where narrative stringency reigns, and trust in the reader's quickness to respond. Mr. Murdstone's head of black hair is after all, or before all, 'beautiful'. Enough said.

Mr. Micawber, the second link, is a figure of the fiercest urban and economic comedy, and of lurking violence. He lives to an extraordinary extent in *oratio obliqua* and reportage:

'Last night, on being childishly solicited for twopence to buy 'lemonstunners'—a local sweetmeat—he presented an oyster-knife at the twins!' (Ch. 49.)

His 'talents'—Mrs. Micawber's word—are those of middleman and private speculator, of dealer in corn and coal; his world has vanished, I feel (for each of us refers great art to his own past, quite irrationally), with those triangular paper bags that held a pennyworth of

sweets—a bag each for the twins. On the one hand Mr. Micawber
drifts in and out untethered to the action of the book, and on the
other he determines, more effectively than anyone else, its characteristic mood of buoyancy, and renders its horrors and indignations so
mysteriously undestroying. We start as if woken from a joyful dream
when David lets fall the judgment that Mr. Micawber is 'slippery'.
And similarly over David's attempt to cancel his articles and recover
his aunt's one thousand pounds, or part thereof, from Mr. Spenlow;
the joke about the absent partner's stubborn opposition to all generous
proposals suddenly turns nasty at this point—I mean the joke turns
nasty, not Mr. Spenlow; for the man continues wrapped in the
Copperfield aura of life-fostering fantasy. And then he has an accident—one of those shameless Dickensian accidents whereby a man
or a building or a marriage is disposed of—and dies; and David
records 'the lazy hush and rest there was in the office' next morning.

Mr. Micawber having been born free, we do wrong to attribute
his pining away when he becomes Uriah Heep's secretary to a
narrowly moral cause. First and foremost this is an unnatural condition in which his vital powers decay; his genius is at last oppressed,
and because his genius has been throughout, in certain essentials, the
genius of the book, our separation of the Portrait of the Artist from
the Trials of David cannot be complete.

Mr. Micawber is also among Dickens's fullest and most vigorous
essays in the shabby-genteel; every critic calls him an inspired
creation, and many critics go on to remark the surpassing brilliance
and variety of the characters in *David Copperfield*. Sometimes the
word voices proves more precise than characters. The book teems
with distinct speech-idioms like that of Mr. Murdstone's friend:

'He having,' Mr. Quinion observed in a low voice, and half turning
round, 'no other prospect, Murdstone.' (Ch. 10.)

and that of Mr. Micawber's nameless creditor ('I think he was a
boot-maker') who found his way into the house at seven in the
morning and bawled up the stairs:

'Come! You aren't out yet, you know. Pay us, will you? Don't hide, you
know; that's mean. I wouldn't be mean if I was you. Pay us, will you?
You just pay us, d'ye hear? Come!' (Ch. 11.)

More than any other novelist, Dickens thrusts the individuations of
character forward and out into utterance, delivering the sinister

pussyfoot (we are told nothing *about* Mr. Quinion) in that delayed
vocative, 'Murdstone'; and the wrathful tradesman in his prose-
clatter tune, and in an obsessively private and also virile sense of
'mean'. These voices people the book and contribute lavishly to its
local flair; so that our endorsing of Dickens's facetious self-appella-
tion, the Inimitable, has a lot to do with them.

Character, as the term is commonly understood and employed,
discovers Dickens at his most inimitably cavalier. If he finds himself
embarrassed by the human image he has been offering, he changes
it. Thus Peggotty's habit, almost her dominant trait, in the early
chapters of the book was to lose buttons from off the back of her
dress 'whenever she made any little exertion'. This is tiresome to keep
up, and so it stops. When David encounters Rose Dartle with
Mrs. Steerforth, the uncomfortable Dartle-tune of insinuation is at
once affirmed: ' "But isn't it though?—I want to be put right, if I
am wrong—isn't it, really?" ' Unfortunately her very promising
rôle is progressively melodramatized, and Dickens sacrifices this
large aspect of her. (The by no means unimpressive attempt to build
a love-hate relationship between her and Steerforth was perhaps an
ambitious after-thought; Rosa is first identified by her tune in the
seventh number plan; while with Steerforth himself we find Dickens
jettisoning a splendid illustration of the villain's power to please, and
doing so for no better reason, apparently, than that the monthly
number, as he had first drafted it, was a little too long: Steerforth
coaxes Mrs. Gummidge into cheerfulness, prevents her from thinking
about the old 'un, by sitting down beside her and confessing that he
is a love lorn creature himself, ' "and everything has gone contrary
with me from my cradle" '.) [1]

No case of changed direction, and hasty re-definition, can compare with that of Miss Mowcher. About her, the Introducer of *David
Copperfield* in the *Oxford Illustrated Dickens* ventures this opinion:
'Of the minor characters I think Miss Mowcher must have had a
living prototype.' A happy guess—and an unnecessary one, since our
knowledge of the grotesque woman dwarf whom Dickens noticed
in the neighbourhood of Devonshire Terrace goes back the best part
of a century, to Forster. She was a chiropodist and manicurist called
Mrs. Seymour Hill, and her appearance was used for Miss Mowcher.

[1] The cancelled passage is printed by Professor John Butt in *Review of English
Studies*, July 1950.

Mrs. Hill read the number and recognized herself and was deeply distressed, and wrote to Dickens to tell him so. In his reply he did not deny—how could he?—the physical resemblance, or the obviously evil bent of Miss Mowcher's nature as he had first conceived it; but he promised to change the character completely in the book's un-written future, leaving readers with a kind of memory of her and sparing Mrs. Hill 'another of those sleepless nights'.

And of course Dickens kept his word, with the result that a bril-liant conception is stifled. In fact worse than stifled: implausibly contradicted. At first Miss Mowcher brings with her a taste of female knowingness and witty corruption, which the world of Doras and Agneses (and equally of Martha Endells: Dickens's bad girls are invulnerably innocent) is stranger to, and which the book as a whole needs most urgently:

'If either of you saw my ankles,' she said, when she was safely elevated, 'say so, and I'll go home and destroy myself.'
'*I* did not,' said Steerforth.
'*I* did not,' said I.
'Well then,' cried Miss Mowcher, 'I'll consent to live.' (Ch. 22.)

Whereas her return is an affair of dismal apologetic, gummed on to the action ('Try not to associate bodily defects with mental, my good friend, except for a solid reason') and articulated in the loud thin voice of Dickens forcing his story:

'Child, child! In the name of blind ill-fortune,' cried Miss Mowcher, wringing her hands impatiently, as she went to and fro again upon the fender, 'why did you praise her so, and blush, and look disturbed?' (Ch. 32.)

He is imagining someone talking and gesturing on a stage. But at Miss Mowcher's first appearance, when she is about to climb up on to the table and dress Steerforth's hair:

'Well, well!' she said, smiting her small knees, and rising, 'this is not business. Come, Steerforth, let's explore the polar regions, and have it over.' (Ch. 22.)

the talk, and the gesture too (compare 'smiting her small knees' with 'wringing her hands impatiently'), are alive.

Walter Gay in *Dombey*, a major character, suffers a more damag-ing *bouleversement* than anyone in *Copperfield*, which is Dickens's next novel. But *Dombey* itself was planned in advance of and during part-issue publication in a way the earliest books were not; hence the picture which has come to dominate some contemporary criticism, of Dickens's steady development in care and self-discipline, with the entertainer losing ground to the artist. The truth about this process is naturally complicated.[1] In at least one instance—that of *Hard Times*—one would cheerfully sacrifice the later tightness of organization for the earlier overspilling vitality that knows itself able to throw away Miss Mowcher, even if under the distant threat of legal proceedings. And in another of the later books—*Little Dorrit* —Dickens has lost vitality (what a weary opening!) without appreciably gaining power to organize. Nor, plainly, is his spendthrift manner always artistically wanton; Miss Mowcher and her like tell us nothing about the picaresque writer's mirroring—itself a principle of organization, and already mastered in *Pickwick*—of life's divine, and less than divine, waste.

And there is one further intricacy, which a final comparison of the Trials of David with the Portrait of the Artist may shed some light on. It concerns two different kinds of happy ending. The subtle truth-to-life of the Trials (the Mrs. Copperfield – Mr. Murdstone – David triangle, for example: M. is a brute, but he does love Mrs. C., but D. confesses ' "I am afraid I liked him none the better for that" ', but . . .) remains unaffected by the fairy-tale cast of David's adventures, leading to the overthrow for ever and for ever of the Murdstone ogres. Somehow this works.

The world of the Portrait, on the other hand, is anything but fairy-tale; it is one in which joyless, calculating, resolute people like Mr. Murdstone may be expected to prosper finally. And Mr. Murdstone does prosper, as little Doctor Chillip recounts. And Julia Mills, the gold-digger, also prospers. She gets her man off-stage, in and through her part of sensibility-specialist, which indicates a very pretty disillusioned wit in her creator. Even Mr. Creakle is sharp enough to keep not merely his head above water, but also society's good opinion. And we leave the resilient pair Heep and Littimer poised for recovery.

---

[1] There is a misleading simplicity about such declarations as that in the preface to *Martin Chuzzlewit*: 'I have endeavoured in the progress of this Tale, to resist the temptation of the current Monthly Number, and to keep a steadier eye upon the general purpose and design.'

So much for the bad people of the Portrait. But its good people are not seen like this at all—a discrepancy which, while it raises wider issues than that of the happy ending, helps to explain why *Copperfield's* closing serenities offend. We are remarking here a deep and widespread failure of convention in the Victorian novel (Jane Austen had been able to place the comfortable run-in of her books within inverted commas of the moral imagination, thereby fencing off those severe fables against damage through a facile solace); and also a specific Dickensian weakness or limitation; for only in his first conclusion to *Great Expectations*, the one which Lytton persuaded him to change and spoil, does he end a late and 'serious' novel adequately.

In considering this matter we perhaps place too much stress, nowadays, on Dickens's sensitiveness to the demands of his public, and not enough on the natural inclination of his talent towards an easy phenomenal art, of the surface but not superficial—rather than towards a static, quasi-architectural apprehension of his material. It may be that we read and criticize too much under the shadow of the Jamesian 'loved object'. Certainly, the perfunctory soft twilight at the end of *Copperfield*, which is a typical novel in this respect, becomes less puzzling when we cease to think of him putting the final (and therefore enormously important) touches to his canvas, and accept instead the image offered in a letter to Forster, of the novelist 'within three pages of the shore'. The end is a time for fond farewell and leave-taking; the book's characters join the writer and his public in an auld lang syne which distances them all from the actualities of the fictional journey and also from those of life.

I am rephrasing the familiar judgment that Dickens thrived on the excitements and pressures of part-issue writing. And this judgment has a converse, less familiar, which is that his attempts to realize an omnipresent and informing Theme, of the kind that floats free of the process of some great novels, are nearly always unconvincing. When he suggests, as he does repeatedly, that *Copperfield* is really about 'the mistaken impulse of an undisciplined heart', we don't believe him; this is a clear case of 'Never trust the artist, trust the tale'—the tale being not an affair of Theme, of subjects, at all.

Observe Dickens trying to make a subject of the great subject, death, at the end of Ch. 1:

. . . and the light upon the window of our room shone out upon the earthly bourne of all such travellers, and the mound above the ashes and the dust that once was he, without whom I had never been.

The iambic thump and the Victorian-Shakespearian diction (*Hamlet* in this case—'bourne of all such travellers'—which Dickens no doubt has at the back of his mind because of his description of Doctor Chillip walking 'as softly as the Ghost in Hamlet', three pages earlier)[1] have no connection with the phenomenon of death in his novels. The Dickensian record may be glancing and unemphatic, as with the nameless male lodger of *Bleak House*:

So the little crazy lodger [Miss Flite] goes for the beadle, and the rest come out of the room. 'Don't leave the cat there!' says the surgeon: 'that won't do!' Mr. Krook therefore drives her out before him; and she goes furtively downstairs, winding her lithe tail and licking her lips. (Ch. 11.)

And at the same time it may touch instincts as remote and deep and powerful as those at work within Sophocles's *Antigone:* instincts concerning the honour of a corpse. To return to our fumbled distinction between the sequential and the thematic imagination, death is interesting in Dickens, but Dickens has nothing of interest to say on the subject of death, for he is not that kind of writer.

[1] Not that it is necessarily a bad thing to plunder Shakespeare, of course. If Dickens got the idea of Barkis going out with the tide from Falstaff's dying 'just between twelve and one, ev'n at the turning o' th' tide', the idea is still a good one.

CHANCE AND DESIGN IN BLEAK HOUSE

W. J. Harvey

TWO APPROACHES to *Bleak House* have been adequately explored. These offer a view of the novel as a social document and as a work of dense, intricate, and powerful symbolism. I wish rather to consider the larger structural properties of the book. This may throw light on the transmutation of social concern into art and may even help us to test the validity of symbolic interpretation. *Bleak House* is so complicated that I shall examine only two aspects of its elaborate architecture. These are Dickens's use of double narration and his use of coincidence.

First, however, I should make explicit the general critical thesis from which this interest stems. Dickens has often been likened to a Jacobean dramatist both for his vivid, exuberant, 'poetic' use of language and for his methods of characterization. There is a third point of likeness. Critics frequently discuss Jacobean plays in terms of 'episodic intensification'. By this they mean the impulse to exploit to the full possibilities of any particular scene, situation or action without too much regard for the relevance of such local intensities to the total work of art. Clearly much of Dickens's fiction is of the same order. To admit this is to risk the displeasure of much modern criticism of fiction which, largely deriving from James, lays great stress on the organic unity of the novel and demands that no part shall be allowed autonomy if this threatens the integrity of the whole.

We can defend in four ways the novel of episodic intensification from such criticism. First, we may admit that in some cases the work may fail as a whole while succeeding in some part. The result may be a dead or crippled work which yet intermittently achieves the

145

vigour of a masterpiece. We may admire what we can and regret the waste of so much else. This, I think, is true of *Barnaby Rudge*. Second, we may deny the fiat of organic unity and maintain that in *some* cases a novel achieves no more than episodic intensification and yet possesses so much vitality that we are content simply to accept its greatness. In James's terms there must be room in the house of fiction for such 'loose, baggy monsters'. With much less certainty I would place *Pickwick Papers* in this category. Third, we may accept the idea of organic unity and yet maintain that by its standards Dickens's novels are entirely successful. Sometimes he achieves an economy, firmness, and clean-cut clarity of control that can only be called classical. This is surely true of *Great Expectations*. Finally, we may accept the idea of organic unity but argue that the criteria by which we judge its presence or absence have been too narrowly conceived and that there exist conventions and methods of organization which are non-Jamesian but still appropriate and effective. (James, unlike some more recent critics, admitted as much.) *Bleak House* is here a relevant example. Indeed, I would say that one of the reasons for its greatness is the extreme tension set up between the centrifugal vigour of its parts and the centripetal demands of the whole. It is a tension between the impulse to intensify each local detail or particular episode and the impulse to subordinate, arrange, and discipline. The final impression is one of immense and potentially anarchic energy being brought—but only just—under control. The fact that the equipoise between part and whole is so precariously maintained is in itself a tribute to the energy here being harnessed.

How well does an examination of the novel's structure support this general view? *Bleak House* is for Dickens a unique and elaborate experiment in narration and plot composition. It is divided into two intermingled and roughly concurrent stories; Esther Summerson's first-person narrative and an omniscient narrative told consistently in the historic present. The latter takes up thirty-four chapters; Esther has one less. Her story, however, occupies a good deal more than half the novel. The reader who checks the distribution of these two narratives against the original part issues will hardly discern any significant pattern or correlation. Most parts contain a mixture of the two stories; one part is narrated entirely by Esther and five parts entirely by the omniscient author. Such a check does, however, support the view that Dickens did not, as is sometimes supposed, use serial publication in the interest of crude suspense. A sensational novelist, for example, might well have ended a part issue with Ch. 31; Dickens subdues the drama by adding another chapter to the number. The obvious exception to this only proves the rule; in the final double number the suspense of Bucket's search for Lady Dedlock is heightened by cutting back to the omniscient narrative and the stricken Sir Leicester. In general, however, Dickens's control of the double narrative is far richer and subtler than this. Through this technique, as I shall try to show, he controls the immense, turbulent, and potentially confusing material of his novel. Indeed, the narrative method seems to me to be part of the very substance of *Bleak House*, expressive of what, in the widest and deepest sense, the novel is about.

Let us first examine the structural functions of Esther Summerson and her narrative. Esther has generally been dismissed as insipid, one of Dickens's flat, non-comic good characters, innocent of imaginative life, more of a moral signpost than a person. Even if we accept this general judgment, we may still find good reasons why Dickens had necessarily to sacrifice vitality or complexity here in order to elaborate or intensify other parts of his novel. If Dickens, far from failing to create a lively Esther, is deliberately suppressing his natural exuberance in order to create a flat Esther, then we may properly consider one of Esther's functions to be that of a brake, controlling the runaway tendency of Dickens's imagination—controlling, in other words, the impulse to episodic intensification.

Can we possibly accept this view? The contrasting styles of the two narratives, while they offer the reader relief and variety, also seem to me evidence of Dickens's control in making Esther what she is, even at the risk of insipidity and dullness. The omniscient style has all the liveliness, fantastication, and poetic density of texture that we typically associate with Dickens. Esther's narrative is plain, matter-of-fact, conscientiously plodding. Only very rarely does her style slip and allow us to glimpse Dickens guiding her pen—as when, for instance, she observes 'Mr. Kenge, standing with his back to the fire, and casting his eyes over the dusty hearthrug as if it were Mrs. Jellyby's biography' (Ch. 4) or when, as Turveydrop bows to her, she could 'almost believe I saw creases come into the white of his eyes' (Ch. 14). Here one may glimpse Dickens chafing at his self-imposed discipline. Such moments apart, any stylistic vivacity or idiosyncrasy in Esther's prose comes from the oddities and foibles of other characters. Dickens imagines them; Esther merely reports them. Even when, at moments of emotional stress, her prose strays into the purple patch one still feels that this is the rhetoric of an amateur, not to be compared, for instance, with the controlled crescendo of Jo's death. Similarly, whenever the straightforward flow of Esther's narrative falters—as in her over-casual mention of Allan Woodcourt at the end of Ch. 14—we prefer to see this as appropriate to her character rather than to spot Dickens signalling a new relationship to us behind her back. That, of course, is precisely what he is doing, but the disguise of style persuades us to focus on Esther and not on her creator. (There is, I think, a corresponding and quite remarkable impersonality about the omniscient narrative. The general impression is of a vast, collective choric voice brilliantly mimicking the varied life it describes, yet able to generalize and comment without lapsing into the idiom of one man, of Dickens himself. Obviously the style exploits and manipulates our sympathies; yet surprisingly rarely do we feel that Dickens is directly button-holing us.)

As I have said, the two narratives are *roughly* concurrent. Deliberately so; Dickens juggles the two chronologies by keeping the details sufficiently vague. Only rarely do we feel any awkwardness in this temporal matching together and any obvious discontinuity generally has a specific narrative or dramatic point. Esther's tale, taken in isolation, plods forward in the simplest kind of sequence. Yet, being autobiographical, it is retrospective and was written, so we are told at the very end, seven years after the main events. This simplicity is rarely disturbed; only occasionally does Esther sound the note of 'If I had known then what I know now'; only occasionally does she throw an anticipatory light forward into the shadowy future of her tale as, for example, she does at the end of Ch. 37. The reason is that, despite the retrospective nature of her story, Esther must *seem* to be living in a dramatic present, ignorant of the plot's ramifications. Dickens is *really* omniscient in the other narrative; god-like he surveys time as though it were an eternal present and Esther must seem to belong to that present. It is a convention most readers readily accept.

In what ways does Esther's tale throw light on its teller? During his later period Dickens showed considerable interest in the possibilities of the first-person narrative. In some cases—*David Copperfield, Great Expectations*—the adult narrator judges, implicitly or explicitly, his growth towards maturity. Esther is clearly not in this category; she swiftly advances from child to woman and scarcely changes at all. We feel that she was 'born old'—a feeling reflected in the nicknames given her, though in fact she is little older than Ada Clare. On the other hand, she cannot be classed with Miss Wade, of *Little Dorrit*, whose story is taken by some critics as an early exercise in that kind of point-of-view technique which dramatizes a limited or crippled consciousness so that what is conveyed to the reader differs radically from the intention of the narrator. Clearly, we are meant to take Esther on trust. If what she tells us is wrong or limited this signifies no moral blind-spot in her, no flaw in her sensibility, but only her necessary innocence of the full ramifications of the plot. Dickens's treatment of Esther is devoid of irony. We have only to imagine what narrative would have resulted if the teller had been Skimpole—or even Richard Carstone—to see that Esther's responses, attitudes, and actions are never qualified or criticized. She is, in short, thoroughly idealized.

One result of the idealizing process is the static nature of Esther's character, the essentials of which we quickly come to know. These never change; her story merely exhibits them in a variety of situations in which she is generally the patient rather than the agent. That is, Esther *does* very little in the sense of initiating a chain of actions by a deliberate choice. Things are done to her or because of her rather than by her. Devastating things happen to Esther from the moment of her birth, but she generally emerges with her usual placidity and acceptance of duty. Indeed, at times Dickens takes care to subdue the effect on the reader of these crises through which Esther as patient must pass. The chapter which deals, for example, with the recognition scene between Esther and her mother closes in fact with Esther's reunion with Ada. The curious thing is the feelings aroused by the Esther-Ada relationship seem more intense—and intensely rendered—than those aroused by the Esther-Lady Dedlock encounter.

Esther then is static, consistent, passive. She is also good. The difficulties of combining these qualities to produce a compelling character are so immense that we should wonder not that Dickens fails, but that his failure is so slight. Still, he does fail. The exigencies of the narrative force him to reveal Esther's goodness in a coy and repellent manner; she is, for instance, continually imputing to others qualities which the author transparently wishes us to transfer to her. Esther's goodness is acceptable when she is least conscious of its effects radiating out to impinge on others. Similarly, her narrative is most acceptable when she is pushed from the centre of the stage by the typical inhabitants of the Dickens world. Happily this is usually so. In other words, Dickens has to reconcile in Esther the demands of a narrator and a main character and he chooses to subdue Esther as a character in the interests of her narrative function. We do not, so to speak, look *at* Esther; we look *through* her at the teeming Dickensian world. This viewpoint is no Jamesian dramatization of a particular consciousness; Esther is as lucid and neutral as a clear window. We look through at a human landscape but we are not, as with James, constantly aware that the window is limited by its frame or that it has a scratch here and an opaque spot there. The penalty Dickens pays for this is the insipidity of Esther's character. But then, *Bleak House* is a thickly populated novel; each character claims his own share of attention and all are connected by a complicated series of interlocking actions. There is no single centre, no Jamesian *disponsible*; rather we have a complex field of force, of interacting stresses and strains. Given this complication it would be too much to ask of the reader that he concentrate on the perceiver as well as the perceived. Were Esther to be complicated the novel would have to be correspondingly simplified and the Dickens world depopulated. Who would wish it so? If the real subject-matter of a novel is a subtly dramatized consciousness then the objects of that consciousness will tend to the sparse refinements of the closest drama. Dickens is the opposite of this; he is to Shakespeare as James is to Racine.

While this, I hope, explains the necessary limitations of Esther's character, it only pushes the real problem one stage farther back. Why was it necessary to have a narrator of this kind at all? Any adequate answer must also take into account the omniscient narrative as well. The two narratives are the systole and diastole of the novel and between them they produce the distinctive effect of *Bleak House*: something that I can only call, in a crudely impressionistic manner, the effect of *pulsation*, of constant expansion and contraction, radiation and convergence.

The famous first chapter of *Bleak House* has had more than its fair share of critical attention; at the risk of tedium, therefore, I wish to isolate two striking features of Dickens's method. The omniscient eye which surveys the scene is like the lens of a film camera in its mobility. It may encompass a large panoramic view or, within a sentence, it may swoop down to a close scrutiny of some character or local detail. Closely related to this mobility is the constant expansion and contraction from the omniscient eye to Esther's single viewpoint. Closely related again is the constant expansion and contraction of the total narrative; now concentrating at great length on some episode, now hustling the plot along with a rapid parade of characters. Dickens's narrative skill is nowhere more evident than in his control of tempo.

All this I mean by *pulsation*. But Ch. I displays yet another related effect. The scene contracts to the Court of Chancery at the heart of the fog but suddenly this process is reversed; Chancery monstrously expands to encompass the whole country:

'This is the Court of Chancery; which has its decaying houses and its blighted lands in every shire; which has its worn-out lunatic in every madhouse, and its dead in every churchyard. . . .'

The heart of Chancery in this respect is Tom-All-Alone's, the breeding-ground of disease (again the radiation of infection). The two are appropriately linked for Chancery *is* a disease and is constantly described in these terms.

This theme is, of course, abundantly worked out in the novel—in Miss Flite, in Gridley, and above all, in Richard Carstone. The idea of corruption radiating out from a rotten centre (Chancery *and* Tom-All-Alone's) is reflected, in geographical terms, in the constant to-and-fro movement between London, Bleak House, and Chesney Wold. But this idea is counterpointed, in plot terms, by the sense one has of convergence, especially the sense of something closing-in on Lady Dedlock. Geography and plot coalesce in the final constriction of the chase and the discovery of Lady Dedlock dead near her lover's tomb.

This pulsation, this interaction of radiation and convergence, is also temporal. The case of Jarndyce and Jarndyce does not merely fan out in the present to enmesh innocent and remote people; it also has a terrible history:

Innumerable children have been born into the cause; innumerable young people have married into it; innumerable old people have died out of it. Scores of persons have deliriously found themselves made parties in Jarndyce and Jarndyce, without knowing how or why; whole families have inherited legendary hatreds with the suit.

Diverse pressures from the past converge to mould the present; Jarndyce and Jarndyce bears down on Richard Carstone; the past

catches up with Esther and finally with her mother. This temporal
convergence is reflected in the structure of the novel as a whole and
locally, in its parts. Thus the first chapter given to Esther (Ch. 3)
quickly brings us from her childhood back to the dramatic present
already described in the omniscient first chapter. Sometimes the
dramatic present is illuminated by a shaft driven back into the past;
thus both Boythorn and Miss Barbary are in some sense enlarged by
the revelation of their abortive love long ago. Or again, the dramatic
present will be left unexplained until time has passed and many
pages have been turned; thus, on a small scale, the mystery of Jo's
disappearance from Bleak House or, on a large scale, Bucket's un-
covering of Tulkinghorn's murderess.

Granted the extremely complicated tangle of effects I have labelled
pulsation, the desirability of a simple, lucid, straightforward narrative such as Esther's should be obvious. It offers us stability, a point
of rest in a flickering and bewildering world, the promise of some
guidance through the labyrinth. The usual novel may be compared
to a pebble thrown into a pool; we watch the ripples spread. But in
Bleak House Dickens has thrown in a whole handful of pebbles and
what we have to discern is the immensely complicated tracery of half-
a-dozen circles expanding, meeting, interacting. Esther—to change
the metaphor—has the stability of a gyroscope; by her we chart our
way.

She is, of course, much more than this. She is, as well, a moral
touchstone; her judgments are rarely emphatic but we accept them.
She can see Richard more clearly than Ada; through her Skimpole is
revealed in his true colours and the Growlery becomes a sign of
Jarndyce's obtuseness. She is also the known constant by which we
judge all the other variables of character. Through her we can see
the horrifyingly vivid notation of decay and infection that signals
the slow process of Richard's destruction. (Among other things, the
intertwining of the two narratives enables Dickens drastically to
foreshorten and mould the *apparent* time sequence here.) Again, by
her consistency Esther contributes to the wonderfully skilful characterization of Sir Leicester and Guppy, who change by fits and starts
throughout the novel. Because these characters demand very different
reactions from us at different times we impute complexity and
development to them. In fact they are not so much complex as discontinuous. Dickens's art lies in masking this discontinuity and
Esther in large part provides a convincing façade; because she is a

simple unity we are conjured into believing that the heterogenity of Guppy or Sir Leicester is a unified complexity.

Finally—and perhaps most important—by intertwining the two narratives Dickens compels us to a double vision of the teeming, fantastic world of *Bleak House*. We—and Esther—are within; we—and the omniscient author—are outside. This double perspective forces us as readers to make connections which because *we* make them have more validity than if Dickens had made them for us. The most crucial instance is Esther's ignorance of so much that surrounds her. What she sees she sees clearly; but she cannot see more than a fraction of the whole. In this she is not alone; one of the triumphs of the novel is the delicacy with which Dickens handles the knowledge, suspicions, guesses, and mistakes of the various characters. Some of them are limited to one or other of the narrative streams; Esther is never seen by the omniscient eye nor does Tulkinghorn ever appear personally in Esther's narrative. This corresponds to their limited knowledge; Tulkinghorn, for all his plotting, never knows of Esther's relation to Lady Dedlock while there is no substantial evidence that Esther knows anything of her father until after her mother's death.

Granted this, the opportunities for dramatic irony are clearly enormous and it is to Dickens's credit as an artist that with great tact he refuses many of the chances for irony offered by the interlocking narratives. How close—all unknowing—is Esther to meeting her father during her first visit to Krook's? Yet we scarcely perceive this, even on a re-reading of the novel. A lesser artist would have wrung dry the irony of such an incident but Dickens is sound in his refusal to do so. For the novel, as it stands, is so taut, so potentially explosive that to expatiate on, or to underline, its implications would make it quite intolerable. Of course the irony is there but it is kept latent and, so to speak, subcritical; it does not explode in the reader's conscious attention. In nothing is Dickens's virtuosity more astonishing than in his control of that aspect of the novel which, together with the double narrative, determines its structure and the quality of its irony. I mean his use of coincidence.

I cannot think of another novel in which coincidence plays so essential a part as it does in *Bleak House*; Hardy's tragedies of circumstance are simple and crude by comparison. As an example we may briefly recall Ch. 24. Richard has decided to join the army and is taking sword-lessons; his teacher turns out to be George Rouncewell, who is thus brought into contact with Esther and

Jarndyce. Thus the various narrative strands converging on George (the reader particularly remembers Smallweed and his interest in Captain Hawdon) begin to tangle with the already tangled strands of Esther's past and future. (This is gently hinted by George's bewilderment at the familiarity of Esther's face; the reader has already encountered something like this when Guppy connected Esther with Lady Dedlock's portrait.) One coincidental connection, acknowledged as such by Esther, is almost immediately made—George's knowledge of Gridley. Esther then goes to the Court of Chancery; coincidentally Guppy is there with Mrs. Chadband, who turns out to be the Mrs. Rachael of Esther's childhood. George appears with a message from Gridley to Miss Flite; providentially Esther is there to introduce them. They go to George's shooting gallery and by chance Bucket turns up at this moment to arrest Gridley on a warrant from Tulkinghorn (one of the few times he is ever mentioned in Esther's narrative); thus Bucket meets Esther for the first time—an important detail since when much later Bucket finds Esther's handkerchief in Lady Dedlock's room he has to ask George where Esther lives in London in order that she may help him search for her mother. In the space of ten pages, then, several chance encounters—most of some consequence for the future of the novel— casually occur.

So casually, indeed, are these quite typical coincidences insinuated into the novel that I doubt whether any relaxed, non-analytical reader would recognize more than one of them (probably Mrs. Rachael— Mrs. Chadband) as coincidental. Certainly one does not feel that the characters are thereby made puppets or that the elaborate plot creaks with obvious contrivance; one accepts coincidence as a natural part of the *Bleak House* world. There are exceptions; Sir Leicester's visit to Jarndyce in Ch. 43 perhaps reveals Dickens in the act of contriving and faking. But by and large, coincidence is to the microcosm of the novel what the law of gravity is to the macrocosm of the real world. We accept both as natural laws and are largely unconscious of their operation.

Only very detailed analysis could properly show how Dickens attains this end. But we may note four main factors combining to merge the various coincidences into the very fabric of the story. The first of these is the interlocking twin narratives we have already examined. Many of the coincidences Esther takes for granted because she is ignorant of something of which the omniscient narrative informs us. But because she takes them for granted and because we trust her, therefore we tend to take them for granted too.

Second, Dickens *does* combine coincidence with a good deal of naturalistic, rational explanation. Clearly in a complex novel dealing so centrally with the consequences, anticipated or unforeseen, of human actions some such explanation will be needed. Dickens had failed badly when faced with this problem early in his career. In *Oliver Twist*, after the mystery of a powerfully imagined Fagin we are offered in an undigested lump the tangled motivations of a feebly imagined Monks. In *Bleak House*, by contrast, such explanations are carefully broken-up, placed, and distributed. Frequently they occur long after the event to be explained has taken place; thus we rarely bother to check their validity. We are never offered too much explanation at one time; thus the Esther-Lady Dedlock relationship is cleared up relatively early. (By this stroke Dickens achieves many ends. He avoids cluttering up the end of the novel with too many climaxes and he misdirects the reader who thinks that the essential mystery is now cleared up and is thus unprepared for the subsequent mystery of Tulkinghorn's death. A similar tactic is central to *Our Mutual Friend* where the reader, having solved the problem of the hero's identity, is liable to take Boffin's pretence at its face value.)

Moreover, what seems coincidental is often the result of plotting and *Bleak House* is full of conspirators. The interesting thing to notice is how often their plots go astray, how often what man proposes is thwarted by the bias of chance, of unforeseen circumstances, of the merely random. No one, not even Bucket, is infallible. Partly because of this, because plotters, plots, and coincidences often cancel each other out, we accept Dickens's scheme of things. Coincidence is not the malign symptom of some metaphysical destiny inexorably hunting down a selected victim; we do not rebel because we feel Fate is unfair; chance reigns with fine impartiality over all.

Finally and paradoxically, it is because coincidence is so extensive in the novel that it becomes so natural. It seems true because it is congruent with the rest of the book. But more important, in the last analysis it expresses a truth about the real world. It expresses our sense that real life blends the casual and the causal, that things are connected and contingent, patterned and random, that we are both free and determined. This sense of life's contradictions is a common sense and we take commonsensically that which, if examined closely, would turn into wonder and mystery, into a world of speculation, dense with *ifs* and *perhapses* and *might-have-beens*. We walk in the real world as Esther walks, through a labyrinth of the conditional; we are surrounded, as she is, by other lives and other narratives; what seems to us a straight path is nothing but a series of cross-roads.

So much is true and trite. Yet Dickens refreshed this cliché, expressed it with such imaginative force that it seems an original and profound intuition about the nature of things. At the heart of his work—beneath his immediate topical or satiric concerns—lie a number of such intuitions, darkly entangled with a number of private obsessions. Together they express something like Dickens's vision of the universal human predicament or, to be more modest and less portentous, the predicament of man in modern industrial society. Such, for instance, is his sense of the fragmented individual. One remembers here the sharp division between public and private, the official and the person; one recalls Bucket the person and Bucket the detective, Vholes the lawyer and Vholes as parent and child. The logical conclusion of this is the happy dichotomy of Wemmick in *Great Expectations*. In a different vein, one remembers Sir Leicester, decent enough but hopelessly locked within the prison of his class and caste; one remembers Lady Dedlock masking her guilt and suffering by a frozen disdain. As with the individual so with the fragmented society; what can the Boodles know of Jo or Jenny when Snagsby, who lives not far away, can be appalled by the unfamiliar hell of Tom-All-Alone's? Against isolation and alienation Dickens poses connection—whether of love, charity, and responsibility or the sinister negations of these, embodied in the infections of Chancery and the slums.

Yet even such basic intuitions as these depend upon that sense of the world I have tried to describe. The most explicit expression of this sense occurs in Forster's frequently quoted report of Dickens:

'On the coincidences, resemblances, and surprises of life Dickens liked especially to dwell, and few things moved his fancy so pleasantly. The world, he would say, was so much smaller than we thought it; we were all so connected by fate without knowing it and people supposed to be far apart were so constantly elbowing each other; and tomorrow bore so close a resemblance to nothing half so much as yesterday.'

This theme is heavily stressed in the opening chapters of *Little Dorrit*; in *Bleak House* it is given only brief and oblique expression by several of the characters. But it is implicit in the whole structure of the novel. Through the double narrative Dickens refracts, reflects, varies, distorts, reiterates his major themes, and the disturbing resonance thus set up is expressive of his deepest sense of what life is like.

'Trust in nothing but Providence and your own efforts. Never separate the two,' Jarndyce tells Richard Carstone and unconsciously sums up this deepest sense of the intricate meshing of chance and choice in the affairs of men. Dickens recognized, of course, that chance is often cruel and that there is a world where Jo and Jenny have no choice but to suffer and die. For them he could see no easy remedy; no trust was to be placed in the Boodles of his world. For the rest of us, all we can do—as Esther would say—is to perform our duty; freedom lies in the recognition of *that* necessity. This, then, is what I take to be the essential substance of *Bleak House* and the form of the novel is expressive of its substance. Here, at the deepest level, the twin narratives and the widespread use of coincidence unite; out of a world of mingled chance and choice Dickens had created the design necessary to a great work of art.

HARD TIMES: A HISTORY AND
A CRITICISM

John Holloway

I

'WITH HIS unbending, utilitarian, matter-of-fact face', Dickens writes of Mr. Gradgrind (I, 15). That *Hard Times* is a novel which embodies a moral problem, an issue between ways of living, is by now familiar knowledge; and so is it, that one side of the issue, in some sense or another, is 'Utilitarianism'. But the ideas and attitudes which that word most readily calls up today prove not to be those which were most prominent in Dickens's own mind or own time; and to trace the exact contour of significance which ran for Dickens himself, as he wrote the book, through the material he handled, will turn out to be a more than merely historical accumulation of knowledge: it determines the critical position which one must finally take with regard to the novel.

Hard Times itself provides the necessary clues plainly enough. But they do not point to Utilitarianism as an ambitious philosophical theory of enlightened and emancipated thinking or of comprehensive social welfare and reform; nor to the genuine (if challengeable) idealism and dedicated high-mindedness of such an education as James Mill designed for his son (Greek at the age of three, and something that could at least pass as the full circle of human knowledge by adolescence). What Dickens seems to have had in mind was something much less far-reaching, and much more mundane and commonplace. The point comes out at once from Dickens's list of possible titles for the novel. This included: 'Two and Two are Four'; 'Simple Arithmetic'; 'A Mere Question of Figures'; and, the first of all, 'According to Cocker'. The last is William Cocker, the seventeenth-century author whose *Arithmetic* was still in use as a school text. 'The celebrated Mr. Cocker', Dickens called him in a speech the year after *Hard Times* appeared.[1]

That Mr. Gradgrind stands for the utilitarian seen not philosophically but arithmetically is made plain elsewhere. 'Let us strike the key-note again . . .' Dickens opens Bk. I, Ch. 8, '. . . by means of addition, subtraction, multiplication, and division, settle everything'. The very next chapter indicates what kind of arithmetic is in question. 'Mr. M'Choakumchild said he would try me again . . . "What is your remark on that *proportion*? (of population dying from starvation);. . . What is the *percentage*?" (of sea-voyagers drowning, etc.)' And at the beginning of this chapter, Mr. Gradgrind is explicit: Dickens's concern is with the often naïve enthusiasm of the earlier nineteenth century for undigested statistics of economic and social advance. '. . . the necessity of infinite grinding at the mill of knowledge as per system, schedule, blue book, report, and tabular statements A to Z'.

That there was something naïve in the use of statistics during the period is not only confirmed by such a modern authority as Schumpeter,[2] but will be clear, even to the comparative layman's eye, from a glance at the tabular statistics of such an author as J. R. McCulloch. In *Hard Times*, in fact, Utilitarianism largely means 'Manchester School' political economy: 'Utilitarian economists, skeletons of schoolmasters, Commissioners of Fact' (II, 6)—there is an implicit reference back to the 'unlucky infants' who are told to 'take everything on political economy' (I, 8).

Dickens had views about McCulloch. Six months before he began *Hard Times* he wrote that a piece submitted for his magazine *Household Words* was '*dreadfully dull* . . . I should have thought the greater part of it by McCulloch edited by Rintoul'.[3] R. S. Rintoul was editor of the *Spectator* from 1828 and (as the *D.N.B.* has it) was 'a model of exact journalism' who 'soon brought round him men like Bentham (and) Mill'. McCulloch is important in the field of political economy not only for his *Principles* (1st ed., 1825)—to which this discussion must revert: it was the standard work until Mill's book of the same name replaced it in 1843—but also, and perhaps

[1] 27 June 1855. See *The Speeches of Charles Dickens*, ed. K. J. Fielding (1960), p. 205.

[2] J. A. Schumpeter, *History of Economic Analysis* (1954), p. 525.

[3] 5 August 1853, to W. H. Wills. See *The Letters of Charles Dickens*, ed. W. Dexter (1938), Vol. II, p. 481.

still more, for encyclopaedic productions like the *Descriptive and Statistical Account of the British Empire*. In these two enormous volumes, amid the laboured elegance of McCulloch's style, and the laborious superabundance of his figures, one may find both what sets the scene for Dickens's novel, and what brings one back to some of the attitudes (those of Bounderby, say) depicted in it. 'Lancashire is the grand seat of the cotton manufacture . . . Manchester, now the second town in the empire, is the principal centre of the manufacture; but it is also carried on, to a great extent, and with astonishing success, at Preston (etc.).'[4] Immediately before this, McCulloch records of the county of Lancashire, '. . . average rent of land in 1842–3, 28s. 11½d. an acre'. This cotton manufacture is 'by far the most wonderful triumph of mechanical genius and invention that the world has ever seen'.[5] In another of McCulloch's encyclopaedias, the *Practical, Theoretical, and Historical Dictionary of Commerce and Commercial Navigation* (1832), we find that for the Lancashire cloth to undersell Indian handloom weavers, though using raw material brought from India, was again 'the greatest triumph of mechanical genius'.[6] The *Dictionary, Geographical, Statistical and Historical, of the Various Countries, Places and Principal Natural Objects of the World* (2 vols., 1841–2), happens to bring out another fact relevant to *Hard Times*. Until only a very few years before this novel was written, no town north of Preston was served by rail from London: Dickens, visiting the town early in 1854 to get first-hand impressions of the cotton lock-out, was indeed penetrating deep into the Other World of the industrial north.

I have given the full titles of these works of McCulloch, because even by themselves they enable one to glimpse the world of naïve but encyclopaedic fact against which Dickens was reacting. As the picture is completed, it leads the attention not towards men of greater intellectual distinction than McCulloch, but towards men still more commonplace, towards now forgotten figures of mid-Victorian popularization. One of these was Charles Knight, Secretary of the Society for the Promotion of Useful Knowledge, and like McCulloch a great compiler of encyclopaedic dictionaries. Knight was for many years a personal friend of Dickens, who was willing to view his factual compilations sympathetically. In 1854 Knight sent him a copy of his *Knowledge is Power*, which was a kind of elementary (and enthu-

---

[4] *op. cit.* (4th ed., 1854), Vol. I, pp. 152–3.
[5] *ibid.*, I, p. 679.   [6] *op. cit.*, 1st ed., 1832, p. 410.

siastic) guide to contemporary processes of commerce and more particularly manufacture; and said he was afraid that Dickens, then
busy writing *Hard Times*, would set him down as 'a cold-hearted
political economist'. Dickens's reply provides useful confirmation of
what is now being argued as the issue in the novel: 'My satire is
against those who see *figures and averages, and nothing else*—the
representatives of the wickedest and most enormous vice of this
time——... Bah! What have you to do with these?' [7]

J. T. Boulton has already suggested that (in spite of this disclaimer
on Dickens's part) *Knowledge is Power* should be seen as the kind
of work which Dickens had in mind in his critique of factualism.[8]
But Dickens's ideas must have been fully formed before he saw a
copy of this work, and a much earlier compilation by Knight, his
Store of Knowledge, seems far more to the point. Indeed, it seems
certain that one of the articles in the *Store of Knowledge* directly
influenced Dickens in respect of *Hard Times*. This is the piece by
William Youatt entitled, baldly, 'The Horse'.[9] On the first page of
this we find a paragraph which begins, 'The teeth of the horse
require some lengthened consideration . . .'; and explains that the
discussion which follows, some 750 words in length, is of value
because the horse's mouth is a sure guide to his age. There seems
reason to think that this must have given Dickens the ideas for
Bitzer's egregious 'definition of a horse':

> Quadruped. Graminiverous. Forty teeth, namely twenty-four grinders,
> four eye-teeth, and twelve incisive. . . . Age known by marks in mouth.
> (Bk. I, Ch. 2.)

Moreover, another article in the *Store of Knowledge* may also have
contributed something to the novel. This is the piece entitled
'Schools' by Dr. Beard, for it contains a remarkable passage from the
evidence given before the 1838 Committee on Education: a passage
which cannot but recall, in detail, the visit of Mr. Gradgrind and
the 'third gentleman' to the school in the opening scene of the novel.
This is the visit which produces Bitzer's model performance, and
the discomfiture of Sissy Jupe:

> . . . certain children are brought prominently forward . . . these frequent
> exhibitions to strangers visiting the school have all an injurious effect

[7] Charles Knight, *Passages of a Working Life* (1873 ed.), Vol. III, pp. 187–8.
[8] *The Dickensian*, 1954, pp. 57 ff.
[9] *Store of Knowledge*, 1841 ed., p. 201.

upon the mind of the child, and also an injurious effect upon the minds of the other children, discouraging and disheartening them.[10]

A careful reading of Beard's article, however, begins to reveal the complexities of the situation Dickens was moving in; for it closes with what is in some ways a most humane and enlightened account of how the education of children should proceed; envisaging it, almost after the manner of *Émile*, as a following of nature and a gradual unfolding of the child's inner powers. I think that this makes clear how one cannot see the issue as a simple one between a humane and enlightened novelist and rigid and hide-bound compilers. That the enlightenment is not on one side only is confirmed by some words of McCulloch's on the subject; words which hint at some of the intricacies of meaning in the word 'utilitarian' itself:

> To render education productive of all the utility that may be derived from it, the poor should, in addition to the elementary instruction now alluded to, be made acquainted with the duties enjoined by morality and religion...[11]

The context of these remarks is thoroughly 'Manchester School', and has its unenlightened side. But the reference to 'utility' gives a little help towards rightly understanding what has often been not understood at all: the standpoint which Dickens takes up in the latter part of the schoolroom scene, the discussion that deals, improbably enough one cannot but remark, with wallpapers and carpets.

II

The fact is, that (as K. J. Fielding has in part made plain, but not, I think, fully enough),[12] Dickens in this section of his book is far from taking up a position which is enlightened. In fact, it is much easier to argue that his satire was directed against the contemporary forces of enlightenment (the whole scene is rich in contemporary reference) and is written from the standpoint of the mid-Victorian middle-class Philistine. This, broadly speaking, is the Dickens who wrote with a low-brow vulgarity about Millais's 'Christ in the Carpenter's Shop' in the Pre-Raphaelite exhibition. The naïveté, in fact, is now on his side. The 'third gentleman' (as Fielding points out)

---

[10] *ed. cit.*, p. 351a.

[11] J. R. McCulloch, *Principles of Political Economy*, 4th ed., 1849, p. 474.

[12] 'Dickens and the Department of Practical Art', *Modern Language Review*, XLVIII, 1953.

represents the views of the 'Department of Practical Art' organized
under the Board of Trade in 1852. But it did not use the word 'Practical' through no-nonsense fact-and-nothing-but-fact Philistinism: it
did so because it sought to function as a growing point in the decorative arts and in industrial design. Those whom it drew together—
John Bell, head of the Normal School of Design at Somerset House;
Owen Jones, the forerunner of Morris in wallpaper design; M. Digby
Wyatt, Secretary of the Executive Committee of the Great Exhibition; Ralph Wornum, compiler of the 1846 National Gallery catalogue; Richard Redgrave; and Henry Cole, Secretary of the
Department of Science and Art from 1853 to 1873, and (since he was
a civil servant) pseudonymous designer of 'Summerly's Art Manu-
factures' from 1847 on—were the most enlightened men in their
field at the time. What they stood for was a repudiation of the crude
and vulgar photographic realism of ignorant factory design—what
might with justice be called 'Bounderby art'—and its replacement by
designs which recognized what would nowadays be universally
accepted as first principles of informed, professional work: the
stylization necessary in decorating a flat surface, the preservation of a
proper balance between empty and filled spaces, and so on. What
they opposed was what Professor Pevsner, writing of design such
as Dickens is defending, called 'the riotous effect of large bouquets
of flowers, rank ferns, and thick whorls'[13]—the carpets, as another
designer having affinities with this group was later to describe them,
'on which ponds of water were drawn with water-lilies floating upon
them, and other absurdities equally offensive to good taste'.[14]

Professor Giedion's important discussion of this group does much
to bring out their contemporary affinities and their essential quality.
First, he points out that in their basic principle of design, fitness for
purpose, 'the intellectual outlook of the circle is more or less in
keeping with Utilitarianism as expounded in its philosophical and
economic aspects by J. S. Mill',[15] a view which does less to damn the
designers than to remind one that Utilitarianism, at its best, had
itself some claim to rank as part of a high civilization. Second, he

[13] N. Pevsner, *High Victorian Design* (1951), p. 98; see also Pevsner's *Pioneers of
Modern Design*, Ch. II.

[14] Christopher Dresser; quoted from the *Penn Monthly*, 1877, by A. Bøe in his *From
Gothic Revival to Functional Form*, Oslo, 1957, p. 68.

[15] S. Giedion, *Mechanization Takes Over* (1948), p. 357. Giedion also refers to a
discussion by Richard Redgrave of 'utility' in art in the *Journal of Design and
Manufacture* (edited by Henry Cole) for 1850; his page reference, however, seems
incorrect (see p. 357 n), and I have not been able to trace this important passage.

mentions that another name must be added to those given above: that of Gottfried Semper. Semper is a forerunner of twentieth-century standards of design. In 1855 Semper left England to become Professor to the Technische Hochschule in Zürich. His main work, *Style in the Technical and Tectonic Arts* (1860–3) was a fundamental work in the theory of design; and by 1910 'the German reform movement in the decorative arts, which took fitness to purpose as its final criterion, regarded him as a basic authority'.[16] Through Semper, the circle which Dickens satirized counts among the forerunners of the Bauhaus.

Like Charles Kent, Henry Cole, perhaps the most active member of the group, was a personal acquaintance of Dickens; and this perhaps explains the difference between the latter's scornful if covert attack on the Department in the novel, and the explicit discussion, in *Household Words*, of the 'Chamber of Horrors', the room full of prize examples of disastrous mid-Victorian taste, which Cole organized for a short time at Marlborough House.[17] Dickens's extent of disagreement with the principles of design represented by Marlborough House is a limited one; and in fact, it would be fair to say that he hardly knows where he stands: 'the whole Hog and nothing but the whole Hog . . . is a little indigestible'. The importance of this article (as of the rather sheepishly inconclusive sentence just quoted) is that it enables one to see the level of thought at which Dickens was operating. Certainly, in both novel and article, he stands in a general way for human feeling against what is doctrinaire and rigid. But there is a sense in which his disagreement is partial or even casual: it does not penetrate to the fundamental issues involved, and one cannot deny that there is at least a hint of the Philistine about it.

III

At present, the reputation of *Hard Times* stands high, and the suggestion that lack of depth, even something of the middle-class Philistine, shows elsewhere in how the book works out its scheme of values, will not carry immediate conviction. The assertion requires proof, of course, with regard to what is in the text itself. Nothing takes the place of that. But it may prove easier to see clearly what is there, if one notices the elements of compromise, of an amiable but casual grasp of the realities, in Dickens's outlook as we can trace it

[16] Giedion, *op. cit.*, pp. 358–9.
[17] 'A House Full of Horrors'; *Household Words*, 4 December 1852.

generally at the very time it was being written. The deficiencies of McCulloch, for example, transpired in his tone—'wonderful triumph of mechanical genius', 'grand seat of the cotton manufacture . . . astonishing success', as much as in his '28s. 11½d.'; we are reminded too closely of the complacent bombast of Mr. Roebuck as Arnold pillories him in *The Function of Criticism at the Present Time*. But it is not easy to find a Roebuckism which excels the following:

> To that great compact phalanx of the people, by whose industry, perseverance, and intelligence, and their result in money-wealth, such places as Birmingham, and many others like it, have arisen—to that great centre of support, that comprehensive experience, and that beating heart— Literature has turned happily . . .

and this is Dickens himself, at a civic dinner in Birmingham exactly a year before he began writing *Hard Times*.[18] All in all, Dickens stood much too near to what he criticized in the novel, for his criticism to reach a fundamental level. This is not a matter of his having a balanced view of the whole situation as between manufacture, labour, and capital; but of his sharing the somewhat naïve enthusiasms, and with them to some extent the brusque middle-class hostilities and presumptions, of those whom he thought he was criticizing. *Household Words*, throughout the early 1850's, is full of enthusiastic accounts of the wonders of Victorian manufacture. Even in February 1854, almost the very moment when he was beginning *Hard Times*, Dickens could write:

> Mighty, indeed, are the dealings of these cotton monarchs. Complicated are their transactions; numberless the interests they affect; and far away and strange the lands they give vitality to, the mouths they feed, the forms they clothe.[19]

A year before, writing then too of the Lancashire mills, he wrote:

> 'the factory itself is certainly not a "thing of beauty" in its externals. But it is a grand machine in its organization—the men, the fingers, and the iron and steel, all work together for one common end'.[20]

The article concludes with a eulogy of the 'captain of industry' (Mr. Titus Salt) who was building new model factories at Saltaire. 'Captain of industry' is of course a phrase of Carlyle's. Dickens dedicated

---

[18] 6 January 1853: *Speeches*, p. 154.
[19] Lancashire Witchcraft': *Household Words*, 4 February 1854.
[20] *Household Words*, 5 February 1853.

Hard Times to that fiery and apocalyptic bourgeois, and assured him that there was nothing in the book with which he would disagree.[21] It is plain that Dickens's whole love-hate relation to Victorian industry was deeply influenced by the writings of the older man.

If this is true, though, how does it show in the novel? It shows in Dickens's treatment of the main situation of the book. For all his opposition to the 'hard fact men' like McCulloch, he subscribes out and out to McCulloch's principle of an ultimate identity of interest between men and masters. 'Those whose interests must be supposed to be identical or must be destroyed', he writes[22]; and the effect of this on the novel is barely less than deliberate falsification of what Dickens knew, from his visit to Preston, to be the facts. For Slackbridge, the 'O my friends' stump-orator (it is wholly in place to appropriate Carlyle's scornful term in *Latter Day Pamphlets*) is based upon a 'professional speaker' whom Dickens actually witnessed on his visit to Preston during the 1853-4 lock-out. He, however, so far from dominating the meeting and getting his way at it, was on Dickens's own testimony suppressed by the Chairman; and when Dickens wrote of that meeting in *Household Words*, what he did was praise the men's

. . . astonishing fortitude and perseverance; their high sense of honour among themselves; the extent to which they are impressed with the responsibility that is upon them of setting a careful example, and keeping their order out of any harm and loss of reputation . . .[23]

IV

If we seek to assess the level of seriousness and insight at which Dickens is working in the novel, it cannot be without significance to notice what he sets against the world of 'addition, subtraction, multiplication, and division' which he rejects. His alternative is neither the determined individuality and, in a certain degree, genuine cultivation of the best masters (as Charlotte Brontë saw this when she depicted Hunsden in *The Professor*, or as Mrs. Gaskell did with John Thornton in *North and South* or indeed, to some extent, Dickens himself with Mr. Rouncewell in *Bleak House*); nor the desperate need, communal feeling, and strengthening responsibility which he saw for himself among the 'hands'. His alternative was something which lay altogether outside the major realities of the

[21] Letter of 29 March 1870.   [22] *Household Words*, 11 February 1854.   [23] *ibid.*

social situation with which he dealt: the circus world of Mr. Sleary.

In principle, perhaps, this world could indeed carry the weight of that 'vital human impulse' to which Dr. Leavis refers as counterpart to the 'utilitarian' ethos that for him is one pole of the novel. The comparison between *Hard Times* and Picasso's 'Saltimbanques' has been made (though it seems obviously extravagant); and occasionally, a phrase in the novel (such as the reformed Mr. Gradgrind's reference to 'the right instinct'—supposing it for the moment to be some quality of that nature) looks as if it could support so ambitious and life-giving an interpretation. Again, however, general indications of how Dickens's mind was working in the period of composition help us to detect the chief impact lying within the text, the main thing which he is setting up in opposition to the 'hard fact men'. It does not seem to be anything even remotely Lawrentian (this was, after all, a pre-Nietzsche novel). On the contrary, it too, like its opposite, operated (for all its obvious common sense and its genuine value) at a relatively shallow level of consciousness, one represented by the Slearies not as vital horsemen but as plain entertainers.

In fact, the creed which Dickens champions in the novel, against Gradgrind's, seems in the main to be that of 'all work and no play makes Jack a dull boy'. How unwilling many will be to admit this! Yet Dickens's letter to Charles Knight when he was writing *Hard Times* takes just this point of view, and turns out to have simply been reworded in the novel.

I earnestly entreat your attention to the point (I have been working upon it, weeks past, in *Hard Times*) . . . the English are, as far as I know, the hardest-worked people on whom the sun shines. Be content if, in their intervals of pleasure, they read for *amusement* and do no worse. They are born at the oar, and they live and die at it. Good God, what would you have of them![24]

In *Hard Times* this becomes (Bk. I, Ch. 10.)

I entertain a weak idea that the English people are as hard-worked as any people upon whom the sun shines. I acknowledge to this ridiculous idiosyncrasy, as a reason why I would give them a little more *play*.

With which one may usefully compare Mr. Gradgrind's 'annihilating the flowers of existence' with his excise-rod and compasses, and Louisa's lament to her brother:

[24] Letter of 17 March 1854.

I don't know what other girls know. I can't play to you, or sing to you. I can't talk to you so as to enlighten your mind, for I never see any *amusing* sights or read any amusing books that it would be a *pleasure or a relief* to you to talk about, *when you are tired*. (Bk. I, Ch. 8.)

One may compare also the decisive closing paragraph of the novel, about the main survivor of the book, Sissy Jupe:

. . . thinking no *innocent and pretty* fancy ever to be despised; trying hard to . . . *beautify* . . . lives of machinery and reality with . . . imaginative graces and delights. (Bk. III, Ch. 8.)

and the concluding words of Mr. Sleary, with their emphasis not on art or gracious vitality, but amusement:

. . . Don't be croth with uth poor vagabonth. People mutht be amused. They can't alwayth be a learning, nor yet they can't be alwayth a working, they an't made for it. You *mutht* have uth, Thquire. Do the withe thing and the kind thing too, and make the betht of uth; not the wurtht! (Book III, Ch. 8.)

From outside the text of the novel, *Household Words* and the *Letters* readily confirm this interpretation. The letter, already quoted, about the 'dreadfully dull' article ran: 'some *fancy* must be got into the number': fancy (the 'tender light of Fancy', as the novel has it: Bk. II, Ch. 9) was the necessary antidote to McCulloch and Rintoul. Finally, the *Household Words* article on the Preston lockout makes the same point, and one must bear in mind that it is one entirely characteristic of Dickens from Mr. Pickwick on:

there must enter something of feeling and sentiment, something which is not to be found in Mr. McCulloch's Dictionary . . . political economy is a mere skeleton unless it has a little human covering and fitting out, a little human bloom on it, and a little human warmth in it.[25]

V

What this discussion seems to me to issue in is a view of the novel's moral intention which accords with the quality and development of Dickens's whole mind. He was not a profound and prophetic genius with insight into the deepest levels of human experience; but (leaving his immense gifts aside for a moment) a man whose outlook was amiable and generous, though it partook a little of the shallowness

[25] *Household Words*, 11 February 1854.

of the merely topical, and the defects of the bourgeois—the word is
not too harsh—Philistine. Ruskin, generations ago, gave the necessary lead over *Hard Times*: 'in several respects the greatest (novel)
he has written', he said, the author is 'entirely right in his main drift
and purpose', but Ruskin himself wishes that he had used 'a severer
and more accurate anaylsis'.[26]

Turn to the detailed presentation, and it is clear that when Dickens
is most preoccupied with his 'idea that laid hold of me by the throat
in a very violent manner',[27] he usually fails. The point is made, and
as it transpires, the life fades away. Sissy's spontaneous, childish
compassionateness becomes a smart debating point:

'. . . in a given time a hundred thousand persons went to sea on long
voyages, and only five hundred of them were drowned or burned to
death. What is the percentage? . . . And I . . . said it was nothing.'
'Nothing, Sissy?'
'Nothing, Miss—to the relations and friends of the people who were
killed . . .' (Bk. I, Ch. 9.)

In the conversation between Louisa and her father when Bounderby has proposed, it is apparent at once that neither character is a
true embodiment of the standpoint—or predicament—which is their
allotted rôle; they are creatures of stick, arguing a case or (with
Gradgrind) obligingly but unconvincingly tongue-tied:

'Father . . . Where have I been? What are my heart's experiences?'
'My dear Louisa,' returned Mr. Gradgrind . . . 'you correct me justly
. . . I merely wished to discharge my duty.'
'What do *I* know, Father . . . of tastes and fancies; of aspirations and
affections; of all that part of my nature in which such light things [the
word "light" should not be overlooked] might have been nourished?
What escape have I had from problems that could be demonstrated, and
realities that could be grasped?' As she said it, she unconsciously closed
her hand, as if upon a solid object, and slowly opened it as though she
were releasing ash.
'My dear,' assented her eminently practical parent, 'quite true, quite
true.' (Bk. I, Ch. 15.)

[26] *Unto This Last* (*Works*, ed. E. T. Cook and A. Wedderburn XVII, p. 31 n).
Compare Ruskin's remarks, very relevant to the account given of *Hard Times* here,
in his letter to C. E. Norton at Dickens's death in 1870: 'The literary loss is infinite
—the political one I care less for than you do—Dickens was a pure modernist . . .
His hero is essentially the iron-master' (*ed. cit.*, Vol. 37, p. 7).
[27] Letter to the Hon. Mrs. Richard Watson, 17 July 1859.

How, frankly, can writing like this (the forced rhetoric, the lack of interchange, the banal image) retain our attention, unless we are enticed by problems but indifferent to art?

Two moments in the working out of the fable seem especially to deserve attention. The first is the moment of anagnorisis for Gradgrind (Bk. II, Ch. 12). The scene is peculiarly significant. It is the resolution of the whole first movement of the fable (and as will become clear, it is fair to say that there is no real second movement). What is the response of a Gradgrind to the moment of discovering that his system is no system at all?—indeed, that it does not even represent what must always have meant most to him, his love for his daughter. Even as we put the question, we notice the extraordinary bias of emphasis which Dickens has given to the chapter. All its weight goes to Louisa. Gradgrind does, and says, virtually nothing. His response to the moment of truth is no response. Mill, in the *Autobiography*, was later to describe such a moment—of total disillusion with the life of the unmitigated intellect—though seen with an amplitude and depth which Dickens did not command, and which (I have argued) was no part of his main intention on the politico-economic side of his book. *Hard Times* does not begin to depict it, and I believe that the limit of the book's achievement is never clearer than it is here. George Eliot, when she showed Rosamund Vincy humiliating herself before Dorothea in the matter of Ladislaw, showed that she had the entry to this world of tortured and intricate psychology. Dickens did not.

It is easy to see the closing chapters of *Hard Times* as an example of what is so common among imperfect novels: the continuation of the plot (after the central idea of the work has been resolved) at the level merely of crisis and adventure. This, however, would do Dickens less than justice. The gradual degeneration of Tom, until the superb moment when, in his ridiculous and degrading disguise, 'he came down, bench by bench [like a monkey] until he stood in the sawdust' (Bk. III, Ch. 8), is barely (as in fact it is treated) related to Dickens's major problems in the book, though it is one of its best things. But Mr. Sleary's decision to stand by Tom, and compound the felony which Bitzer will not compound, is a major landmark in the whole fable, and the second of the two 'moments' which I mentioned above. For, after all, it is the key point (along with the 'discovery' of Bounderby's mother and her devotion) at which the fable creates its picture of the lengths to which untutored kindness

JOHN HOLLOWAY

and unreasoned feeling can go, and how they look as they go to these
lengths. It is, or could be, the second great test of the values of the
book. Yet Dickens does not come up to the scratch; nor, after all, has
Mr. Sleary ever been a character that his creator could really hope to
steer through a revelatory moral crisis. The moment is left as one of
lively, but not meaningful, excitement.

'The Thquire thtood by you, Thethilia, and I'll thtand by the Thquire.
More than that: thith ith a prethiouth rathcal, and belongth to that
bluthtering Cove that my people nearly pitht out o' winder. It'll be a dark
night . . .' (Bk. III, Ch. 8.)

As a 'moral fable' *Hard Times* is a vigorous and good-hearted
book, but if 'shallow' is unduly severe with regard to the level of
insight with which it proceeds, Dr. Leavis, in writing that here 'the
creative exuberance is controlled by a *profound* inspiration' has conceded just the word which requires to be withheld.

At which point, when the smugness that too easily attends passing
critical *fiats* is (it may be) about to descend, we open the novel at
random and find, it may be, this:

'. . . she never had a lover, and the governor proposed old Bounderby, and
she took him'.
'Very dutiful in your interesting sister,' said Mr. James Harthouse.
'Yes, but she wouldn't have been as dutiful, and it would not have
come off as easily,' returned the whelp, 'if it hadn't been for me.'
The tempter merely lifted his eyebrows; but the whelp was obliged to
go on.
'*I* persuaded her,' he said, with an edifying air of superiority. 'I was
stuck into old Bounderby's bank . . . and I knew I should get into
scrapes . . . so I told her my wishes, and she came into them . . . It was
very game of her, wasn't it?'
'It was charming, Tom!'
'Not that it was altogether so important to her as it was to me,' continued Tom coolly, 'because my liberty and comfort, and perhaps my
getting on, depended on it . . . but still it was a good thing in her.'
'Perfectly delightful. And she gets on so placidly.'
'Oh,' returned Tom . . . 'She's a regular girl. A girl can get on anywhere . . . I have often known her sit and watch the fire—for an hour at
a stretch.'
'Ay, ay? Has resources of her own,' said Harthouse, smoking quietly.
'Not so much of that as you may suppose . . .' (Bk. II, Ch. 3.)

How splendid that is, in its crisp vitality and observation, and how

172

copiously yet exactly it contributes, at every point, to the movement of the book! The hint of theatricality that is never quite absent in Dickens seems here only to add to the energy. Elsewhere, too, Harthouse figures in scenes which the author manages admirably—as in the critical conversation between him and Louisa :

'I will confide to you my doubt whether he has had many advantages. Whether—forgive my plainness—whether any great amount of confidence is likely to have been established between himself and his most worthy father.'
'I do not,' said Louisa, flushing with her own great remembrance in that wise, 'think it likely.'
'Or, between himself, and—I may trust to your perfect understanding of my meaning, I am sure—and his highly-esteemed brother-in-law.'
She flushed deeper and deeper, and was burning red when she replied in a fainter voice, 'I do not think that likely, either.'

The moment of the decisive revelation runs :

'. . . When I married, I found that my brother was even at that time heavily in debt. Heavily for him, I mean. Heavily enough to oblige me to sell some trinkets. They were no sacrifice. I sold them very willingly. I attached no value to them. They were quite worthless to me.'
Either she saw in his face that he knew, or she only feared in her conscience that he knew, that she spoke of some of her husband's gifts. She stopped, and reddened again. If he had not known it before, he would have known it then . . . (Bk. II, Ch. 7.)

No one can miss the mounting emotion, created in the increasing bluntness, of the very words of Louisa's speech; nor the shrewd insight into psychology, and dexterous use of it for drama, in the author's comment which follows.

Perhaps the most vividly memorable part of the whole novel is that of Mrs. Sparsit spying on Louisa and Harthouse, and following the fleeing Louisa, through the thunderstorm, to the railway station and to Coketown. It is the culmination of one of the great imaginative strokes of the book, Dickens's likening of her temptation to the descent of a great staircase, into chaos at its foot. He extracts the image, with great skill and economy, from Louisa's own 'What does it matter?' then imposes it on Mrs. Sparsit, and modulates it, with a truly poetic movement, into the 'deep water' and universal deluge of the railway scene. This whole scene of the flight, in its fluent modulation of imagery and its melodrama charged with human weight, is Dickens at his most characteristic and his best.

In fact, if what is best in this novel is reviewed generally, it cannot but suggest reflections which extend beyond itself. For the passages in *Hard Times* where Dickens most shows his genius, is most freely himself, are not those where he is most engaged with his moral fable or intent (if we think, mistakenly, that he is so at all) on what Dr. Leavis called 'the confutation of Utilitarianism by life'. Rather, they appear when he comes near to being least engrossed with such things; when he is the Dickens who appears throughout the novels [28]: the master of dialogue that, even through its stylization, crackles with life, perception, and sharpness, the master of drama in spectacle and setting and action. And one possibility that the novel suggests is that we can pay too high a price for the moral fable, for such undertakings as 'the confutation of Utilitarianism'. We can pay the price of impairing a large free-ranging consciousness of the outward spectacle and psychic life of men. We assume, it may be, as we turn from the picturesqueness and picaresqueness of Dickens's earlier work to a novel like *Hard Times*, that in organizing his work round a moral issue he will enjoy a deeper apprehension and produce a richer result. On second thoughts, this may prove the reverse of true. The 'peculiarly insistent moral intention' (the words are again Dr. Leavis's, and to me they seem wonderfully disquieting and unacceptable) is one thing; and a moral because simply a total apprehension on the writer's part, a capacity in him to consume and register, in full, the buoyant abundance and endless variation of reality, is another. Henry James has already made the point: 'The essence of moral energy is to survey the whole field . . . try to catch the colour of life itself'.[29] Perhaps we are too much inclined to demand the all-embracing moral structure in fiction, to take its mere presence as its success, to forget that what is all-embracing may also be all-consuming, and in some measure to forgo the free life, the unconstrained movement, the inexhaustible wealth of fiction, for the chiaroscuro of moralism and tyranny of theme.

[28] Cf. Monroe Engel, *The Maturity of Dickens* (1959): 'The greatest virtues of *Hard Times* are Dickens's characteristic virtues, but less richly present in this book than in many others . . . the crude but forceless simplicity of Gradgrind can scarcely be said to represent the complexity and solidity of Bentham's influential contribution to English thought': a similar view was expressed by Humphry House: '(Dickens) did not understand enough of any philosophy even to be able to guy it successfully' (*The Dickens World*, 1941, p. 205).   [29] 'The Art of Fiction', 1884.

LITTLE DORRIT

John Wain

'A family with the wrong members in control—that, perhaps, is
as near as one can come to describing England in a phrase.'
—GEORGE ORWELL

THE PURPOSE of this essay is to argue that *Little Dorrit*, in addition
to its already acknowledged status as one of the greatest novels of the
nineteenth century, has also the distinction of occupying a special
place in the *œuvre* of Dickens. It is his most stationary novel; its
impact is even less dependent on 'plot' than is customary throughout
Dickens's work; its development is by means of outward radiation,
rather than linear progression. As everyone who has read it atten-
tively has seen, it is built up on two metaphors, the prison and the
family.

If the plot of this novel is tedious and artificial to a degree rarely
found even in Dickens, it is also true that the fact can be ignored,
without having recourse to special pleading. For *Little Dorrit* is, in
essence, a plotless novel. For all the scurry of event on its surface, it
never for a moment suggests genuine movement. It is an intricate
labyrinth, designed so that the reader, on whatever path he sets out,
will always be brought back to the point where one or other of the
two principal metaphors is confronting him. It does not matter at
what point we enter this labyrinth. Obviously Dickens could not be
expected to flout literary convention so thoroughly as to dispense
with plot altogether; it is hardly likely that any such idea would have
crossed his mind. But his heart lay in the devising of the labyrinth;
from that, and not from the plot with its pallid ingenuities, nor even
from the incidental felicities, comes the power which keeps the book
so strongly alive in the memory of every reader.

Little Dorrit is Dickens's most tragic novel. It deals tragically both with society and with personal relationships; and it is engineered so as to convey, ineffaceably, that the two are inextricably blended. The determination with which Dickens interweaves the two themes is not, I think, a mere matter of artistic unity (though this would have been a sufficient reason); it arises from his belief that when a society becomes oppressive, human relationships within that society become warped. There is, for once, no 'happy ending', though the difficulties are resolved as well as can be expected under the circumstances—by which one means, as usual, that the author marries off his principal couple. These consist of a girl who has put all her energies into relieving the sufferings of her weak and selfish father, and as a result is left in a permanently disabled psychological state in which the relationship of father and daughter is the only one she can think of as real; and a man whose emotional life has been stifled by the harshly repressive behaviour of his mother, so that for years he has been in the habit of thinking that a normal marriage is something he can no longer hope for. By seeing these two as far as the altar, and not forgetting to add that the future holds a good deal of foster-parental responsibility ('to give a mother's care, in the fullness of time, to Fanny's neglected children no less than to their own'), Dickens is coming as near to a final-curtain blaze of good luck as the all-pervading truthfulness of the story will allow him.

The Clennams will get along; they will treat each other decently and with gratitude; and anything more resplendent would be false to the book's central import, which is that nineteenth-century England is a place where genuine happiness is impossible. It is a prison, in which all the convicts are members of one family. Alternatively, it is a family which organizes its life after the fashion of a prison.

Before taking any more steps, let us have before us the outline of the plot, as given in that *vade mecum* of the novel-reader, *The Oxford Companion to English Literature*:

William Dorrit has been so long in the Marshalsea prison for debtors that he has become the 'Father of the Marshalsea'. He has had the misfortune to be responsible for an uncompleted contract with the Circumlocution Office (a satiric presentment of the government departments of the day, with their incompetent and obstructive officials, typified in the Barnacles). His lot is alleviated by the devotion of Amy, his youngest daughter, 'Little Dorrit', born in the Marshalsea, whose diminutive stature is compensated by the greatness of her heart. Amy has a snobbish sister, Fanny, a theatrical dancer, and a scapegrace brother, Tip. Old Dorrit and Amy are befriended by Arthur Clennam, the middle-aged hero, for whom Little Dorrit conceives a deep passion, at first unrequited. The unexpected discovery that William Dorrit is heir to a fortune raises the family to affluence. Except Little Dorrit, they become arrogant and purse-proud. Clennam, on the other hand, owing to an unfortunate speculation, is brought in turn to the debtors' prison, and is found in the Marshalsea, sick and despairing, by Little Dorrit, who tenderly nurses and consoles him. He has meanwhile learned the value of her love, but her fortune stands in the way of asking her hand. The loss of this makes their union possible, on Clennam's release.

With this main theme is wound the thread of an elaborate mystery. Clennam has long suspected that his mother, a grim old puritanical paralysed woman, living in a gloomy house with a former attendant and present partner, Flintwich, has done some wrong to Little Dorrit. Through the agency of a stagy villain, Rigaud alias Blandois, this is brought to light, and it appears that Mrs. Clennam is not Arthur's mother, and that her religious principles have not prevented her from suppressing a codicil in a will that benefited the Dorrit family.

After this noble effort of disentanglement, the summarizer feels impelled to touch upon the wealth of material which, as far as the plot is concerned, remains unassimilated:

There are a host of minor characters in the work of whom the most notable are the worthy Pancks, rent-collector to the humbug Casby; Casby's voluble daughter, Flora, the early love of Arthur Clennam; her eccentric relative 'Mr. F's Aunt'; Merdle, the swindling financier, and Mrs. Merdle, who 'piques herself on being society'; Affery, the villain Flintwich's wife; 'Young John' Chivery, the son of the Marshalsea warder; and the Meagles and Gowan households. The Marshalsea scenes have more reality than the rest of the story, for Dickens's father had been immured in that prison.

Of course Dickens's plots are always the weakest point in his novels, so much so that one is generally driven to push them to one side and go ahead with a purely thematic analysis. In *Little Dorrit*, for the most part, Dickens seems to be co-operating fully with any wish of this kind; 'theme' is so much in the foreground, 'plot' so much in the background. Still, having taken the trouble to think up a plot that runs very steadily parallel to the theme, there are moments when he cannot resist nudging the reader to make sure that the more obvious links are not being overlooked. When Clennam, visiting

William Dorrit, does not get out of the Marshalsea fast enough and is obliged to spend the night within its walls, Dickens explains in the baldest manner just why the episode was introduced.

A swift thought shot into his mind. In that long imprisonment here, and in her own long confinement to her room, did his mother find a balance to be struck? I admit that I was accessory to that man's captivity. I have suffered for it in kind. He has decayed in his prison; I in mine. I have paid the penalty. (Bk. I, Ch. 8.)

Actually Dickens has laced the two themes together so well that there was no real need for this flourish; that Mrs. Clennam had been *personally* involved in William Dorrit's financial ruin, and thus made it necessary for the pair of them to go to prison for life, hardly matters, in view of the book's insistence that we are all involved one with another. So long as England is 'a family with the wrong members in control', everything is bound to go wrong in both public and private life.

It hardly matters where we begin. Little Dorrit is the child of a father whose mind has been rotted by imprisonment, and she has reacted towards him as strongly as her brother and sister, by going to the bad, have reacted away from him. Her life is mainly spent among the poor; and in Bleeding Heart Yard she is surrounded by the same pattern of twisted parent-child relationships. One of her special protégées, the half-witted girl Maggy, addresses her always as 'Little Mother'. Old Casby, the extortionate landlord, manages, by dint of deputing the thumb-screwing to Pancks, to appear in the light of a father to his tenants, and is known as 'the Patriarch'. The one really harmonious family in the book, the Plornishes, are deprived of their genuine Patriarch, Mrs. Plornish's father, by the fact that poverty has driven him into the workhouse; all they can do is to make heart-rendingly much of him on his infrequent days off. Meanwhile, on a slightly higher social level, Mr. and Mrs. Meagles are systematically ruining their daughter's chances of happiness by smothering her in kindness and protecting her from life to such an extent that she will presently arrive at womanhood with no more knowledge of herself than to marry a cad who will make her miserable. The cad himself, Henry Gowan, is expressly shown as the product of another distorted family relationship; his history is sketched so as to imply that he could hardly have turned out any better than he did:

Pursuing his inquiries, Clennam found that the Gowan family were a very distant ramification of the Barnacles; and that the paternal Gowan, originally attached to a legation abroad, had been pensioned off as a Commissioner of nothing particular somewhere or other, and had died at his post with his drawn salary in his hand, nobly defending it to the last extremity. In consideration of this eminent public service, the Barnacle then in power had recommended the Crown to bestow a pension of two or three hundred a year on his widow; to which the next Barnacle in power had added certain shady and sedate apartments in the Palace at Hampton Court, where the old lady still lived, deploring the degeneracy of the times, in company with several other old ladies of both sexes. Her son, Mr. Henry Gowan, inheriting from his father, the Commissioner, that very questionable help in life, a very small independence, had been difficult to settle; the rather, as public appointments chanced to be scarce, and his genius, during his earlier manhood, was of that exclusively agricultural character which applies itself to the cultivation of wild oats. At last he had declared that he would become a Painter; partly because he had always had an idle knack that way, and partly to grieve the souls of the Barnacles-in-chief who had not provided for him. So it had come to pass successively, first, that several distinguished ladies had been frightfully shocked; then, that portfolios of his performances had been handed about o' nights, and declared with ecstasy to be perfect Claudes, perfect Cuyps, perfect phænomena; then, that Lord Decimus had bought his picture, and had asked the President and Council to dinner at a blow, and had said, with his own magnificent gravity, 'Do you know, there appears to me to be really immense merit in that work?' and, in short, that people of condition had absolutely taken pains to bring him into fashion. But somehow it had all failed. The prejudiced public had stood out against it obstinately. They had determined not to admire Lord Decimus's picture. They had determined to believe that in every service, except their own, a man must qualify himself by striving early and late, and by working heart and soul, might and main. So now Mr. Gowan, like that worn-out old coffin which never was Mahomet's nor anybody else's, hung midway between two points: jaundiced and jealous as to the one he had left: jaundiced and jealous as to the other that he couldn't reach. (Bk. I, Ch. 17.)

Mr. Meagles, a man of good heart and, in most matters, good understanding, is prevented from seeing through Gowan because he has 'a weakness which none of us need go into the next street to find, and which no amount of Circumlocution experience, could long subdue in him'. That weakness, snobbery, is one of the chief binding materials used in the book, and as such it is more important than any amount of contrived plot links. Not only is it the reason why the Tite Barnacles are allowed to carry on their pseudo-paternalistic muddling; it is also the reason why the life of the Dorrits is no less prison-like after they come into money and leave the Marshalsea; it even provides the toehold which Blandois has in the story, since his method of getting people to accept him is to insist continually that he is a gentleman.

Pet Meagles, her will-power coddled away, and her natural womanly shrewdness given no chance to develop, is then offered up by her tearful parents on the altar of snobbery, which is seen consistently as a perverted form of family sentiment; she is thus, like Little Dorrit, a victim of both kinds of *malaise*, that in the heart of the family and that in society at large. And, while she is forced by this distortion into a loveless marriage, her companion Tattycoram, whom her parents had adopted partly as a substitute for her dead sister, is forced by the general distortion of relationships, and by her own unstable temperament, beyond the reach of normal emotions altogether. In case any reader, even in the 1860's, failed to pick up the point that Miss Wade has drawn Tattycoram into a perverted sexual relationship, Dickens has Mr. Meagles go to see her and accuse her of it point-blank: 'I don't know what you are, but you don't hide, can't hide, what a dark spirit you have within you. If it should happen that you are a woman, who, from whatever cause, has a perverted delight in making a sister-woman as wretched as she is (I am old enough to have heard of such), I warn her against you, and I warn you against yourself.' (Bk. I, Ch. 27.)

The marriage of Pet Meagles and Gowan brings us into the world of the Tite Barnacles, but the direct impingement of the fashionable and governing-class world on the world of the Dorrits is provided, of course, by the infatuation of Edmund Sparkler with Fanny Dorrit. Dickens is usually supposed not to be able to manage characters from 'high life', but it is hard to see how he could have improved on the wonderful scene (Bk. I, Ch. 20) where Mrs. Merdle, plunging and rearing, is humiliated by Fanny, who forces her to recount for Little Dorrit's benefit how she was compelled to intercede and rescue her son from the entanglement. The parrot, crawling about malevolently on the wires of its cage, provides a focus for a good deal of the emotion that is generated, since it is a blend of the arrogantly 'natural', interrupting the conversation with sardonic screams, and the exotic. This is no mere flourish, as Dickens's bonus details are apt to be, since the whole theme of the conversation is that all of them are living in a society which has become so unnatural that no one can any longer trust his own spontaneous feelings:

'My sister, ma'am,' said Fanny, in whom there was a singular mixture of deference and hardihood, 'has been asking me to tell her, as between sisters, how I came to have the honour of knowing you. And as I had engaged to call upon you once more, I thought I might take the liberty of bringing her with me, when perhaps you would tell her. I wish her to know, and perhaps you will tell her?'

'Do you think, at your sister's age——' hinted Mrs. Merdle.

'She is much older than she looks,' said Fanny; 'almost as old as I am.'

'Society,' said Mrs. Merdle, with another curve of her little finger, 'is so difficult to explain to young persons (indeed is so difficult to explain to most persons), that I am glad to hear that. I wish Society was not so arbitrary, I wish it was not so exacting—— Bird, be quiet!'

The parrot has given a most piercing shriek, as if its name were Society and it asserted its right to its exactions.

'But,' resumed Mrs. Merdle, 'we must take it as we find it. We know it is hollow and conventional and worldly and very shocking, but unless we are Savages in the Tropical seas (I should have been charmed to be one myself—most delightful life and perfect climate I am told), we must consult it. It is the common lot. Mr. Merdle is a most extensive merchant, his transactions are on the vastest scale, his wealth and influence are very great, but even he—— Bird, be quiet!'

The parrot had shrieked another shriek; and it filled up the sentence so expressively that Mrs. Merdle was under no necessity to end it. (Bk. I, Ch. 20.)

The first glimpse we have of the parrot is 'on the outside of a golden cage holding on by its beak with its scaly legs in the air, and putting itself into many strange upside-down postures'. Mrs. Merdle, on entering, composes herself 'in a nest of crimson and gold cushions, on an ottoman near the parrot'. It is a familiar Dickensian strategy, to make her enter the same area of vicious unreality as the parrot; but it is used far more effectively here than in the earlier novels. The scene has so much power because all the metaphors are pointing in the same direction.

Distorted family relationships, then, and particularly those between parent and child, make up one side of the coin. The other side is the related theme of imprisonment. Having got as far as Mrs. Merdle, we might as well use her husband, the philanthropic financier, as the bridge from one theme to the other. He is, on a large scale, what

Casby is on the scale of Bleeding Heart Yard: a fake patriarch, the result of whose operations is to rob people of their money. He is also the counterpart of William Dorrit, being a prisoner in his own house. His manner, throughout, is that of a convict; the Chief Butler is his turnkey, and even when he has managed to escape for a moment from the man's contemptuous eye, he still stands 'with his hands crossed under his uneasy coat-cuffs, as if he were taking himself into custody'. The Chief Butler is to Mr. Merdle what the parrot is to his wife; the complementary detail which both robs and bestows reality. When Merdle has committed suicide, the Butler is duly there to drain the event of any human significance:

'Mr. Merdle is dead.'
'I should wish,' said the Chief Butler, 'to give a month's notice.' (Bk. II, Ch. 25.)

To judge from the number of overt references he makes to this imprisonment-theme, Dickens was determined that no reader should overlook it. No one can ever have missed the moral of the whole story of the Dorrit family's Grand Tour; on being released from the debtors' prison, they set off on a journey across Europe which bears no more relation to freedom than does 'exercise in the yard'; the place of the Warden of the Marshalsea being taken, for a consideration, by Mrs. General (the military title is significant). No reader, as I say, can ever have missed the point; but just in case anyone's attention might wander, Dickens provides a sustained overt comparison in which all is made explicit:

It appeared on the whole, to Little Dorrit herself, that this same society in which they lived, greatly resembled a superior sort of Marshalsea. Numbers of people seemed to come abroad, pretty much as people had come into the prison; through debt, through idleness, relationship, curiosity, and general unfitness for getting on at home. They were brought into these foreign towns in the custody of couriers and local followers, just as the debtors had been brought into the prison. They prowled about the churches and picture-galleries, much in the old, dreary, prison-yard manner. They were usually going away again tomorrow or next week, and rarely knew their own minds, and seldom did what they said they would do, or went where they said they would go: in all this again, very like the prison debtors. They paid high for poor accommodation, and disparaged a place while they pretended to like it: which was exactly the Marshalsea habit invariably. A certain set of words and phrases, as much belonging to tourists as the College and the Snuggery belonged to the jail, was always in their mouths. They had precisely the same incapacity for settling down to anything, as the prisoners used to have; they rather deteriorated one another, as the prisoners used to do; and they wore untidy dresses, and fell into a slouching way of life: still, always like the people in the Marshalsea. (Bk. II, Ch. 7.)

But of course not only the fashionable Continental resorts but every locale mentioned in the book is a prison, or is capable of becoming one, just as every relationship is, potentially or actually, familial. The opening scene establishes the achingly real physical contrast between the blistering heat of Marseilles and the dank rottenness of the prison in which we find ourselves with Rigaud and John Baptist. The first words spoken in the book, Rigaud's 'To the devil with this Brigand of a Sun that never shines in here!' are invested with a significance that gradually builds up as the story progresses. One of the main abstract facts for which the metaphor of imprisonment provides a concrete embodiment, is the fact of repression; the emotions bundled away out of sight and left to fester until the whole organism is infected. One of the things that makes a prison prison-like is precisely that the sun never shines into it. The whole novel is organized to show what this means in detail. It is no accident, for instance, that the next scene of the book should echo this initial contrast between the fierce, uncompromising sunshine and the vaporous dungeon; for the switch of scene is to London, not actually in a pea-soup fog (that would be *too* obvious) but on a rainy Sunday evening. The London scene is immediately described in terms that establish its prison-like character:

Everything was bolted and barred that could by possibility furnish relief to an overworked people. No pictures, no unfamiliar animals, no rare plants or flowers, no natural or artificial wonders of the ancient world—all *taboo* with that enlightened strictness, that the ugly South Sea gods in the British Museum might have supposed themselves at home again . . . Miles of close wells and pits of houses, where the inhabitants gasped for air, stretched far away towards every point of the compass. (Bk. I, Ch. 3.)

Altogether, the opening scene is an essential induction to the main body of the novel, since it introduces not only the physical contrast between prison and the world outside, but also the disfiguring social relationships that create such prisons, embodied in the difference between the food the gaoler brings to the two men in the same cell.

The gaoler's daughter, with her gentle pity for the 'poor birds', is, so to speak, a miniature preliminary emblem of Little Dorrit herself.

As if eager to plant the imprisonment-theme deeply in the reader's mind at once, Dickens throws in another variant on it before we leave Marseilles for London, by showing us the group of travellers that includes Clennam, the Meagles family, and Miss Wade, held in quarantine and chafing to continue their journey. What is more, they are made to reveal their characters in a discussion on this very theme:

The reserved Englishwoman took up Mr. Meagles in his last remark.
'Do you mean that a prisoner forgives his prison?' said she, slowly and with emphasis.
'That was my speculation, Miss Wade. I don't pretend to know positively how a prisoner might feel. I never was one before.' (Bk. I, Ch. 2.)

Miss Wade's problem, of course, is that her sexual emotions have buckled up and become perverted. In other words, she is suffering from a disease engendered by imprisonment, on the psychological level. This links her with that *motif* which finds its most direct expression in the figure of Mrs. General. Just as Dickens is surprisingly explicit on the subject of Miss Wade's Lesbianism, he insists quite tenaciously on the point that Mrs. General is the enemy of the instinctual, including the sexual, side of human life. She herself is 'a cool, waxy, blown-out woman, who had never lighted well', and this is the condition to which she seeks to reduce her charges.

Mrs. General was not to be told of anything shocking. Accidents, miseries, and offences, were never to be mentioned before her. Passion was to go to sleep in the presence of Mrs. General, and blood was to change to milk and water. The little that was left in the world, when all these deductions were made, it was Mrs. General's province to varnish. In that formation process of hers she dipped the smallest of brushes into the largest of pots, and varnished the surface of every object that came under consideration. The more cracked it was, the more Mrs. General varnished it. (Bk. II, Ch. 2.)

This distrust of the instinctual and spontaneous is common to all the unsympathetic characters in the book. Mr. Tite Barnacle, for instance, was

a buttoned-up man, and consequently a weighty one. All buttoned-up men are weighty. All buttoned-up men are believed in. Whether or no the reserved and never-exercised power of unbuttoning, fascinates mankind; whether or no wisdom is supposed to condense and augment when buttoned up, and to evaporate when unbuttoned; it is certain that the man to whom importance is accorded is the buttoned-up man. Mr. Tite Barnacle never would have passed for half his current value, unless his coat had always been buttoned up to his white cravat. (Bk. II, Ch. 12.)

Mrs. Merdle, again, is continually spoken of as the possessor of a celebrated Bosom—and we are reminded no less continually that the only use to which she ever puts this Bosom is to hang jewellery on it. Mrs. Clennam is actually reduced to invalidism by what we should now call psycho-somatic means; at the end of the book, Dickens underlines this by having her leave her wheel-chair and walk through the streets; her limbs are set in motion by that same mental power which paralysed them.

As we should expect, the sympathetic characters all show a contrasting spontaneity and naturalness. But Dickens was in too bleak a mood to allow of his drawing any neat, compensatory contrast. Setting aside Clennam and Little Dorrit, whose happy ending consists barely of saving their souls alive, the 'good' characters are conceived mainly in pastoral terms. John Baptist, with his unfailing and unforced cheerfulness, is the Anglo-Saxon's view of the sympathetic Latin—the obverse of the scowling, knife-carrying dago of the adventure story. The Plornishes, like all working-class characters in Dickens, are seen from above, in a way that diminishes their essential reality. Maggy is an actual idiot, her mind smashed by early cruelty and privation; this (to say the least) neutralizes the fact that she is almost the only character in the book who cannot be imagined as feeling any resentment or self-pity. Affery Flintwich is beautifully presented, in her first conversation with Clennam, as having a mind so disorganized that she is inarticulate except when she can call in the aid of movement. Her movements are not gestures, like John Baptist's; each one is part of the never-ending drudgery of her lifetime :

'Affery, you were not married when I went away.'
She screwed her mouth into the form of saying 'No', shook her head, and proceeded to get a pillow into its case.
'How did it happen?'
'Why, Jeremiah, o' course,' said Affery, with an end of the pillow-case between her teeth.
'Of course he proposed it, but how did it all come about? I should have thought that neither of you would have married; least of all should I have thought of your marrying each other.'

'No more should I,' said Mrs. Flintwich, tying the pillow tightly in its case.

'That's what I mean. When did you begin to think otherwise?'

'Never begun to think otherwise at all,' said Mrs. Flintwich.

Seeing, as she patted the pillow into its place on the bolster, that he was still looking at her, as if waiting for the rest of her reply, she gave it a great poke in the middle, and asked, 'How could I help myself?' (Bk. I, Ch. 3.)

There, I believe, my immediate task ends. What this essay has been trying to do is simply to present the evidence for claiming that *Little Dorrit* has a balance and logic sufficient to avert that loss of energy which is so evident in Dickens's early novels. Everyone now realizes that Dickens was a great novelist, and that his greatness lay in his inexhaustible imaginative fertility, his promptness with dabs of unforgettable detail, and his breadth of human sympathy. At the same time it is generally conceded that his earlier output is marred by a curiously facile optimism and by a tendency to build his imaginative structures on perfunctory foundation. Sometimes defenders of Dickens try to evade these two charges by presenting him as first and foremost a poet. It is true that Dickens had more of the spirit of poetry in him than most of the verse-poets of his day; he created a unified imaginative world by an unprecedented use of the pathetic fallacy which caused the inanimate to rise and engulf the animate; he is always giving us people who resemble pieces of furniture and furniture that resembles people, so that we soon become aware of inhabiting what Miss Dorothy Van Ghent (with a wealth of illuminatingly chosen detail) calls 'The Dickens World' (*Sewanee Review*, LVIII, 3). It is also true that Dickens saw the inherent poetry of the big city and gave it memorable expression before that poetry became one of the commonplaces of Western European literature. Nevertheless, when we come to make distinctions of merit among Dickens's novels, we shall, I think, be driven to the conclusion that the best ones are those which show not only these poetic qualities but novelistic ones besides: to me, *Little Dorrit* is the most satisfying of his books because it is both grand and apocalyptic, setting out a vision of human society that includes nearly everything of importance, and also lovingly shaped, his most solid attempt at solving the specific problems of long fictional narrative.

A TALE OF TWO CITIES

John Gross

A Tale of Two Cities ends fairly cheerfully with its hero getting killed; Dickens's previous novel, *Little Dorrit*, ends in deep gloom with its hero getting married. Violence offers Dickens a partial release from the sense of frustration and despondency which crept over him during the eighteen-fifties; the shadow of the Marshalsea lifts a little with the storming of the Bastille, and everyone remembers *A Tale of Two Cities* above all for the intoxication of its crowd-scenes. In fact they take up less space than one supposes in retrospect, and for the most part the atmosphere is every bit as stifling as that of *Little Dorrit*. Dickens originally thought of calling the book *Buried Alive*, and at its heart lie images of death and, much less certainly, of resurrection: themes which foreshadow *Our Mutual Friend*.

The story opens with the feeblest of resurrections, the recall to life of Doctor Manette. His daughter is afraid that she is going to meet his ghost, a fear that is almost justified when she actually sees his spectral face and hears his voice, so faint and lacking in life and resonance that it is 'like the last feeble echo of a sound made long and long ago . . . like a voice underground'. (Bk. I, Ch. 6.) The whole novel is thronged with ghosts; from the mist moving forlornly up the Dover Road 'like an evil spirit seeking rest and finding none' to the gunsmoke which as it clears suggests Madame Defarge's soul leaving her body, there are scores of references to spectres, phantoms, and apparitions. The penniless émigrés haunt Tellson's like familiar spirits; Lorry sees the likeness of the Lucie whom he once knew pass like a breath across the pier-glass behind her; the fountains of the château show ghostly in the dawn—but it would be tedious to compile a catalogue.

Such ghostliness suggests, first of all, a sense of unreality, of the death in life to which men are reduced by imprisonment, psychological or actual. To Darnay, the prisoners in La Force, going through the motions of elegance and pride in the midst of squalor, are ghosts all, 'waiting their dismissal from the desolate shore', and the scene simply 'the crowning unreality of his long unreal ride'. (Bk. III, Ch. 1.) But ghosts are also the creatures of false or, at any rate, imperfect resurrection: the grave gives up its dead reluctantly, and the prisoner who has been released is still far from being a free man. The inmates of the Bastille, suddenly given their liberty by 'the storm that had burst their tomb', are anything but overjoyed: 'all scared, all lost, all wondering and amazed, as if the Last Day were come, and those who rejoiced around them were all lost spirits'. (Bk. II, Ch. 21.) Even the phlegmatic Darnay, after his Old Bailey acquittal, 'scarcely seems to belong to this world again'. As for Doctor Manette, he has been as deeply scarred by his prison experience as William Dorrit. Lucie's love is not enough in itself to stop him from retreating into his shoe-making, and it takes a symbolic act of violence to complete the cure; he is fully restored to himself only after Mr. Lorry has hacked to pieces his cobbler's bench, 'while Miss Pross held the candle as if she were assisting at a murder'. (Book II, Ch. 19). But by this time the centre of interest in the book has shifted unmistakably to Sydney Carton.

The prison and the grave are linked in Dickens's mind with the idea that 'every human creature is constituted to be that profound secret and mystery to every other'. We live in essential isolation; in each heart there is, 'in some of its imaginings, a secret to the heart nearest it. Something of the awfulness, even of death itself, is referable to this . . . In any of the burial-places of this city through which I pass, is there a sleeper more inscrutable than its busy inhabitants are, in their innermost personality, to me, or than I am to them?' (Bk. I, Ch. 3.) On his journey to greet the newly released Manette, Mr. Lorry feels as if he is going to unearth a secret as well as dig up a dead man; in his dream the grave is confused with the underground strong-rooms at Tellson's, and he fancies himself digging 'now with a spade, now with a great key, now with his hands'. In his hotel room, the two tall candles are reflected on every leaf of the heavy dark tables, 'as if *they* were buried in deep graves of dark mahogany, and no light to speak of could be expected of them until they were dug out'. (Bk. I, Ch. 4.)

This oppressive sense of mystery generates suspicion and fear. 'All secret men are soon terrified', Dickens tells us in connection with Barsad, the police spy; but we are in a world where everyone is a secret man, a world of whispers and echoes. On the Dover Mail 'the guard suspected the passengers, the passengers suspected one another and the guard, they all suspected everybody else'; when Darnay returns to France, 'the universal watchfulness so encompassed him, that if he had been taken in a net, or were being forwarded to his destination in a cage, he could not have felt his freedom more completely gone'. (Bk. III, Ch. 1.) Even in the haven established for Doctor Manette near Soho Square there is foreboding in the air, in the echoes which Lucie makes out to be 'the echoes of all the footsteps that are coming by and by into our lives'. An accurate enough premonition of the noise of feet and voices pouring into the Paris courtyard which first draws her attention to the bloodstained grindstone, or of the troubled movement and shouting round a street-corner which herald the Carmagnole. Carton's last impression, too, is to be of 'the pressing on of many footsteps' on the outskirts of the crowd round the guillotine. Footsteps suggest other people, and in *A Tale of Two Cities* other people are primarily a threat and a source of danger. The little group around Doctor Manette is as self-contained as any in Dickens, but it enjoys only a precarious safety; the emblematic golden arm on the wall at Soho Square is always capable of dealing a poisoned blow.

A Tale of Two Cities is a tale of two heroes. The theme of the double has such obvious attractions for a writer preoccupied with disguises, rival impulses, and hidden affinities that it is surprising that Dickens didn't make more use of it elsewhere. But no one could claim that his handling of the device is very successful here, or that he has managed to range the significant forces of the novel behind Carton and Darnay. Darnay is, so to speak, the accredited representative of Dickens in the novel, the 'normal' hero for whom a happy ending is still possible. It has been noted, interestingly enough, that he shares his creator's initials—and that is pretty well the only interesting thing about him. Otherwise he is a pasteboard character, completely undeveloped. His position as an exile, his struggles as a language-teacher, his admiration for George Washington are so many openings thrown away.

Carton, of course, is a far more striking figure. He belongs to the line of cultivated wastrels who play an increasingly large part in

Dickens's novels during the second half of his career, culminating in Eugene Wrayburn; his clearest predecessor, as his name indicates, is the luckless Richard Carstone of *Bleak House*. He has squandered his gifts and drunk away his early promise; his will is broken, but his intellect is unimpaired. In a sense, his opposite is not Darnay at all, but the aggressive Stryver, who makes a fortune by picking his brains. Yet there is something hollow about his complete resignation to failure: his self-abasement in front of Lucie, for instance. ('I am like one who died young . . . I know very well that you can have no tenderness for me . . .') For, stagy a figure though he is, Carton does suggest what Thomas Hardy calls 'fearful unfulfilments'; he still has vitality, and it is hard to believe that he has gone down without a struggle. The total effect is one of energy held unnaturally in check: the bottled-up frustration which Carton represents must spill over somewhere.

Carton's and Darnay's fates are entwined from their first meeting, at the Old Bailey trial. Over the dock there hangs a mirror: 'crowds of the wicked and the wretched had been reflected in it, and had passed from its surface and this earth's together. Haunted in a most ghastly manner that abominable place would have been, if the glass could ever have rendered back its reflections, as the ocean is one day to give up its dead.' (Bk. II, Ch. 2.) After Darnay's acquittal we leave him with Carton, 'so like each other in feature, so unlike in manner, both reflected in the glass above them'. Reflections, like ghosts, suggest unreality and self-division, and at the end of the same day Carton stares at his own image in the glass and upbraids it: 'Why should you particularly like a man who resembles you? There is nothing in you to like: you know that. Ah, confound you! . . . Come on, and have it out in plain words! You hate the fellow.' (Bk. II, Ch. 4.) In front of the mirror, Carton thinks of changing places with Darnay; at the end of the book, he is to take the other's death upon him. Dickens prepares the ground: when Darnay is in jail, it is Carton who strikes Mr. Lorry as having 'the wasted air of a prisoner', and when he is visited by Carton on the rescue attempt, he thinks at first that he is 'an apparition of his own imagining'. But Dickens is determined to stick by Darnay: a happy ending *must* be possible. As Lorry and his party gallop to safety with the drugged Darnay, there is an abrupt switch to the first person: 'The wind is rushing after us, and the clouds are flying after us, and the moon is plunging after us, and the whole wild night is in pursuit of us; but so far, we are pursued by nothing else.' (Bk. III, Ch. 13.) *We* can make our escape, however narrowly; Carton, expelled from our system, must be abandoned to his fate.

But the last word is with Carton—the most famous last word in Dickens, in fact. Those who take a simplified view of Dickens's radicalism, or regard him as one of nature's Marxists, can hardly help regretting that *A Tale of Two Cities* should end as it does. They are bound to feel, with Edgar Johnson, that 'instead of merging, the truth of revolution and the truth of sacrifice are made to appear in conflict'. A highly personal, indeed a unique crisis cuts across public issues and muffles the political message. But this is both to sentimentalize Dickens's view of the revolution, and to miss the point about Carton. The cynical judgment that his sacrifice was trifling, since he had nothing to live for, is somewhat nearer the mark. Drained of the will to live, he is shown in the closing chapters of the book as a man courting death, and embracing it when it comes. 'In seasons of pestilence, some of us will have a secret attraction to the disease—a terrible passing inclination to die of it. And all of us have like wonders hidden in our breasts, only needing circumstances to evoke them.' (Bk. III, Ch. 6.) It is Carton rather than Darnay who is 'drawn to the loadstone rock'.[1] On his last walk around Paris, a passage which Shaw cites in the preface to *Man and Superman* as proof of Dickens's essentially irreligious nature, his thoughts run on religion: 'I am the Resurrection and the Life.' But his impressions are all of death: the day comes coldly, 'looking like a dead face out of the sky', while on the river 'a trading boat, with a sail of the softened colour of a dead leaf, then glided into his view, floated by him, and died away'. (Bk. III, Ch. 9.) His walk recalls an earlier night, when he wandered round London with 'wreaths of dust spinning round and round before the morning blast, as if the desert sand had risen far away and the first spray of it in its advance had begun to overwhelm the city'. (Bk. II, Ch. 5.) Then, with the wilderness bringing home to him a sense of the wasted powers within him, he saw a momentary mirage of what he might have achieved and was reduced to tears; but now that the city has been overwhelmed in

[1] Darnay, who only comes to life in the face of death, is nevertheless obsessed with the guillotine. He has 'a strange besetting desire to know what to do when the time came, a desire gigantically disproportionate to the few swift moments to which it referred; a wondering that was more like the wondering of some other spirit within his, than his own'. (Bk III, Ch. 13.) Carton's spirit, perhaps; through the exigencies of the plot, Dickens has got the wires crossed.

earnest, he is past thinking of what might have been. 'It is a far, far
better thing that I do, than I have ever done'—but the 'better thing'
might just as well be committing suicide as laying down his life for
Darnay. At any rate, he thinks of himself as going towards rest, not
towards resurrection.

By this time the revolution has become simply the agency of death,
the storm that overwhelms the city. Or rather, all the pent-up fury
and resentment that is allowed no outlet in the 'personal' side of the
book, with Carton kow-towing to Stryver and nobly renouncing
Lucie, boils over in revolutionary violence: Dickens dances the
Carmagnole, and howls for blood with the mob. Frightened by the
forces which he has released, he views the revolution with hatred
and disgust; he doesn't record a single incident in which it might be
shown as beneficent, constructive or even tragic. Instead, it is
described time and again in terms of pestilence and madness. Dickens
will hear nothing of noble aspirations; the disorder of the whole
period is embodied in the dervishes who dance the Carmagnole—'no
fight could have been half so terrible'. Confronted with the crowd,
Dickens reaches for his gun; he looks into eyes 'which any un-
brutalized beholder would have given twenty years of life, to have
petrified with a well-directed gun'. (Bk. III, Ch. 2.) That 'well-
directed' has the true ring of outraged rate-paying respectability,
while the image seems oddly out of place in a book which has laid so
much stress on the stony faces and petrified hearts of the aristocracy.
Dickens can only deal with mob-violence in a deliberately pictur-
esque story set in the past. But *A Tale of Two Cities*, written by a
middle-aged man who could afford a longer perspective at a time
when Chartism was already receding into history, is not quite
analogous to *Barnaby Rudge*. There, however contemptible we are
meant to find the world of Sir John Chester, the riots are an explosion
of madness and nothing more. But the French Revolution compels
Dickens to acquire a theory of history, however primitive: 'crush
humanity out of shape once more, under similar hammers, and it will
twist itself into the same tortured forms'. (Bk. III, Ch. 15.) The
revolutionaries return evil for evil; the guillotine is the product not
of innate depravity but of intolerable oppression. If Dickens's sympathies shift towards the aristocrats as soon as they become victims,
he can also show a grim restraint; he underlines the horror of
Foulon's death, strung up with a bunch of grass tied to his back (how

his imagination pounces on such a detail!), but he never allows us to forget who Foulon was. Nor does he have any sympathy with those who talk of the Revolution 'as though it were the only harvest under the skies that had never been sown', although he himself is at times plainly tempted to treat it as an inexplicable calamity, a rising of the sea (the gaoler at La Force has the bloated body of a drowned man, and so forth) or a rising of fire: the flames which destroy the château of St. Evrémonde 'blow from the infernal regions', convulsing nature until the lead boils over inside the stone fountains. But cause and effect are never kept out of sight for long; Dickens is always reminding himself that the Revolution, though 'a frightful moral disorder', was born of 'unspeakable suffering, intolerable oppression, and heartless indifference'. Society was diseased before the fever broke out: the shattered cask of wine which at the outset falls on the 'crippling' stones of Saint Antoine is scooped up in little mugs of 'mutilated' earthenware.

But to grasp a patient's medical history is not to condone his disease, and Dickens is unyielding in his hostility to the crowd. The buzzing of the flies on the scent for carrion at the Old Bailey trial and the mass-rejoicing at Roger Cly's funeral are early indications of what he feels. The courtroom in Paris is also full of buzzing and stirring, but by this time the atmosphere has become positively cannibalistic; a jury of dogs has been empanelled to try the deer, Madame Defarge 'feasts' on the prisoner, Jacques III, with his very Carlylean croak, is described as an epicure.

Whatever Dickens's motives, a good deal of this is no doubt perfectly valid; morbid fantasies can still prompt shrewd observations, as when we are shown Darnay, the prisoner of half an hour, already learning to count the steps as he is led away to his cell. In particular, Dickens recognizes the ways in which a period of upheaval can obliterate the individual personality; there is no more telling detail in the book than the roll-call of the condemned containing the names of a prisoner who has died in jail and two who have already been guillotined, all of them forgotten. Insane suspicion, senseless massacres, the rise to power of the worst elements: in the era of Gladstonian budgets Dickens understands the workings of a police state.

But it would be ludicrous to claim very much for the accuracy of Dickens's account of the French Revolution as such. There are scarcely any references to the actual course of events, and no suggestion at all that the revolution had an intellectual or idealistic

content, while the portrayal of fanaticism seems childish if we compare it even with something as one-sided as *The Gods are Athirst*. For
the purposes of the novel, the revolution is the Defarges, and although
Carton foresees that Defarge in his turn will perish on the guillotine,
he has no inkling of how the whole internecine process will ever
come to a halt. As for Madame Defarge, she is as much driven by
fate as the stony-hearted Marquis, with his coachmen cracking their
whips like the Furies: the time has laid 'a dreadfully disfiguring
hand upon her'. Her last entry is her most dramatic. Miss Pross is
bathing her eyes to rid herself of feverish apprehensions, when she
suddenly appears—materializes, one might say—in the doorway:

The basin fell to the ground broken, and the water flowed to the feet of
Madame Defarge. By strange stern ways, and through much staining
blood, those feet had come to meet that water. (Bk. III, Ch. 14.)

We are reminded, by rather too forcible a contrast, of the broken
cask of red wine which prefaces Madame Defarge's first appearance
in the novel. Her element, from the very start, is blood.

Still, *A Tale of Two Cities* is not a private nightmare, but a work
which continues to give pleasure. Dickens's drives and conflicts are
his raw material, not the source of his artistic power, and in itself the
fact that the novel twists the French Revolution into a highly personal
fantasy proves nothing: so, after all, does *The Scarlet Pimpernel*.
Everything depends on the quality of the writing—which is usually
one's cue, in talking about Dickens, to pay tribute to his exuberance
and fertility. Dickens's genius inheres in minute particulars; later we
may discern patterns of symbolism and imagery, a design which lies
deeper than the plot, but first we are struck by the lavish heaping-up
of acute observations, startling similes, descriptive flourishes, circum-
stantial embroidery. Or such is the case with every Dickens novel
except for the *Tale*, which is written in a style so grey and unadorned
that many readers are reluctant to grant it a place in the Canon at all.
Dickens wouldn't be Dickens if there weren't occasional touches like
the 'hospital procession of negro cupids, several headless and all
cripples', which Mr. Lorry notices framing the mirror in his hotel
(or the whitewashed cupid 'in the coolest linen' on the ceiling of his
Paris office, which makes its appearance three hundred pages later).
But for the most part one goes to the book for qualities which are

easier to praise than to illustrate or examine: a rapid tempo which never lets up from the opening sentence, and a sombre eloquence which saves Carton from mere melodrama, and stamps an episode like the running-down of the child by the Marquis's carriage on one's mind with a primitive intensity rarely found after Dickens's early novels, like an outrage committed in a fairy-tale.

But it must be admitted that the *Tale* is in many ways a thin and uncharacteristic work, bringing the mounting despair of the eighteen-fifties to a dead end rather than ushering in the triumphs of the 'sixties. In no other novel, not even *Hard Times*, has Dickens's natural profusion been so drastically pruned. Above all, the book is notoriously deficient in humour. One falls—or flops—back hopefully on the Crunchers, but to small avail. True, the comic element parodies the serious action: Jerry, like his master, is a 'Resurrection-Man', but on the only occasion that we see him rifling a grave it turns out to be empty, while his son's panic-stricken flight with an imaginary coffin in full pursuit is nightmarish rather than funny. As comic characters the Crunchers are forced and mechanical; such true humour as there is in the book is rather to be found in scattered observations, but settings and characters are colourful rather than grotesque. Obviously Dickens's humour is many things, but it is usually bound up with a sense of almost magical power over nature: to distort, exaggerate, yoke together or dissolve is to manipulate and control external reality. In Dickens people are always taking on the qualities of objects with which they come into contact, and *vice versa*: a basic Dickensian trick of style, which makes its appearance as early as the opening pages of *Sketches by Boz*, where there is a fine passage ('Our Parish', Chapter VII) on the 'resemblance and sympathy' between a man's face and the knocker on his front door. Such transformations are not unknown in *A Tale of Two Cities*— there is the obstinate door at Tellson's with the weak rattle in its throat, for example—but they occur less frequently than in any other Dickens novel, and there is a corresponding lack of power for which a neatly constructed plot is small compensation.

Contrary to what might be expected, this absence of burlesque is accompanied by a failure to present society in any depth. *A Tale of Two Cities* may deal with great political events, but nowhere else in the later work of Dickens is there less sense of society as a living organism. Evrémondes and Defarges alike seem animated by sheer hatred; we hear very little of the stock social themes, money, hypocrisy, and snobbery. Tellson's, musty and cramped and anti-quated, makes an excellent Dickensian set-piece, but it is scarcely followed up. Jarvis Lorry, too, is a sympathetic version of the fairy-godfather, a saddened Cheeryble who repines at spending his days 'turning a vast pecuniary mangle', but this side of his character is only lightly sketched in. He may glance through the iron bars of his office-window 'as if they were ruled for figures too, and every-thing under the clouds were a sum', but he is more important as a protective, reassuring figure: in times of revolution Tellson's musti-ness becomes a positive virtue.

The lack of social density shows up Dickens's melodrama to dis-advantage. This is partly a question of length, since in a short novel everything has to be worked in as best it can: Barsad will inevit-ably turn out to be Miss Pross's long-lost brother, Defarge has to double as Doctor Manette's old servant, and so forth. But there is a deeper reason for feeling more dissatisfaction with the artificial plot here than one does with equally far-fetched situations elsewhere in Dickens. Where society is felt as an all-enveloping force, Dickens is able to turn the melodramatic conventions which he inherited to good use; however preposterous the individual coincidences, they serve an important symbolic function. The world is more of a piece than we suppose, Dickens is saying, and our fates are bound up, however cut off from one another we may appear: the pestilence from Tom-all-Alone's really will spread to the Dedlock mansion, and sooner or later the river in which Gaffer Hexam fishes for corpses will flow through the Veneering drawing-room. In a word, we can't have Miss Havisham without Magwitch. But without a thick social atmo-sphere swirling round them, the characters of *A Tale of Two Cities* stand out in stark melodramatic isolation; the spotlight is trained too sharply on the implausibilities of the plot, and the stage is set for Sir John Martin-Harvey and *The Only Way*. So, too, the relentless workings of destiny are stressed rather clumsily by such a bare presentation; Madame Defarge points the finger of fate a little too vigorously, and there is a tendency towards heavy repetitions and parallelisms, brought out by the chapter-headings, 'A Hand at Cards' and 'The Game Made', 'Dusk' and 'Darkness', and so forth.

Yet despite the dark mood in which it was conceived, the *Tale* isn't a wholly gloomy work; nor is the final impression which it leaves with us one of a wallow of self-pity on the scaffold. We are told of Darnay in the condemned cell (or is it Carton?) that his hold on life was strong, and it was very, very hard to loosen; by gradual efforts and degrees unclosed a little here, it clenched the tighter there; and when he brought his strength to bear on that hand and it yielded, this was closed again. There was a hurry, too, in all his thoughts, a turbulent and heated working of his heart, that contended against resignation. (Bk. III, Ch. 13.)

And near the end, as Miss Pross grapples with Madame Defarge, Dickens speaks of 'the vigorous tenacity of love, always so much stronger than hate'. The gruesome events of the book scarcely bear out such a judgment, yet as an article of faith, if not as a statement of the literal truth, it is curiously impressive. For all the sense of horror which he must have felt stirring within him when he wrote *A Tale of Two Cities*, Dickens remained a moralist and a preacher, and it was his saving strength. But if the author doesn't succumb with Carton, neither does he escape with Darnay. At the end of the book 'we' gallop away not to safety and Lucie, but to the false hopes of Pip, the thwarted passion of Bradley Headstone, the divided life of John Jasper. Nothing is concluded, and by turning his malaise into a work of art Dickens obtains parole, not release: the prison will soon be summoning him once more.

GREAT EXPECTATIONS

Christopher Ricks

THE MOST important things about *Great Expectations* are also the most obvious—a fact that is fortunate for the book, but unfortunate for the critic. The greatly deplored deficiency of modern criticism is its inability to deal adequately with what is at the heart of most novels: 'scenes, actions, *stuff*, people' (Christopher Caudwell). That is, in a way as specific as is usual in the discussion of poetry, relying more on cognition and less on ejaculation than did an earlier generation. Yet at the heart of *Great Expectations* are all those obvious sorts of greatness which embarrass the modern critic—convincing and often profound characterization, a moving and exciting story, and a world observed with both literal and moral fidelity. More particularly, a boy is corrupted by great expectations into becoming an ungrateful snob, but is eventually saved by his love for the convict who had been his unknown patron. There needs no explicator to tell us what is primarily great about Miss Havisham and her decaying house, or about so explicit a scene as Pip's coldly unknowing reception of the returned Magwitch, cold until 'I saw with amazement that his eyes were full of tears'. Tears such as Magwitch weeps leave us moved and shamed.

If the critic quiets his conscience, more or less ignores 'scenes, actions, *stuff*, people', and turns instead to symbols and themes, he does at any rate know where he is. Naturally such an approach can tap more of some novels than others—or rather leave less untapped. Not a very great deal about *Little Dorrit* has to be left unsaid if the *prison* is comprehensively discussed. But *Great Expectations*, though it too may at many points be read symbolically, has a different centre of gravity, is even, perhaps, more old-fashioned. Its symbols are striking, and strikingly used, but the novel could have managed without them; to ignore them would mar but not ruin the novel. Admittedly, this is partly because, at their best, Dickens's symbols do not make the fundamental mistake of appearing to owe their presence to their symbolic function. It is not difficult to design consciously or erupt obsessively a pattern of cross-connecting themes or symbols; and the virtue of cross-connection is felt only when the *raison d'être* of the separate moments is something other than that they will be connected. The important image or gesture or word should owe its existence to some non-symbolic necessity (as it almost always does in Shakespeare)—to plausible characterization, say, or likely incident. 'We hate poetry that has a palpable design upon us'. and we dislike such symbols too. At any rate, we see no real reason to *believe* them—they have just been put there. At their worst, Dickens's cross-connections are notable examples of how not to do it; in *Our Mutual Friend*, Eugene and Lightwood are drinking at the riverside pub:

Lightwood helped him to some more of that stuff, but it had been cooling, and didn't answer now.

'Pooh,' said Eugene, spitting it out among the ashes. 'Tastes like the wash of the river.'

'Are you so familiar with the flavour of the wash of the river?'

'I seem to be to-night. I feel as if I had been half drowned, and swallowing a gallon of it.'

'Influence of locality,' suggested Lightwood.

'You are mighty learned to-night, you and your influences,' returned Eugene. (Ch. 13.)

The combination of the stilted and the jocular only draws attention to the gross manipulation; and sure enough ten pages later we are confronted with the drowned body of Gaffer Hexam. The river in *Our Mutual Friend* is often finely used, but sometimes the pattern is achieved only by violating the integrity of the individual incident 'Only connect' will not really do, either for author or critic.

But at his best, Dickens can make the separate moments true in themselves, so that the cross-connection is not only beautiful, but, what is even better, convincing. Magwitch's first act of gratitude to Pip for saving him from starvation is to send two pound notes to him *via* a discharged convict—'Nothing less than two fat sweltering one-pound notes that seemed to have been on terms of the warmest intimacy with all the cattle markets in the county.' Simply as description, it is vivid and plausible; but its subterranean energy comes out clearly when Pip, still thinking that Miss Havisham is his great benefactor, tries to pay back the returned Magwitch:

> 'Like you, I have done well since, and you must let me pay them back. You can put them to some other poor boy's use.' I took out my purse.
> He watched me as I laid my purse upon the table and opened it, and he watched me as I separated two one-pound notes from its contents. They were clean and new, and I spread them out and handed them over to him. Still watching me, he laid them one upon the other, folded them longwise, gave them a twist, set fire to them at the lamp, and dropped the ashes into the tray. (Ch. 39.)

Here too the account of the notes is apt to Pip and his station; and then the descriptions ignite, and we see in a flash the parable of Pip and his money. For him the money from the convict, fat and sweltering from the cattle markets, is a very different thing from that of Miss Havisham, 'clean and new'. But he is wrong about his benefactor, and he is wrong in thinking that some money is mysteriously cleaner than other money. When Magwitch burns the clean money, Dickens means more by it than Magwitch does. Magwitch means to shock and waken Pip, but he also burns Pip's dreams of a clean gentlemanly fortune.

Tolstoy, casually, has a similar thrust at those who enjoy the clean spending of money while prissy about the dirty side of it:

> 'This is what I want, my dear fellow,' said the count to the deferential young man who had entered. 'Bring me . . .' he reflected a moment, 'Yes, bring me seven hundred rubles, yes! But mind, don't bring me such tattered and dirty notes as last time, but nice clean ones for the countess.'
> 'Yes Dmítri, clean ones, please,' said the countess, sighing deeply.[1]

The incident rings true, and so especially does the countess, generous and lachrymose. Unlike Dickens, Tolstoy did not need here the cross-connection, the past and the present, the illusion and the disillusion. Not that either Tolstoy or Dickens is superior in his handling of the notion. If Dickens's seems the weightier of the two, that is simply because it is closer to the centre of his book, because it focuses more of what he wants to say. And it is plain that he was well aware of the importance of seeing such juxtapositions and changes: 'We left

---

[1] *War and Peace* (tr. L. and A. Maude, 1942), p. 59.

him [Magwitch] on the landing outside his door, holding a light over the stair-rail to light us down-stairs. Looking back at him, I thought of the first night of his return when our positions were reversed, and when I little supposed my heart could ever be as heavy and anxious at parting from him as it was now.' (Ch. 46.) Or of the changed Pumblechook: 'This reminded me of the wonderful difference between the servile manner in which he had offered his hand in my new prosperity, saying, "May I?" and the ostentatious clemency with which he had just now exhibited the same fat five fingers.' (Ch. 58.)

Yet cross-connections, symbols or themes do not really grapple with the book. Humphry House did, when he said that

The final wonder of *Great Expectations* is that in spite of all Pip's neglect of Joe and coldness towards Biddy and all the remorse and self-recrimination that they caused him, he is made to appear at the end of it all a really better person than he was at the beginning. It is a remarkable achievement to have kept the reader's sympathy throughout a snob's progress.[2]

How then *does* Pip keep our sympathy? It is a crucial question, and some of the more general answers are obvious enough—indeed they throng in. That our first sight of him in the churchyard shows him not only defenceless but also compassionate and generous; that he is ill-treated by his sister Mrs. Joe and by all the visitors to the house, especially Pumblechook; that he early shows what is surely a praiseworthy wish to get on, and a willingness to spend his time and his pocket-money on learning to read and write—and all that before he has met Estella and caught her 'infectious' contempt for his commonness: all these dispose us well towards him. And even when he has become a snob, our feelings are tempered by the fact that even snobbery pales besides the murderous violence of the savage Orlick, the dark crimes of the hypocritical Compeyson, and the brutal arrogance of the surly Drummle. Moreover, we are disinclined to pursue vengefully a sinner who gets so little pleasure out of his sin; remorse at his ingratitude to Joe, fear and insecurity about his great expectations, and hopeless yearning for Estella, all combine to make him appropriately unhappy. 'We were always more or less miserable.' At the profoundest level, Pip's feelings of guilt (as Mr. Julian Moynahan has imaginatively and convincingly shown [3]) can be compared

[2] *The Dickens World*, p. 156. [3] *Essays in Criticism*, January 1960.

to Dostoievsky, with reservations but without absurdity. Yet in a more elementary way, Pip's unhappiness is one of the strongest reasons why we keep our sympathy for him. And without that sympathy the novel could not begin to express its darker purpose.

Not that it is only Pip's behaviour and state of mind which control our feelings. If Pip thinks that it is Miss Havisham who is making his fortune, that is more because he has been deceived by others than self-deceived. The very first time Pip is to go to Satis House, his sister and Pumblechook insist 'that for anything we can tell, this boy's fortune may be made by his going to Miss Havisham's'. It is never forgotten that it is they who stuff Pip's head with 'nonsensical speculations about Miss Havisham, and about what she would do with me and for me'. Nor is this the limit of the mitigation; Pip is the victim not only of the chatter of his sister and Pumblechook, but also of the deliberate intrigue of Miss Havisham and Jaggers—and he 'deep as Australia', a man against whom no one has a chance. Pip's mistaken guess is precipitated by Jaggers's mention of Miss Havisham's relations the Pockets, and by Miss Havisham's own gloating knowledge of his new fortune and its conditions. She herself admits that she deliberately let Pip go on in his mistake, and we are not to believe her when she flashes out 'You made your own snares. *I* never made them.' At the very least, Pip's wishful thinking had been swollen by others, by ignorant speculations and by knowing deceptions. And even beyond this mitigation is our sympathy for Pip's bad luck. That Jaggers is both Miss Havisham's and Magwitch's lawyer, say, or that the Magwitch met in the opening pages should be the father of the Estella met soon at Satis House—these improbabilities are gross enough, but it is one of the few things to be said for them that they do help us to stay sorry for Pip rather than disgusted by him. The odds against him are shown to be pretty terrifying.

Yet not even these extenuations really explain why we feel so little malice towards Pip, who has behaved so badly. Perhaps only one thing can make us accept as likeable a boy so ungrateful and snobbish, and that is that he should admit it—which is of course just what Pip's first-person narrative does. The effect of using the first-person is completely to reverse the normal problem about keeping a reader's sympathy. We do not, in the ordinary way, have much difficulty in liking someone who tells us how bad he has been; we are perhaps less sympathetic to someone who talks about his good deeds. And, conversely, we are likely to feel sympathy with a man seen from the outside as acting well, but not otherwise. Goodness should not talk about itself, but badness may be absolved, or mitigated, by doing so. Not that there are no problems for the novelist who lets his bad character confess; but they are the opposite of what would ordinarily be suggested by Humphry House's remark. The real difficulties are two: can his confession always ring true, and not sound like disingenuous breast-beating?; and can he keep our sympathy even when he is telling us of his good actions?

Dickens's task here is made easier since Pip does very few good actions—and we are less suspicious about a good action when it comes after a frank admission of so many bad ones. To think of *David Copperfield* or of *Bleak House* is to see how different, and in some ways how much smaller, Dickens's difficulty is here. A lot of the time David Copperfield is telling us how good he was—sometimes he sounds goody-goody. Esther Summerson never sounds anything else: 'I don't know how it is, I seem to be always writing about myself. I mean all the time to write about other people, and I try to think about myself as little as possible, and I am sure, when I find myself coming into the story again, I am really vexed and say, "Dear, dear, you tiresome little creature, I wish you wouldn't!" but it is all of no use.' (Ch. 9.)

Yet since, within limits, we tend to like people who admit faults, we must be convinced that they are not admitting the faults only as a way of getting us to like them, meanwhile securely complacent. Most of the time Dickens gets exactly the right tone for Pip—open but not abased, willing to admit faults but not positively enjoying it. At its best, such a confession has a briskness, an unwillingness to luxuriate, which renders it immediately authentic: 'Whatever [learning] I acquired, I tried to impart to Joe. This statement sounds so well, that I cannot in my conscience let it pass unexplained. I wanted to make Joe less ignorant and common, that he might be worthier of my society and less open to Estella's reproach.' (Ch. 15.) Brief and simple, that is all that is said. Or, when Pip hears that Joe is coming to see him in London:

Let me confess exactly, with what feelings I looked forward to Joe's coming.

Not with pleasure, though I was bound to him by so many ties; no; with considerable disturbance, some mortification, and a keen sense of incongruity. If I could have kept him away by paying money, I certainly would have paid money. (Ch. 27.)

Again it is dry and terse, convincing and therefore likeable.

To discuss the less convincing confessions means first granting with pleasure that there are few of them, and that they do throw into relief the innumerable times when the poise is perfect. There is a spectrum of unsatisfying moments, ranging from the faintly uneasy to the hotly embarrassing. So Pip tells us that 'I know right well that any good that intermixed itself with my apprenticeship came of plain contented Joe, and not of restless aspiring discontented me'; where uneasiness might focus on the staunchness of 'I know right well', on the condescension in 'plain contented Joe', and on the heightened self-reproach of 'restless aspiring discontented me' (three adjectives to the two that Joe gets). Brevity is the soul of confession, or we start to see the shadow of the impure motive. But the example is admittedly not a gross one; it is not, for example, Pip's final expiation : 'Don't tell him, Joe, that I was thankless; don't tell him, Biddy, that I was ungenerous and unjust; only tell him that I honoured you both, because you were both so good and true, and that, as your child, I said it would be natural to him to grow up a much better man than I did.' (Ch. 58.) Pip is overdoing it, and there is even more to come. *Qui s'excuse s'accuse.*

Midway between such moments are those when Dickens is clever but dishonest, when the admission is slick but too evidently exists to be likeable. So when at the end of the book Pip joins the firm of Clarriker's, he tells us that

we owed so much to Herbert's ever cheerful industry and readiness, that I often wondered how I had conceived that old idea of his inaptitude, until I was one day enlightened by the reflection, that perhaps the inaptitude had never been in him at all, but had been in me. (Ch. 58.)

Charming, yes—but there is charm and charm. And when we look back at 'that old idea of his inaptitude', we find that it was not really an idea about *inaptitude* at all, rather, 'something that at the same time whispered to me he would never be successful or rich', 'that odd impression that Herbert Pocket would never be very succcessful or rich'. In that early scene Herbert talks with airy and attractive silliness about his plans as 'a capitalist—an Insurer of Ships'; ' "I think I shall trade, also," said he, putting his thumbs in his waistcoat pockets, "to the West Indies, for sugar, tobacco, and rum. Also to Ceylon, especially for elephants' tusks".' It is really from Herbert's mouth that we can tell that he will never be 'very successful or rich', and it is clearly *not* merely a matter of an inaptitude in Pip. And when Pip winningly tells us later on that it *was*, the winningness is too obtrusive—he sounds not humble but 'umble.

Dickens's skill in such a case is at the service of a miscalculation, one to which first-person narration is liable. The last two sentences of George Orwell's 'Shooting an Elephant' tell us: 'Afterwards I was very glad that the coolie had been killed; it put me legally in the right and it gave me a sufficient pretext for shooting the elephant. I often wondered whether any of the others grasped that I had done it solely to avoid looking a fool.' But is this really the truth? or is it a shrewdly calculated determination to sound grimly authentic at the close? Orwell knows that we are likely to believe someone who is so brutally frank about himself; but to look back five pages at the deeply compassionate description of the 'crucified' coolie is to think it very improbable that Orwell *was* so brutally 'very glad that the coolie had been killed'. And in the same way it doesn't look from the rest of the essay as if the shooting was done 'solely' to avoid looking a fool. Is it possible that *no* part was played by his knowing that one life had been lost, that the elephant 'might charge if you went too close to him', through the 'soft mud into which one would sink at every step'? Orwell has overdone the brutal frankness of his closing sentences; and his essay, like Dickens's novel, is marred (though certainly not spoilt) by the disingenuousness.

But most of the time Dickens catches the right tone for Pip's admissions. His handling of the other difficulty, Pip's good actions, is just as skilful. The three important ones are his secret act of kindness in buying Herbert a partnership, his final refusal to accept money from Miss Havisham or from Magwitch, and his love for Magwitch. And the greatest of these three is love, which redeems him.

At first sight the incident of Herbert's partnership is not perhaps quite satisfactory. The early mentions of it are plausible enough, but verge on the mawkish: 'I did really cry in good earnest when I went to bed, to think that my expectations had done some good to somebody.' But what strengthens and elevates it is simply the fact that Pip is unable to complete the good act casually himself, since he no longer has any money. He has to go to Miss Havisham and ask a favour, one which runs the risk of being misunderstood both by her and by Jaggers. (Her instructions to him were 'evidently intended to absolve me from any suspicion of profiting by the receipt of the money'.) The incident succeeds not merely because Pip does not go on about it, but also because it means that he must ignore his proud wish to be independent of the woman who tricked him.

During that visit comes her offer to help him. Dickens's tact here is at its finest. In a way, this moment ought to be the long-awaited answer to Pip's dreams; all along he has thought of his 'great expectations' from Miss Havisham, and now at last they can be realized. Yet the power of this incident comes precisely from the fact that Dickens, who is so often over-explicit, does not need to mention how Pip's dreams are here finally destroyed. By leaving the rest unsaid, and by not at any point showing Pip meditating on such an offer or on his refusal of it, Dickens makes the incident all the more moving. And the simple dignity of Pip's refusal is a far truer evidence of his maturity than is the self-abasement before Joe:

'Can I only serve you, Pip, by serving your friend? Regarding that as done, is there nothing I can do for you yourself?'
'Nothing. I thank you for the question. I thank you even more for the tone of the question. But, there is nothing.' (Ch. 49.)

That comma after 'But' must be the least careless comma in Dickens —the decent mystery of leaving the rest unsaid.

Pip's refusal to take any more money from Magwitch is plainly right. One should not take money from someone whom one finds repugnant. And by the time that Pip loves Magwitch, the convict's fortune has been forfeited to the Crown. It was easy enough for Dickens to make convincing Pip's early shrinking from the money; the latter attitude needed to be more delicately handled. What happens is not a grand renunciation of the money, but a firm resignation to losing it; the firmness makes Pip admirable, the resignation instead of renunciation makes him plausible. Jaggers

did not conceal from me that although there might be many cases in which forfeiture would not be exacted, there were no circumstances in this case to make it one of them. I understood that very well. I was not related to the outlaw, or connected with him by any recognisable tie; he had put his hand to no writing or settlement in my favour before his apprehension, and to do so now would be idle. I had no claim, and I finally resolved, and ever afterwards abided by the resolution, that my heart should never be sickened with the hopeless task of attempting to establish one. (Ch. 55.)

'I *finally* resolved . . .': those are the words not of a plaster saint, but of a decent man who manages not to repine.

But of all Pip's good deeds it is his loyal love for Magwitch which most matters. It more than counterbalances his ingratitude to Joe and Biddy, partly for the good reason that Pip's love for Magwitch is so strongly felt, partly for the bad reason that Joe and Biddy, despite all their occasional vividness, remain characters sadly insubstantial compared with Magwitch (or at any rate *become* so as soon as Pip grows up). The fact that, when Magwitch first returns, Pip feels nothing but repugnance for him, is not only the most powerful reason why his final love is so moving, but also the most powerful reason why it is so convincing. It is likely enough that Pip would shrink from Magwitch; the danger for Dickens here is that this may topple the reader over into disliking Pip. What retrieves the situation is the stroke of having Herbert Pocket react at first in just the same way to Magwitch—Herbert, the simple, unsnobbish and good-natured:

I saw my own feelings reflected in Herbert's face, and, not least among them, my repugnance towards the man who had done so much for me . .
[Magwitch's] chair remaining where it had stood, Herbert unconsciously took it, but next moment started out of it, pushed it away, and took another. He had no occasion to say, after that, that he had conceived an aversion for my patron, neither had I occasion to confess my own. We interchanged that confidence without shaping a syllable. (Ch. 41.)

That first repugnance for Magwitch, convincing yet (because of Herbert) not disgusting, is Dickens's shrewdest move to authenticate the final love; and it is not forgotten at the deepest moment of the love:

For now my repugnance to him had all melted away, and in the hunted wounded shackled creature who held my hand in his, I only saw a man who had meant to be my benefactor, and who had felt affectionately, gratefully, and generously, towards me with great constancy through a series of years. (Ch. 54.)

'Who held my hand in his': Pip's love for Magwitch is not a matter of confessing or verbalizing—it is as simple and faithful as a smile and shake of the hand. There is nothing self-regarding in the telling of it: in court, 'with his hand in mine'; and on his death-bed, 'I pressed his hand in silence', 'a gentle pressure on my hand', 'a stronger pressure on my hand', 'he raised my hand to his lips'. The joined hands of Pip and Magwitch have their loving dignity enhanced by their contrast with the absurdly sycophantic shakes of the hand from Pumblechook ('May I?'), and with the one-sided relationship when Magwitch first returns: 'I reluctantly gave him my hands. . . . Once more he took me by both hands and surveyed me with an air of admiring proprietorship.'

The other stroke which makes the love convincing is simply Dickens's awareness that love means stopping thinking about oneself. Throughout the book, Pip has been shown as in the grip of 'these matters that with myself I too much discuss, too much explain'. Not that he has been always selfish or complacent; but guilt is self-centred. But when the day for escaping down the river with Magwitch begins, 'a veil seemed to be drawn from the river, and millions of sparkles burst out upon its waters. From me, too, a veil seemed to be drawn, and I felt strong and well'. And in the astonishing Ch. 54 which follows (telling of the attempt to escape and Magwitch's capture), Pip's attention is all on Magwitch. The first-person narrative ceases to be a way of thinking, however honestly, about oneself, and instead manages to combine a narrator's direct love with a simple attention to an accelerating narrative which involves almost complete abnegation of the narrator's self. The effect is all the more striking since, until this great chapter, the narrator's self has been so continually before our eyes. As Gissing insisted, 'no story in the first person was ever better told'.

It would be silly to give the impression that retaining our sympathy for Pip was at all an end in itself. What really matters is that Pip loves Magwitch; but this could never have come alive if Dickens had not so finely controlled our attitude to Pip.

Not that *Great Expectations* is flawless; rather, it is that compared with Dickens's other novels it has less flaws. It is a pity that Joe is not so credible or touching a figure as Magwitch, since Pip's ingratitude never quite strikes home; and it is a pity that Wopsle, the church-clerk turned actor, not merely is a throw-back to an earlier comic vein, but lacks the sheer comic vigour of that vein. It is more than a pity that the coincidences on which the plot depends (Jaggers being the lawyer of both Miss Havisham and Magwitch, and Magwitch being Estella's father) should not be revealed until almost the end of the novel. *Données* are not usually looked in the mouth; but when they are offered as late as this it is easy to feel that they exist not, legitimately, as a means to writing the novel, but, illegitimately, as a means to rounding it off. And it is a matter for at least dismay that Dickens changed the original ending and allowed Pip to marry Estella; everything that we know of Miss Havisham and her bringing up of Estella is made hollow by this softening of Estella, since we find, not that we must forgive the tragic Miss Havisham, but that there was not really anything to forgive.

Such flaws are mainly technical, though some of them are serious. But there is one flaw of sympathy which is more grave. In the early scenes, the villain Compeyson is seen with the same compassionate realism as Magwitch:

This man was dressed in coarse grey, too, and had a great iron on his leg, and was lame, and hoarse, and cold, and was everything that the other man was; except that he had not the same face, and had a flat, broad-brimmed, low-crowned felt hat on. (Ch. 3.)

But as soon as Compeyson disappears from our sight, he becomes merely a villain, and the villainy is rather hollowly denounced: 'that evil genius, Compeyson, the worst of scoundrels among many scoundrels'—'They fell into deeper shame and degradation—if there can be deeper—and ruin.' The denouncing words are too empty to weigh much in the scale against that 'flat, broad-brimmed, low-crowned felt hat'. Such villainy is often as insubstantial as Luke's in *Michael*:

> Meantime Luke began
> To slacken in his duty; and, at length,
> He in the dissolute city gave himself
> To evil courses: ignominy and shame
> Fell on him, so that he was driven at last
> To seek a hiding-place beyond the seas.

It is not that some people are not wickeder than others; rather that the loose melodrama with which Compeyson is treated exerts an unwanted pressure on Magwitch. It puts the novel in danger of saying, not that Magwitch is a criminal whom we must love, but that he is not really a criminal. Real criminals we are left free to hate as before.

Not that this is anything like the total impression which the book in fact makes. There *is* a failure of compassion in the treatment of Compeyson ('tumbling on the tides, dead'), but it is almost as nothing when set against the love of Pip and Magwitch. That love is made compellingly real; the whole novel is perhaps Dickens's most straightforwardly realistic; and even the fairy-tale elements look slightly different if one remembers that James Joyce received a letter from Slack Monro Saw & Co.:

Dear Sir,

We are instructed to write to you on behalf of an admirer of your writing, who desires to be anonymous, to say that we are to forward you a cheque for £50 on the 1st May, August, November, and February next, making a total of £200, which we hope you will accept without any enquiry as to the source of the gift.

Dickens's fiction is not stranger than truth.

OUR MUTUAL FRIEND

Arnold Kettle

MOST PEOPLE today who take Dickens seriously as a writer would probably agree with what was, in 1937, the minority view expressed by T. A. Jackson when he wrote, referring to the later novels:

Dickens sought, by means of the incident-plot of his novels, to achieve a moral-plot indicative of and symbolizing a politico-ethical criticism of the social life of his time. [1]

There may be, perhaps, from the metaphysicians and myth-critics a certain jibbing at 'politico-ethical' and even 'social', but even from such quarters there will be agreement that Dickens's plots are 'more than' plots and that the later novels, especially, embody a more complex and profound level of organization and significance than most early literary criticism of Dickens, however enthusiastic, recognized.

This is not to suggest that there is anything abstract or even allegorical about the conception of a novel like *Our Mutual Friend*. About *Hard Times* and even *Great Expectations* there is indeed a certain recognizable background of abstract thinking which emerges, interestingly, in their very titles; but by and large the images around and through which Dickens worked are not conceived in at all an abstract way. What he mostly thought about was, indeed, his plots and characters; but to get these plots and characters 'right', to satisfy the essential, not necessarily fully formulated, end he was after, required, as he went on, their more and more careful subordination to a whole, and in that whole a moral view and purpose is predominant.

More critical notice has been taken of the grammar of the title of *Our Mutual Friend* than of its significance. This is not altogether surprising, for a consideration of Dickens's titles is not always re-

[1] T. A. Jackson, *Charles Dickens: The Progress of a Radical* (1937), p. 203.

warding. It is hard to make much of *Martin Chuzzlewit* as a title and *Little Dorrit* is a good deal less interesting than its rejected alternative *Nobody's Fault*. Yet it is perhaps significant that in this big, ambitious, eminently serious novel Dickens should have underlined in his title the rôle of John Harmon. It is of course obvious that in the incident-plot (hereinafter referred to simply as plot) John Harmon, alias Handford, alias Rokesmith, is the king-pin. It is his inheritance and his supposed murder that sets the whole thing going; he is indeed the Beginning of the story, 'the man from nowhere'. But, without overdoing Harmon/Rokesmith's significance (he doesn't really bear too much loading with that commodity) I think it is worth noticing that his part in the moral-plot (hereinafter the pattern) is also important. For his function within the novel is to link not only diverse characters but diverse areas. Not least important is the actual topographical link he supplies, for it is he who brings the mounds or dust-heaps into relation with the river and this, as we shall see, is fundamental to the imagery of *Our Mutual Friend*. But there is another respect, thematic rather than concrete, in which Harmon/Rokesmith forms a vital link. He connects the area of wealth with the area of poverty. And this is fundamental to the conception of the novel. T. A. Jackson puts it quite correctly: 'Class-contrast and class-antagonism, class-hatred and class-contempt are woven into the innermost texture of *Our Mutual Friend*.' [2]

The idea of mutuality as involving more than the isolable *personal* relationships of individual characters is, of course, very deep in Dickens. There is a deeply-felt moment in *Bleak House*, more important in the pattern of that book than is generally recognized, when Esther Summerson tries to sum up her feelings and Ada's about their first ghastly visit, with Mrs. Pardiggle, to the brickmakers' cottage:

We both felt painfully sensible that between us and these people there was an iron barrier, which could not be removed by our new friend (Mrs. Pardiggle). By whom, or how, it could be removed we did not know; but we knew that. (Ch. 8.)

All Dickens's novels might be described on one level as explorations into the human effects of this iron barrier and the ways of removing it, and *Our Mutual Friend* is perhaps the most profound and consistent of these explorations. What underlies Mr. Boffin's description

[2] *ibid.*, p. 204.

of Harmon/Rokesmith as 'our mutual friend' (he is talking to Mrs. Wilfer) is that character's part in bridging and, in a sense, loosening up the class-relationships of the whole world of the novel. For not merely does Harmon/Rokesmith connect the Boffins with the Wilfers but he is also the unwitting means of introducing Eugene Wrayburn to Lizzie Hexam, a connection just as important to the pattern of *Our Mutual Friend*.

In the Boffin–Wilfer relationship class-antagonism as such does not arise, though there is a great deal of caste-antagonism and caste-contempt. Mrs. Wilfer is every bit as snobbish as Lady Tippins, but the joke is, of course, that her snobbery has no real social basis: she is a tragedy-queen out of a tenth-rate repertory company. And Bella's mercenariness, though almost fatal, is in an important sense unlike the mercenariness of Podsnappery, based on shares and exploitation; hers is a working-class mercenariness, not much different in essence from that of Richardson's Pamela, based simply on the bitter experience of what not having money involves. What is fought out in the Boffin–Rokesmith–Wilfer area of the novel is a moral battle which is a class-battle in the quite fundamental sense that it hinges on class-values. Is the way out of poverty the way of Podsnappian acquisitiveness? Bella at first thinks it is. She learns better through the example of the apparent corruption of Mr. Boffin.

This episode, which has often been objected to as improbable or clumsy, seems to me one of Dickens's happiest inspirations. It serves a double purpose, not in the facile sense of getting two effects for the price of one but in the rarer way of revealing simultaneously two sides of the same coin. Bella is tested and changed by her experiences, graduating in the school of nineteenth-century heroines from the status of a Dora (in *David Copperfield*) to somewhere approaching that of a Nora (in *The Doll's House*); and at the same time the possibilities of corruption inherent in the Boffin-situation are triumphantly revealed. Dickens gets it both ways: the alternative possibilities before Boffin are both dramatized and the degrading horror of the one throws into relief the humane excellence of the other. These alternative possibilities of corruption and human decency are underlined meanwhile within the Boffin area of the book by the respective paths of Messrs. Wegg and Venus. The relationship between Boffin and Wegg seems to me extraordinarily well done. Not only Wegg's meanness but Boffin's own vulnerability emerge in episodes as psychologically subtle as they are funny. There is more than a touch of the nastier kind of unease in Boffin's naïve dealings with his literary man. Because he is in the position of patron he begins behaving like a patron—he who so hates patronage (it is a recurring theme of consideration throughout the book). One understands Wegg's irritation, even though his basic reactions are of course unforgivable. And it must also be said that Dickens's plot, towards the end of the Boffin–Wegg strand, gets him into one of those rare situations in which he is not quite on top of things. Boffin's dissimulation is fair enough in relation to Bella, but when the golden dustman has simultaneously to unravel the complicated machinations of Wegg and Venus it is not always clear in which persona he is performing or who is leading whom up the dust-heap or why.

The question that both Bella and the Boffins have to face is whether, given the opportunity, they want to 'rise', i.e. emerge morally from the working-class world into the world of Podsnap the bourgeois. This, it is worth stressing, is the real issue, an issue not of money as such but of values. The corrupting force in *Our Mutual Friend* is not money but bourgeois attitudes to it. That is why critics who take the superficial view that class is simply a matter of birth or level of income can make little of the pattern of *Our Mutual Friend* and are likely to end by presenting an image of Dickens as a comfortable middle-class do-gooder with vulgar tastes and a soft spot for the deserving poor.

The question that both Bella and the Boffins have to face is Hexams' and the Veneerings' problem as well as the Wilfers' and the Boffins'. One of the central aspects of the problem is—as in so much Victorian literature and thinking—that of education. Almost the first thing Mr. Boffin does when he gets his money is to employ Wegg to improve his education. Again, one recalls the importance of books in preserving David Copperfield's integrity and the wonderful moment in *Bleak House* when old Krook is found teaching *himself* to read and write because he cannot trust anyone else to teach him right. To insist that Dickens was keen on education is to miss half the point. What he also recognized was that in a class-divided society education itself has a double tendency, to corrupt as well as to liberate. At the school where Charley Hexam learns and Bradley Headstone teaches—a 'temple of good intentions' Dickens calls it—'an exceptionally sharp boy exceptionally determined to learn, could learn something' and the worth of that something is not underestimated. But the *values* which Charley Hexam imbibes are also part of his educa-

tion and they, of course, are not merely snobbish in the more superficial sense, making him socially contemptuous of Lizzie and her
friends, but infected at the core with anti-working-class attitudes,
especially the idea of 'getting up in the world'. The imagery used to
describe Bradley Headstone's mind is extraordinarily telling:

> From his early childhood up, his mind had been a place of mechanical
> stowage. The arrangement of his wholesale warehouse, so that it might
> be always ready to meet the demands of retail dealers—history here,
> geography there, astronomy to the right, political economy to the left . . .
> this care had imparted to his countenance a look of care. (Bk. II, Ch. 1.)

Not only is the educational system as such here linked with the processes of capitalist economy, but Headstone's own personal neuroses
connected organically with the socio-intellectual system of which he
is a cog, a system which is revealed as inhuman not only in its underlying values—commercial and mechanical—but in its division of
knowledge and experience into isolated compartments. In a single
sentence Dickens is indeed, in terms entirely relevant to the personal
situation he is depicting, producing a profound humanist critique of
the modern British educational system.

'Rising' is a desperate danger in the world of *Our Mutual Friend,*
for to 'rise' is to enter the sphere of the Podsnaps and the Veneerings.
Charley Hexam does not enter that sphere financially but spiritually
he does, and his spiritual corruption is inseparable from his social
ambitions, his undeviating, fanatical determination to make himself
'respectable in the scale of society'. And when, in his nauseating complacency, he finally turns on the wretched Headstone, his tone and
language are those of Mr. Podsnap. Charley's final judgment on his
sister (Bk. IV, Ch. 7) and Podsnap's (Bk. IV, Chapter the
Last), though made from socially different positions, are interchangeable. For level of income is not the determining feature of Podsnappery and an increase in income is not the same as 'rising'. Lizzie
Hexam will not be corrupted by becoming Mrs. Eugene Wrayburn
any more than Mrs. Boffin is spoiled by her innocent enthusiasm for
Fashion and her frank enjoyment of the pleasures of wealth.

Does this mean that Dickens makes a simple division between
'good' and 'bad' characters and that the 'good', irrespective of social
status or class position, resist corruption while the 'bad' are drawn
under, like Rogue Riderhood drawn under the treacherous waters of
the Thames? I do not think such an assessment stands up to a

thorough-going examination. Obviously Dickens is not, in a crude sense, a social determinist; he does not imply that the social 'background' of a character is inescapable. Lizzie and Charley Hexam grow up in the same house, subjected to the same general social influences, but turn out quite differently. Lizzie, so to speak, moves upstream, Charley down. But Charley's deterioration is bound up, not just with 'character' in an isolated, unchanging sense, but with specific social choices, including Lizzie's own ambitions for him as opposed to her lack of ambition for herself. We understand why Lizzie wants to get Charley away from the riverside and we respect her for it, but we are forced to recognize, as she herself never quite does, that she has, in all innocence, made a frightful error in judgment, an error which, faced with a temptation of her own, she manages to avoid. Lizzie refuses to be drawn into corruption, just as Jenny Wren and Mr. Riah and Mr. Venus do, and though the refusal costs each of them something, what is maintained is moral independence. These people, despite their poverty, decline to 'rise' by grasping 'opportunities' that will undermine their humanity.

This is the significance of the Betty Higden episode which is all too easily seen as merely a bit of doubtless well-intentioned propaganda against the workhouses and their 'honourable boards', a not very relevant return to the preoccupations of *Oliver Twist*. In naturalistic terms old Betty is no doubt overdone (rather in the way Firs, the old servant in *The Cherry Orchard*, can be felt to be overdone), yet her uncompromising and obsessional determination to be beholden to no one, even the undemanding Mrs. Boffin, is an important, and I think necessary, strand in the pattern of Dickens's presentation of the problems of poverty and working-class morality. To accept patronage is to lose independence, to drift into the arms of the 'honourable boards' is to accept human degradation. It is notable that in *Our Mutual Friend* it is not the idea of social services that is attacked: Dickens goes out of his way to praise the children's hospital and to show that old Betty's suspicions of it are groundless. He is not holding up Mrs. Higden's sturdy independence as something preferable to the acceptance of a decently conceived system of planned social welfare. What he is underlining is a moral embedded deep in this novel: that a genuine emancipation or even amelioration involves the maintenance of their moral independence by working-class people and that such independence is incompatible either with 'rising' or with the acceptance of the sort of charity which has bourgeois strings attached.

For of all of Dickens's novels this is the one most deeply and consistently impregnated with a consciousness of the power of the bourgeoisie. How essential the 'society' chapters—set in the homes of the Podsnaps and Veneerings—are to the basic conception of the novel is emphasized by the nature and positioning of Chapter the Last, which is very different from the usual final chapter of a Victorian novel, tying up loose ends and adding more or less irrelevant information about the future careers of the characters. 'The Voice of Society' it is called and it is clear that Dickens is using the word 'society' with deliberate and effective ambiguity; for though the voice referred to is in fact 'society' in the narrower sense of those who people the 'society columns' of the newspapers, it is the implication of the whole novel that their voice is the one which dominates society as a whole and that their values are in a precise sense the ruling values of the world of *Our Mutual Friend*. These values get their fullest and most insistent symbolic expression in the novel in the recurring emphases on dust and shares. The dust-heaps are the dominant visual image of the accumulation of wealth and power; but it is a feature of that power that it operates not openly but mysteriously, through bits of paper: wills, promissory notes, the offer of reward which Rogue Riderhood clutches, above all, through shares.

As is well known to the wise in their generation, traffic in Shares is the one thing to have to do with in this world. Have no antecedents, no established character, no cultivation, no ideas, no manners; have Shares. Have Shares enough to be on Boards of Direction in capital letters, oscillate on mysterious business between London and Paris, and be great. Where does he come from? Shares. Where is he going to? Shares. What are his tastes? Shares. Has he any principles? Shares. What squeezes him into Parliament? Shares. Perhaps he never of himself achieved success in anything, never originated anything, never produced anything! Sufficient answer to all; Shares. O mighty Shares! (Bk. I, Ch. 10.)

Such a passage, quoted out of context, may give the impression of an aside, a perhaps not quite legitimate intrusion of one of Dickens's hobby-horses. In fact it is fully integrated into the structure of the novel. The immediate occasion of it is the approaching marriage of the Lammles, one of the minor triumphs of the book and a brilliant advance on Thackeray's treatment of a similar theme in the 'how to live on nothing a year' part of *Vanity Fair*, because the emotional nature of the Lammles' impasse is suggested in a way Thackeray cannot reach. But it is not simply the Lammles' career that the passage touches: it is the whole operation of Podsnappery, from the honourable boards that terrify Betty Higden and the honourable debt that almost ruins Mr. Twemlow to the whole marvellously funny career of the Veneerings who emerge from nothing and disappear into nothing, but take in a seat in Parliament on their way, people from nowhere, spreading a sort of doom.[3]

It is, I suppose, the uncompromising nature of this insight, so fundamental to *Our Mutual Friend* of the null and friendless nature of the Podsnap world, that has led, as much as anything, to the underestimating of this novel. Henry James's unfavourable contemporary review in *The Nation*, though it does its author less than justice (the later James would have been more generous, though whether he would have been as frank is perhaps more doubtful), centres on this very question.

What a world were this world if the world of *Our Mutual Friend* were an honest reflection of it! . . . Society is maintained by natural sense and natural feeling. We cannot conceive a society in which these principles are not in some manner represented. Where in these pages are the depositories of that intelligence without which the movement of life would cease? Who represents nature? [4]

The tone of sophisticated outrage is arresting and straightway illuminates the gap between the worlds of, say, George Eliot, Matthew Arnold, and Henry James on the one side and Dickens on the other. Who represents nature indeed? One recalls Mr. Squeers's rich philosophical aside to the effect that nature is a rum'n. Or perhaps the simplest reply is to ask: whose nature? It is of the very essence of *Our Mutual Friend* that Podsnappery does represent a significant area of nature—bourgeois nature—and that for 'natural sense and natural feeling' this particular area of aspiration, to use an expressive phrase of the Artful Dodger's, 'ain't the shop'.

The Jamesian shift, in the passage just quoted, from 'natural sense and natural feeling' to 'depositories of intelligence' is in itself interesting. Clearly it is because he is unable to see the Boffins as the

[3] Mr. Hillis Miller, in an interpretation of *Our Mutual Friend* which strikes me as being, by and large, of almost ludicrous irrelevance, makes an excellent point when he refers to the 'nullity' of the Veneerings. (*Charles Dickens, The World of his Novels*, 1958, p. 297).   [4] *The House of Fiction* (ed. L. Edel, 1957), p. 255.

depositories of the kind of intelligence which he, Arnold-like, associates with those whose destiny it is to set standards for society and spread sweetness and light, that Henry James cannot even recognize their natural sense and natural feeling. James sees the Boffins as eccentrics. Whereas to Dickens it is they, above all, who are the representatives of the sort of nature he was most interested in—popular nature in the true nineteenth-century sense of popular, expressive of the worth and potentiality of the People as opposed to those who rule and exploit them.[5]

The two most important concrete visual images in *Our Mutual Friend*, as everyone recognizes, are the mounds and the river. It is worth emphasizing that they are not, in any abstract or schematic sense, symbols, but straightforward poetic images, embodying in the richness of their relevant qualities and the manifold 'rightness' of their relationship to one another, the central content and meaning of the novel. Several critics, especially perhaps Humphry House, have helped us to see the full importance of the dust-heaps, not merely as historical phenomena, actual outcrops on the face of Victorian London and specific examples of capital accumulation and speculation, but in the nature of their content of waste and even excrement.[6] The mounds get their effect in the novel in a number of ways working simultaneously. Visually they are huge, ugly, barren, man-made, yet in their operation there is a kind of perverse fertility about them, the fertility of manure and—the connection is not arbitrary—dividends. They keep the system going. To own them is not merely to be rich but to control the processes of social continuity. And the poor live within their shadow and their stench.

The mounds are connected with the river in several ways. Visually or geographically they rear up as a sort of artificial Primrose Hill, overlooking North London. In terms of the plot it is, as I have already suggested, Harmon/Rokesmith who links the two areas and a subsidiary link is provided by the ludicrous romance of Mr. Venus and Pleasant Riderhood. An interesting associative connection has been suggested in the form of the Houses of Parliament ('the national cinder-heap') which stand by the river.[7] But though this may be a trifle far-fetched, the main relationship is clear. It is the filth of Lon-

---

[5] Dickens's clearest expression of his conscious commitment to the 'popular' side in precisely this sense is to be found in the famous speech at Birmingham, 27 Sept. 1869 (*The Speeches of Charles Dickens*, ed. K. J. Fielding, 1960, p. 407).

[6] *The Dickens World* (1942 ed.), pp. 166 ff.

[7] Edgar Johnson, *Charles Dickens, His Tragedy and Triumph* (1953), p. 1030.

don, itself one vast fog-infested dust-heap, that pollutes the river and turns it from a pleasing and refreshing stream into a flowing sewer of filth and refuse. There is indeed a grim and significant parallel between the image of old Harmon (and Silas Wegg) fishing his wealth out of the dust of commercial London and Gaffer Hexam fishing his sordid living out of the polluted waters of the chartered Thames.

Rivers nowadays always seem to tempt the Jungians to their most absurd excesses and no one familiar with the ways of twentieth-century American criticism especially will be surprised to find the Thames of *Our Mutual Friend* saddled with every conceivable kind of ritual significance. Unfortunately for these interpretations, on the only occasion really conducive to such an emphasis—the rescue and revival of Rogue Riderhood—Dickens goes out of his way to laugh at any such idea as the restorative power of drowning. Pleasant Riderhood is visited by

some vague idea that the old evil is drowned out of him, and that if he should happily come back to resume his occupation of the empty form that lies upon his bed, his spirit will be altered. In which state of mind she kisses the stony lips, and quite believes that the impassive hand she chafes will revive a tender hand, if it revive ever.

Sweet delusion for Pleasant Riderhood. . . . (Bk. III, Ch. 3.)

It is quite true of course that Eugene's conversion follows his immersion in the river; but here the point is no more 'mythic' than in the case of the unconverted Riderhood. The reason that Eugene has to be rescued in that particular way is simply that this is the sphere in which Lizzie, the female waterman, is uniquely capable of achieving such a rescue.

Not that one would wish to under-emphasize the importance of the Thames in *Our Mutual Friend*. It is, in the early reaches of the book and the lower ones of the river, the very mainstream of corruption and wretchedness. This is a persistent image in Dickens's work. The prostitute Martha in *David Copperfield* is drawn towards the river:

'I know it's like me!' she exclaimed. 'I know that I belong to it. I know that it's the natural company of such as I am! It comes from country places, where there was once no harm in it—and it creeps through the dismal streets, defiled and miserable—and it goes away, like my life, to a great sea that is always troubled—and I feel that I must go with it.' (Ch. 47.)

Even here, though, the corruption and wretchedness are not in the least mysterious, let alone metaphysical. The filth is the actual filth of London, the wretchedness is poverty. Almost all the poor characters of *Our Mutual Friend* live around the river, and when Charley Hexam is trying to persuade Lizzie to marry Headstone and get away from the house in Smith Square he argues that she 'would at last get quit of the river-side and the old disagreeables belonging to it'. (Bk. II, Ch. 15.)

Even the upper reach of the river, the idyllic Berkshire valley, takes on a sinister colour when the inhabitants of the corrupted lower river, Riderhood and Headstone, invade it. But by and large it is a place of sweet contrast and it is obviously not fortuitous that the model factory should be placed here or that Betty Higden should escape westwards in her flight from the honourable boards. It is to Chertsey, Walton, Kingston, and Staines that Betty goes.

In those pleasant little towns on Thames, you may hear the fall of the water over the weirs, or even, in still weather, the rustle of the rushes; and from the bridge you may see the young river, dimpled like a young child, playfully gliding away among the trees, unpolluted by the defilements that lie in wait for it on its course . . . (Bk. III, Ch. 8.)

If one is to talk of 'waste-land' imagery in connection with this novel it must be in a very naturalistic and precise sense.

Between the mounds and the river the complex, cunningly interwoven dramas of *Our Mutual Friend* are worked out, merging into a single drama in which the values of humanity struggle against those of Podsnappery. That it is in the profoundest sense a class struggle would be clear even if the 'moral' were not underlined in the final chapter where, with the greatest analytical candour, the personal relationships involved in the plot are examined and judged in the light of the moral preoccupations which control the novel's pattern. The bourgeois class delivers its judgment on the marriage of Lizzie and Eugene, and Mr. Twemlow, the dim little aristocrat, who has learned at any rate something from his dealings with the Lammles and Fascination Fledgeby, dissociates himself from it, standing up even to the veiled threat of Podsnap to tell Lord Snigsworth of his class-apostasy. Perhaps the most significant moment of the whole scene is the judgment of 'the Contractor, of five hundred thousand power':

It appears to this potentate * that what the man in question should have done, would have been to buy the young woman a boat and a small annuity, and set her up for herself. These things are a question of beef-steaks and porter. You buy the young woman a boat. Very good. You buy her, at the same time, a small annuity. You speak of that annuity in pounds sterling, but it is in reality so many pounds of beefsteaks and so many pints of porter. On the one hand, the young woman has the boat. On the other hand, she consumes so many pounds of beefsteaks and so many pints of porter. Those beefsteaks and that porter are the fuel to that young woman's engine. She derives therefrom a certain amount of power to row the boat; that power will produce so much money; you add that to the small annuity; and thus you get at the young woman's income. That (it seems to the Contractor) is the way of looking at it. (Bk. IV, Chapter the Last.)

It is particularly telling, not only because of the brutal connections it reveals between the Contractor's morals and his social position, but because it echoes Eugene's own cynical morality of his unregenerate days. Then he was able to say to Jenny Wren:

'I think of setting up a doll, Miss Jenny.'
'You had better not,' replied the dressmaker.
'Why not?'
'You are sure to break it. All you children do.'
'But that makes good for trade, you know, Miss Wren,' returned Eugene. 'Much as people's breaking promises and contracts and bargains of all sorts, makes good for *my* trade.'
'I don't know about that,' Miss Wren retorted; 'but you had better by half set up a penwiper, and turn industrious and use it.'
'Why, if we were all as industrious as you, little Busy-Body, we should begin to work as soon as we could crawl, and there would be a bad thing!'
'Do you mean,' returned the little creature, with a flush suffusing her face, 'bad for your backs and your legs?'
'No, no, no,' said Eugene; shocked—to do him justice—at the thought of trifling with her infirmity. 'Bad for business, bad for business. If we all set to work as soon as we could use our hands, it would be all over with the dolls' dressmakers.'
'There's something in that,' replied Miss Wren; 'you have a sort of an idea in your noddle sometimes.' Then, in a changed tone: 'Talking of ideas, my Lizzie,' they were sitting side by side as they had sat at first, 'I wonder how it happens that when I am work, work, working here, all alone in the summer-time, I smell flowers.' (Bk. II, Ch. 2.)

* Cf. Mr. Venus's early description of Pleasant Riderhood: 'She is worthy of being loved by a Potentate.'

I think this is a most interesting and subtle passage, revealing very strikingly the profundity of Dickens's moral control of his plot. Here the essential conflict of values at the heart of *Our Mutual Friend* is expressed simply, yet in the most richly complex terms. Eugene's attitudes emerge in all their crudity. The doll is obviously Lizzie, though its 'setting up' can also imply the bribing of Jenny, and Eugene has no hesitation in discussing the whole affair in terms of the morality of trade. But even he is shocked when Jenny puts the working-class case in equally crude and personal terms, associating her own infirmities with her class position. And Jenny herself is forced to acknowledge that, in the competitive world she lives in, 'there's something in' Eugene's cynical morality. But she is unconvinced and turns to Lizzie (who seems, incidentally, to understand nothing of the implications of the conversation) with her thought about smelling flowers, a theme that is then developed at sufficient length to associate Jenny's dreams and her morality with the nature-imagery of the upper-Thames sections of the book. What Jenny is granting in this passage is the short-term expediency of the Wrayburn/Contractor morality, while clinging to a scale of values and aspiration not only more humane but altogether more 'natural'. And it is only when Eugene himself comes to accept those values—the popular values of those who work with their hands, as opposed to the ruling-class values of Podsnappery—that the conflict within the novel can be resolved and Mortimer Lightwood can fare to the Temple, gaily.

It is only those who, like George Orwell, wear blinkers which prevent a recognition of what Dickens is saying and of what class-conflict really is, who fail to see the profundity and consistency of the artistic structure of *Our Mutual Friend*. I think Jack Lindsay is doing the novel no more than justice when he describes it as one of the greatest works of prose ever written, a work which finally vindicates Dickens's right to stand, as no other English writer can stand, at the side of Shakespeare.[8]

[8] *Charles Dickens* (1950), p. 308.

EDWIN DROOD: EARLY AND
LATE DICKENS RECONCILED

A. O. J. Cockshut

I

In Rusholme, Manchester, near where I live, there is a dingy barber's shop; and outside it is a rotting plywood figure, approximately human in size and form, which bears the caption, 'Shave, sir'. One of the main reasons why we admire Dickens, I think, is that he has so far been the only English writer (with the possible exception of Lawrence) who has given artistic meaning to sights like these. And we know that this is no superficial gift of impressionism, but an outward sign of his wonderful use of the material of industrial civilization, which other novelists have found intractable, or have ignored. The railways and the commerce of *Dombey and Son*, the mounds in *Our Mutual Friend*, the disused mines in the country outside Coketown, the treatment of income from investment in *Great Expectations*—these things now seem to be his greatest and most characteristic achievement. No doubt fashion, and the reaction from the Chestertonian coaching Dickens, play some part in this; but on the whole this preference seems to me justified.

The fact that all this is absent from *Edwin Drood* is one reason why we are apt to feel uneasy with it. Cloisterham is very fine, the cathedral and elms are fine, but they are in a well-worn tradition of fictional settings. They are not quite a sufficient substitute, we may feel, for the Marshalsea, or for the rotting Thames of *Our Mutual Friend*.

A second reason for uneasiness is fortuitous, but can, nevertheless, be important. As the book is a mystery story, and unfinished, it attracts the type of critical attention which is given by those who do not care for literature at all. The people who are most eager to invent a new theory about Drood's murder are the same as those who wish to prove that the *real* old curiosity shop was in the Brompton Road, or to disentangle the topical references in *romans à clef*. Those of us who do not share this kind of interest are put off.

A third handicap to the full enjoyment of *Drood* is linked with the first. It seems to be in some ways a regression to the author's more superficial early style. Durdles seems at first sight (I hope to show that he is not) a stock early Dickens eccentric like Dick Swiveller. The moral evil associated with Jasper and Honeythunder seems purely external and melodramatic, like that of Ralph Nickleby or Quilp. We have no sense of uneasily watching the portrayal of our own vices and shortcomings, as we do when we read about Pip. Still less do we feel that the author is comprehending and defining his own moral weaknesses as he does when he portrays Harold Skimpole. If the late Dickens is the best, as I believe it is, his last book may at first sight look very like the second childhood of his talent. The very names of the characters point to this, with their reversion to early Dickensian fantasy, and in some cases, their obvious allegorical suggestions—Honeythunder, Crisparkle, Rosa Budd. Both the name and the nature of the crusty, jocular old uncle, Grewgious, remind us very much of the high jinks and Christmassy pseudo-benevolence of some of the worst early passages. He is not as bad as the Cheeryble brothers, but he is much inferior as a guardian angel to Joe Gargery.

Of course, all this may seem, even if its general truth is accepted, to be disparaging the early Dickens too much. If so, we can point to Sapsea's monument:

ETHELINDA
Reverential Wife of
Mr. THOMAS SAPSEA,
AUCTIONEER, VALUER, ESTATE AGENT, &c.
OF THIS CITY,
Whose Knowledge of the World,
Though somewhat extensive,
Never brought him acquainted with
A SPIRIT
More capable of
LOOKING UP TO HIM.
STRANGER, PAUSE
And ask thyself the question,
CANST THOU DO LIKEWISE?
If Not,
WITH A BLUSH RETIRE   (Ch. 4.)

This is early Dickens at his exuberant best. This is the humour of Mrs. Gamp and Pecksniff, the humour that escapes satire, and creates unanswerable new absurdities that no living person could ever really contemplate. When a mature artist reverts to the style of his early popular successes, we are apt to diagnose fatigue and loss of interest; particularly, perhaps, when we know that his health was failing and that he died with the book unfinished.

II

A first glance at the plot may yield a similar result. I take it to be established by scholarship, ignorant though I am myself on the subject, that every indication points to the presence of Indian thuggery in the story. The following indications among others have been noticed: Jasper's black scarf, the call of a rook in sight of a river, the fact that the murdered man is a traveller and is treated by the probable murderer with great kindness just before the deed. So, even if any doubt remains about the murderer's identity, it is clear that Dickens set out to produce a flavour of Eastern mystery, that he used opium addiction mainly for this purpose, that Jasper is an addict and that he goes through many of the rituals which were supposed to be performed by the Indian thug. Now this choice of plot is obviously important. It is true, and we have often been reminded, that Dickens's friend Wilkie Collins had recently published *The Moonstone*, which has a superficial similarity as a story of Eastern mystery. But the word 'influence' is apt to be misleading when applied to Dickens. It would seem that he was incapable of being influenced except in the way he wanted to go. His imaginative system could not assimilate matter alien to it; it was one of the benefits he derived from his anti-intellectualism. George Eliot paid the penalty for being an intellectual open to wide cultural influences in *Romola*.

And so the Eastern plot is very surprising. Dickens had always been so very English in the settings of his novels. The Paris of *A Tale of Two Cities* is a solitary exception which proves the rule. For after Carlyle the French Revolution had come to be regarded as a great event in English history. Apart from this, I can only recall the very 'English, grand tour' Italian travels of the Dorrit family. It looks as if the man is fatigued, is wearily seeking for factitious novelty, is deserting the field of his triumphs because the effort of true artistic creation is too great. For Dickens may have read and heard a lot about Indian thuggery. But he could not really have known about it in the way he knew the subjects with which he had achieved his most brilliant successes, the Thames, railways, money, dirt, prisons. He knew these with penetrating eyes, with memories of childhood agony and joy. Why travel so far from these obsessive and fruitful interests?

Weariness is the obvious diagnosis, and it would seem there was something to be said for Bernard Shaw's summary, 'only a gesture by a man three quarters dead'. Though I believe this plausible judgment to be quite mistaken about the book as a whole, I fancy that I do detect some weariness in the last four or five chapters, though it is difficult to be quite sure that one is not unconsciously influenced by the knowledge that Dickens collapsed and died shortly after writing the words 'fall to with an appetite'. But whether or not we diagnose a weary searching after novelty in the choice of opium-dens and thuggery, it is certain that such an explanation is totally incomplete. Consider the opening passage:

An ancient English Cathedral Tower? How can the ancient English Cathedral tower be here! The well-known massive grey square tower of its old Cathedral? How can that be here! There is no spike of rusty iron in the air, between the eye and it, from any point of the real prospect. What is the spike that intervenes, and who has set it up? Maybe it is set up by the Sultan's orders for the impaling of a horde of Turkish robbers, one by one. It is so, for cymbals clash, and the Sultan goes by to his palace in long procession. Ten thousand scimitars flash in the sunlight, and thrice ten thousand dancing-girls strew flowers. Then follow white elephants caparisoned in countless gorgeous colours, and infinite in number and attendants. Still the Cathedral Tower rises in the background, where it cannot be, and still no writhing figure is on the grim spike. Stay! Is the spike so low a thing as the rusty spike on the top of a post of an old bedstead that has tumbled all awry? (Ch. 1.)

This brilliant simultaneous evocation of the split mind, and of one culture superimposed upon another, perfectly introduced the whole text that we have. Taking the hint from it, we can see that *Drood* was never just a story with a titillating spice of Eastern mystery for jaded English palates, like *The Moonstone*. It was going to set the known and the unknown side by side, to reveal the value or the decadence (or both) of English society by means of the intrusion of an alien and destructive ethos. No doubt Dickens was wise, or lucky, in his choice of India, rather than (say) Italy, and not merely on the tactical ground that it would be more unfamiliar and exciting to his readers. The elementary John Bull in Dickens, as in later Arabophiles and Bengal Lancers, was far more at home with something truly alien than with the repudiated and misunderstood roots of our common European culture. Dickens could have written an excellent Asiatic travel book, but he only revealed his limitations in *Pictures from Italy*.

A startling contrast of cultures, and the split minds that go with it —that is the theme, and once that is understood, we are in a better position to evaluate the reversion to early Dickens humour, early Dickens macabre and murder, and early Dickens Christmas conviviality. Take the cathedral, for instance. Here no doubt nostalgic boyhood memories mingle with his new purpose. On the whole a cathedral does not seem a promising subject for Dickens. His Anglicanism was sincere enough, despite heretical tendencies towards Unitarianism. But he lacked several qualities needed to make the most of a cathedral as a symbol and of the Close as a social fact. He lacked a sense of history. The mediaeval past, of which cathedrals are the abiding monument, was to him an object of ignorant distaste and contempt. We remember that revealing row of dummy books he was so proud of—'The Wisdom of our Ancestors' series, all with titles like 'The Rack' and 'Disease'. One would expect the life of the Close to forfeit all his sympathy. Whether it is thought of as a life of old-world gentlemanly ease, or as a life of prayer, liturgical devotion, and scholarship, Dickens the 'practical', low-church philanthropist, despised, ignored, misunderstood both. Ancient churches had, for many years past, made few appearances in his work. He had given in *Our Mutual Friend* a word of praise to Mr. Milvey, the hard-working and impoverished guardian of a slum parish. But that is a different matter. That was an aspect of the new, swarming proletarian society of the nineteenth century. That was (as Dickens, like his own Mr. Meagles, would have said) 'practical'. On the other hand, when, many years before in *The Old Curiosity Shop* he had used the ancient peace and charm of the English village church, the presentation had been devoid of religious content. It had only been a sentimental setting for the enjoyment of the factitious agonies of Little Nell. The precedents were certainly not encouraging. And in the light of them Dickens's achievement in the treatment of the cathedral here becomes impressive. Not only is it solid, truly observed, not only is its setting of dripping elm trees and fallen leaves memorable, but it has an unexpectedly powerful symbolic force as well.

It seems as if the superimposition upon the cathedral of the mysteries of Eastern civilization and of the opium dream helped Dickens to see its positive aspects for the first time; and hence eventually its negative aspect also. For the cathedral is dreary and decaying; it is the home of the dead; it almost becomes in the end a monument to a dying civilization; dying, unregretted. We are very far from the smart sneering of dummy books, though the new message may be no more comforting in the last resort for supporters of conservative Anglicanism.

The book is full of little hints of decay and of split mind: 'Mr. Crisparkle, minor canon and good man, lately "Coach" upon the chief Pagan high roads, but since promoted by a patron (grateful for a well-taught son) to his present Christian beat.' An ordinary enough point; nothing is more likely than that a canon would have been a tutor in Latin and Greek. But in the context of the split mind and bestial pagan tendencies of the musical director of the cathedral's worship such little points are significant.

The past of Cloisterham is seen as a patchwork of ill-connected traditions, hence the description of its stones:

Fragments of old wall, saint's chapel, chapter-house, convent, and monastery, have got incongruously or obstructively built into many of its houses and gardens, much as kindred jumbled notions have become incorporated into many of its citizens' minds. All things in it are of the past. (Ch. 3.)

The choir has white robes but they are sullied. Jasper is in the middle of them. The old ways are in decline. 'Not only the day is waning but the year.' It seeems at first like the disintegration which precedes death.

And so we come to the importance of Durdles. It is here that we can see most clearly how the old and new Dickens are united in an exciting new pattern. The distinction I make between the early and the late Dickens is in no way original and can be briefly summarized In books like *Pickwick* and *Nicholas Nickleby* we have a spirited macabre and humorous development of the traditions of English melodrama. Grotesque fantasy of plot and character is made tolerable by that marvellous gift which never deserted Dickens throughout his career, his obsessive power of communicating the reality of physical objects. But in *Little Dorrit, Great Expectations,* and *Our Mutual Friend*, we have controlled symbolic comment on society, largely conveyed through the development of simple ideas which haunted him throughout his life—dirt, money, prisons, and the like. On the whole, except in *David Copperfield*, which is a rather unsatisfactory special case, there is little mingling of the two methods, and certainly no earlier satisfactory synthesis.

When we first meet Durdles we could easily mistake him for an inhabitant of the crude world of *Nicholas Nickleby:*

He often speaks of himself in the third person; perhaps, being a little misty as to his own identity, when he narrates; perhaps impartially adopting the Cloisterham nomenclature in reference to a character of acknowledged distinction. Thus he will say, touching his strange sights: 'Durdles came upon the old chap', in reference to a buried magnate of ancient time and high degree, 'by striking right into the coffin with his pick'. The old chap gave Durdles a look with his open eyes, as much as to say, 'Is your name Durdles? Why, my man, I've been waiting for you a devil of a time!' And then he turned to powder. (Ch. 4.)

But the meaning is deepened when we come to passages like this, in which Mr. Grewgious is shown the crypt:

Old Time heaved a mouldy sigh from tomb and arch and vault; and gloomy shadows began to deepen in corners; and damps began to rise from green patches of stone; and jewels, cast upon the pavement of the nave from stained glass by the declining sun, began to perish. Within the grill-gate of the chancel, up the steps surmounted loomingly by the fast-darkening organ, white robes could be dimly seen, and one feeble voice, rising and falling in a cracked monotonous mutter, could at intervals be faintly heard. (Ch. 9.)

Durdles, as a character, is bizarre early Dickens. As a symbol of the decay of the cathedral, of the collapse of the civilization of the country town, he is comparable in his symbolic status to the river in *Our Mutual Friend*. Such a synthesis is perhaps not completely unprecedented. A case could be made for Rogue Riderhood and Gaffer Hexam in *Our Mutual Friend* as achieving it partially. But Durdles is at any rate the most developed case. And it was a difficult achievement to synthesize two periods of a great career.

Durdles may be said to represent, too, both the two poles round which the novel historically turns—the intellectual, symbolical, 'artistic' type of Flaubert, James, etc., and the realistic, social-critical type of Balzac and Tolstoy. The few great masters who have achieved a synthesis have done so only occasionally in their careers. *Moby Dick* achieves it, but not *Pierre* or *The Confidence Man*. Durdles's death-obsession is much more than a psychological quirk. We can now examine briefly the way in which the other characters fit into this synthesis or opposition of early and late Dickens's styles. Deputy, Durdles's young imp, is another fine example of synthesis. As a character he might come straight from the pages of *Pickwick*. He is vivid, superficial, redolent, in spite of the Cloisterham setting, of the London streets on which Dickens had brooded for so long. Durdles explains how Deputy earns a halfpenny a day by driving him home with stones when he is drunk. Jasper comments: 'I wonder he has no competitors', and Durdles replies: 'He has plenty, Mr. Jasper, but he stones 'em all away.' A subtler, briefer, and more blistering comment even than is to be found in *Hard Times* upon the Manchester school, the commercial greatness of England, and the 'immutable laws of supply and demand'.

In Honeythunder, the synthesis of old and new is not successfully achieved. He has all the vigorous memorability of an early Dickens hypocrite. But the moral criticism of the uncharitable type of philanthropic temperament is crude. His ill-temper and rudeness become simply incredible, and his hypocrisy is vague, general, and improbable. It is a comedown from the brilliant portraits of Bounderby and Harthouse in *Hard Times*, each with his special, calculated, and entirely credible type of hypocrisy lurking behind certain agreed social stereotypes.

Bounderby, the self-made man, feeds on the Smiles myth of industry triumphant over early poverty and degradation, so that he invents a fairy-tale gutter to be born in, and denigrates the character of his worthy mother in order to justify his brutality and magnify his triumph. At the same time we see clearly from his delight in keeping a 'distressed gentlewoman' as housekeeper, how the source of his myth is inverted snobbery. Harthouse feeds on the myth of the weary, cynical, unambitious aristocrat. He knows that the snobbery of the utilitarians will award him a higher place in their counsels than he could obtain elsewhere if he adopted a political system usual to men of his class. This brief account of a complex matter will be enough to show that Honeythunder, however amusing, represents a disappointing reversion to the early style.

Of Drood himself little need be said; he is a workmanlike hero, colourless perhaps by the author's intention. The Landless family and the amusing Miss Twinkleton contain little that is original. But the character of Crisparkle reveals a new respect for the priestly office, and, though not a profound character study, he is conceived with a balanced sympathy which the early Dickens had lacked.

But, of course, Jasper is the prime example of the successful synthesis of old and new. Here, clearly, there was much more to come; and we must speak tentatively. It would seem that he is a genuine split personality, not a melodramatic hypocrite. And so, he draws together in his person the threads of a story of clashing civilizations. He has his crude, early-Dickensian moments, as when he shows his jealousy of Rosa. But the mesmeric effect of his personality rings true. We cannot tell how the author would have resolved the apparent contradiction of motives. (Jasper shows signs of being at the same time a psychopath, and a conscientious devotee of thuggery.) But a reconciliation of these two strains is not impossible. It seems that Dickens had partly achieved at his death, and might have fully achieved, had he lived, the feat he had so often failed to achieve, the feat Dostoevsky, after learning from him, triumphantly achieved, the total analysis of the murderer's soul.

There are lapses, then, in this synthesis of old and new, and there are special problems, which are due to the work's unfinished state. But when we consider the extraordinary difficulty of telescoping the achievements of a great career, we may be amazed at the degree of success achieved. One thing is certain; whatever the effect on him as a man, Dickens as artist had not been spoiled by success. He refused to do over again what the public expected. As ill-health strengthened its hold, he was still seeking that true originality which includes and develops the achievements of the past.

III

Let us now examine briefly some of the hints which the text gives about the working-out of the plot. Perhaps the most obvious is given when Grewgious, Rosa's guardian, presents Drood with the ring which belonged to Rosa's mother (Ch. 11). The understanding is that Drood will either place it solemnly on Rosa's finger as a sign of irrevocable promise of marriage, or return it to Grewgious, if the engagement is brought to an end. Grewgious says, 'I charge you once more, by the living and by the dead, to bring that ring back to me.' 'By the dead' means literally Rosa's dead parent. But it is scarcely a large assumption that it would have had an ironic meaning, in that the ring would have returned from Drood's dead body into Grewgious's possession, and (probably) given a clue to the identity of the murderer. There is partial confirmation of this in Forster's account of his conversation with Dickens on the subject. In spite of various more subtle theories, it still seems overwhelmingly probable that Jasper really was the murderer; but it is just conceivable that he was not, *although he thought he was*. That is, moving into a world of illusion through opium, he began to conform to the thug rituals, until he imagined that he had really committed another man's crime. In either case, it is relevant that it was contrary to the thug doctrine to murder a man with gold in his possession. Perhaps we have here something more than a melodramatic device for detecting a criminal. We may be in that late Dickens world where material objects glow with a strange sacramental power—where things which, in the early Dickens would have been mere convenient coincidences, now testify to a vaguely-conceived but powerfully felt conviction of divine power and destiny. Such, for instance, is the destroying and healing power of the prison in *Little Dorrit* and of the river in *Our Mutual Friend*. A start is made towards achieving this in the following passage, which immediately succeeds Drood's decision to tell Rosa nothing about the ring he received from Grewgious, now that their engagement is at an end:

Let them be. Let them lie unspoken of, in his breast. However distinctly or indistinctly he entertained these thoughts, he arrived at the conclusion, Let them be. Among the mighty store of wonderful chains that are for ever forging, day and night, in the vast ironworks of time and circumstance, there was one chain forged in the moment of that small conclusion, riveted to the foundations of heaven and earth, and gifted with invincible force to hold and drag. (Ch. 13.)

The quick-lime and the hidden chamber in the cathedral provide an obvious clue about the disposal of the body; and if the clue is not misleading, we can take it that another reinforcing version of death-in-life in the cathedral was in preparation. Finally we have a broad hint in the title of Ch. 14, 'When shall these three meet again?' The three are Jasper, Drood, and Neville Landless, who dine together on Christmas Eve. One can only assume that some sort of terrible dramatic tableau had been planned. The most likely form of it would have been this: Jasper (the murderer) is revisiting the dead body of Drood (? in the crypt), perhaps for the purpose of recovering the neglected ring from the body, when Neville Landless, wrongly suspected of the murder, catches him in the act. No doubt there are other possible variants which the reader may like to amuse himself by supplying.

Speaking tentatively, we may say that in the plot, also, we have a synthesis of early and late Dickens, though the early features predominate here more than they do in the characters or in the symbolism of the cathedral. The plot is intensely melodramatic, just as much so as that of *Oliver Twist*. The old unbalanced excitement about murder, strong at all stages of Dickens's career, but softened in his best later books, is back again in its full force. The masked villain is there, and preparations are going on for a thrilling discovery scene. Yet there is something, less obtrusive and less easy to characterize, which is 'late'. Signs are already present, and destined perhaps to be stronger in the complete work, of a deeper meaning behind the melodrama and coincidence. In the early Dickens, if an opium addict had been a respected servant of a cathedral, it could only have been for the sake of disguise and the device of 'the most unlikely person'. Now it is more. It is a comment on the traditional cathedral world. There is a deadly irony in

Mr. Jasper is in beautiful voice this day. In the pathetic supplication to have his heart inclined to keep this law, he quite astonishes his fellows by his melodious power. He has never sung difficult music with such skill and harmony, as in this day's anthem. His nervous temperament is occasionally prone to take difficult music a little too quickly; to-day, his time is perfect. (Ch. 14.)

There is even a point in the effects of the storm, which tore off the hands of the cathedral clock. The cathedral is being contaminated; official Christianity is losing touch with the time. The European way of life is losing its cultural purity. Jasper is, in his way, prophetic of 'Les Demoiselles d'Avignon'.

One crucial question remains, and I can only ask it, not answer it. What, in the last resort, is Dickens's attitude to all the things he collectively symbolized by the cathedral? What I have just said, and indeed any detailed analysis of all the images of death and decay associated with the cathedral, might suggest the author really believed that the old way of life was dead, and official Christianity with it. Yet I am not satisfied that this is the final impression the reader receives. It is not merely that Eastern and pagan influences are presented in their most repellent form, so that old English things, even if stupid and out-of-date, seem by comparison attractive. It is not only that, at the political and social level, as George Orwell and others have shown, Dickens is nearly always much more conservative than he thinks he is. It is more a question of a new development in his religious sensibility—as if the cathedral, rotting within, and wracked with storms without, had at last become for Dickens a convincing image of the Christian civilization he had so long ignored or sneered at, or misunderstood. The storm comes at a great festival of the Church, Christmas, as if to emphasize the danger; but it emphasizes also the value of what is threatened. And in the last few pages that Dickens ever wrote, there is a passage which hints at the revival of the cathedral life:

A brilliant morning shines on the old city. Its antiquities and ruins are surprisingly beautiful, with a lusty ivy gleaming in the sun, and the rich trees waving in the balmy air. Changes of glorious light from moving boughs, songs of birds, scents from gardens, woods, and fields—or, rather, from the one great garden of the whole cultivated island in its yielding time—penetrate into the Cathedral, subdue its earthy odour, and preach the Resurrection and the Life. (Ch. 23.)

Or is this too far-fetched? Would the images of death and decay have dominated in the end? In writing of this strange book, mysterious in intention, and still more mysterious in its unfinished state, I make no apology for ending with a question mark.

INDEX

I. GENERAL

239

II. CHARACTERS

See also under the novels in which they occur

INDEX OF CHARACTERS